Ideologies of Globalization

D0153828

"Globalization" is a term that dominates much political discussion at the start of the twenty-first century and is accepted by many as an inevitable process. However, as recent protests in the United States and elsewhere have demonstrated, there is considerable disagreement as to the significance of globalization and much popular opposition to the vaunted "New World Order."

This book provides a critical interpretation of ideological and political struggles over the meaning and future of "globalization"—especially as these have unfolded in the nexus between the US and the world political economy. Examining key debates about globalization, it provides a detailed and incisive analysis of the contradictions, tensions, and possibilities that animate various positions in these struggles. It explores the social meanings attached to globalization, the ideologies in terms of which it is assigned political significance, and the political projects that these ideologies envision and enable.

Subjects covered include:

- the historical context of the development of globalization and its relation to structures of US political economy in the postwar period;
- the emergence of progressive opposition movements through resistance to the North American Free Trade Agreement (NAFTA), the General Agreement on Tariffs and Trade (GATT), and the World Trade Organization (WTO);
- nationalist responses to globalization from Buchananites, militia groups, and others on the far right;
- the ambiguities and democratic possibilities of the populist backlash against neoliberal globalization;
- recent moves by advocates of liberalization to present "globalization with a human face."

Timely, informative, and controversial, this book is essential reading for all those seeking to understand the intersection of American politics and the global political economy.

Mark Rupert is Associate Professor of Political Science at Syracuse University, USA.

Routledge/RIPE Studies in Global Political Economy
Series editors: Otto Holman, Marianne H. Marchand
(Research Centre for International Political Economy,
University of Amsterdam) and Henk Overbeek
(Free University, Amsterdam)

This series, published in association with the *Review of International Political Economy*, provides a forum for current debates in international political economy. The series aims to cover all the central topics in IPE and to present innovative analyses of emerging topics. The titles in the series seek to transcend a state-centered discourse and focus on three broad themes:

- the nature of the forces driving globalization forward
- resistance to globalization
- the transformation of the world order.

The series comprises two strands:

Routledge/RIPE Studies in Global Political Economy is a forum for innovative new research intended for a high-level specialist readership, and the titles will be available in hardback only. Titles include:

1. **Globalization and Governance**
   Edited by Aseem Prakash and Jeffrey A. Hart

2. **Nation-States and Money**
   The past, present and future of national currencies
   Edited by Emily Gilbert and Eric Helleiner

3. **The Global Political Economy of Intellectual Property Rights**
   The new enclosures?
   Christopher May

The *RIPE Series in Global Political Economy* aims to address the needs of students and teachers, and the titles will be published in hardback and paperback. Titles include:

Transnational Classes and International Relations
Kees van der Pijl

Gender and Global Restructuring
Sightings, sites and resistances
Edited by Marianne H. Marchand and Anne Sisson Runyan

Global Political Economy
Contemporary theories
Edited by Ronen Palan

Ideologies of Globalization
Contending visions of a New World Order
Mark Rupert

Ideologies of Globalization

Contending visions of a
New World Order

Mark Rupert

London and New York

First published 2000 by Routledge
11 New Fetter Lane, London EC4P 4EE

Simultaneously published in the USA and Canada
by Routledge
29 West 35th Street, New York, NY 10001

Routledge is an imprint of the Taylor & Francis Group

© 2000 Mark Rupert

Typeset in Sabon by
The Running Head Limited, Cambridge
Printed and bound in Great Britain by Clays Ltd, St Ives plc

British Library Cataloguing in Publication Data
A catalogue record for this book is available from the British Library

Library of Congress Cataloging in Publication Data
Rupert, Mark.
 Ideologies of globalization: contending visions of a new world order / Mark Rupert.
  p. cm.
 Includes bibliographical references and index.
 1. United States–Foreign economic relations. 2. Free trade–United States. 3.
 International economic relations–Political aspects. 4. Globalization–Moral and ethical
 aspects. I. Title.
 HF1455.R78 2000
 337.73—dc21   00–038258

ISBN 0–415–18924–1 (hbk)
ISBN 0–415–18925–X (pbk)

For Anna Elise and her world

Contents

Series editors' preface

In April, 2000, some 10,000 demonstrators tried to shut down the spring meetings of the International Monetary Fund (IMF) and World Bank in Washington, D.C. Most of them were members of one of the activist groups and non-governmental organizations which together formed the *Mobilization for Global Justice*. This umbrella organization coordinated the so-called second Battle of Seattle from the "Convergence Space," the organization's campaign headquarters. All the participating groups "converged" in their opposition to "globalization" and, indeed, capitalism. More specifically they protested—in a non-violent way—against "global violence," i.e., the active role of the "unholy trinity of undemocratic institutions" (the IMF, World Bank, and World Trade Organization) in maintaining poverty, furthering environmental degradation, etc. It was noticed that most of the protesters were students, on the one hand, and elderly people, on the other, those in their thirties and forties being conspicuous by their absence. This group was sitting at home that weekend, nail-biting and anticipating yet another attack on capitalism, albeit from another side: a further collapse of the world's stock exchanges. Meanwhile, the demonstrations were effectively crushed by police forces with the aid of pepper spray, tear gas, and heavy rains.

These developments in the third weekend of April 2000 form a good illustration of what Mark Rupert refers to as the process of re-articulating relations between local sites and the world economy. After a decade or more in which the neoliberal narrative successfully presented the comprehensive program of macro-economic austerity, economic deregulation, and labor market flexibilization as the only way forward, organized opposition is becoming stronger and stronger. And it is the accompanying narrative of globalization, and its defence of global free trade and finance, that these organized forces oppose. In *Ideologies of Globalization: Contending Visions of a New World Order* Rupert analyses competing ideologies of globalization in terms of contests being waged over popular common sense. Next to the dominant discourse of economic liberalism or hyper-liberalism, at least two alternative narratives can be discerned in recent years. On the one hand there is the "new populism," exemplified *inter alia* by Pat

Buchanan's assertive nationalism, which draws upon the resources of popular common sense sensitive to the articulation of liberal individualism with masculinist, religious, and racial identities. In the United States, the far-right anti-globalists seek to legitimize the protection of particularistic economic interests at the national level by constructing "an image of American exceptionalism as a bastion of white, male, Christian privilege." At the other side of the political spectrum, we find "progressive" groups not necessarily opposed to globalization per se, and hence not necessarily in favor of renationalization of economic policies; instead, these groups question the way the United States presently participates in globalization. Here the keyword is not identity but democracy. It is through a profound democratization of the decision-making structures in the world economy that a more socially and environmentally inspired global policy must be realized.

Recent debates in the Unites States on NAFTA, GATT/WTO, and presidential Fast Track authority in negotiating trade agreements show a growing opposition to globalization, which in turn has prompted a reaction from leading business circles and political elites. Rupert convincingly shows that the recent pleas for "globalization with a human face" (for example from President Clinton, the World Bank or the World Economic Forum) are a clear but merely rhetorical reaction to the perceived threat stemming from these oppositional forces. The very fact that this orchestrated reaction of the "global power bloc" is transnational in nature suggests that this opposition to the present form of globalization is by no means restricted to the United States. Both the contesting narratives that Rupert discerns in the United States can also be found in the European context: from far-right, xenophobic anti-globalism in (for instance) Austria to the recent upsurge of anti-Americanism in France and left-wing anti-capitalist clashes in London. In the latter cases, opposition is not so much directed against global integration per se but against the unregulated nature of present-day globalization. If these progressive and cosmopolitan groups in the United States, Europe, and elsewhere can unite forces along transnational lines, then the "predominant transnational capitalist bloc" that underpins neoliberal restructuring might be challenged. It is this perspective of transformation that makes Mark Rupert's book essential reading for those citizens in global society who feel uneasy with dominant neoliberal narratives but do not want to relapse into dangerous experiments with constructing alternative identities or revamping old ones.

Otto Holman
Marianne Marchand
Henk Overbeek
Amsterdam, May 2000

Foreword

I want to express my gratitude to those whose work has provided the inspiration for this book: the people of the Central New York Fair Trade Coalition who organized against NAFTA during 1993, and the many others who continue the worldwide struggle against neoliberal globalization.

I am pleased to acknowledge a special intellectual debt to Mark Laffey, whose intelligence and persistence have succeeded in teaching me important things about politics and ideology which, at first, I did not especially want to see. I am very grateful to Chip Berlet of Political Research Associates who took time to provide this neophyte with tutorials on the topography of the radical right, and provided me with open access to PRA archives of far-right publications. My colleague Michael Barkun has also generously shared his knowledge of the radical right. Hazel Smith has provided helpful feedback and encouragement while also pointing out my incorrigible yank-o-centrism. Jean-Christophe Graz gave me acute criticism of an earlier version of this argument. This project has also benefited from the critical thinking of several of the PhD students at Syracuse University: I am especially grateful to Scott Solomon, Marian Paules, and Nicole Lindstrom. Any errors of fact or interpretation, of course, are my own.

My attempts to understand the reasoning behind New World Order ideology were aided by representatives of the John Birch Society, and by subscribers to the patriot movement listserv, *USA Forever*, who helped me access documents circulating within the patriot and militia movements. Gene Kapp of the Christian Broadcast Network provided partial transcripts of *700 Club* programs dealing with trade and globalization. I have benefited from extensive conversations with Richard Osborn, who was intimately involved with Chuck Harder's *For the People* radio network; Richard also arranged for me to receive the complete print run of *For the People*'s tabloid. Sid Shniad of Berkeley e-mails progressive-oriented news to me (and many others) on a daily basis, and there are numerous news stories which have found their way into this book as a result of his efforts.

I am grateful to the following for their collective willingness to act as a sounding board for development of the ideas which have found their way into this book: Stephen J. Rosow and the Political Science Department of the State University of New York at Oswego; Martha Lee and the Political Science Department of the University of Windsor, Ontario; Craig Murphy and the Workshop on Globalization and Egalitarian Movements, Wellesley College; Mark Laffey, Tarak Barkawi, and the workshop on Democracy, the Use of Force and Global Social Change, University of Minnesota; Judith-Maria Buechler, Linda Robertson, and the symposium on Gender and Globalization at Hobart and William Smith College; David Richardson and the Global Political Economy Research Consortium at Syracuse University's Maxwell School.

Parts of this book have previously appeared in the following publications: *Review of International Political Economy*; Stephen Gill and James Mittelman (eds), *Innovation and Transformation in International Studies* (Cambridge University Press, 1997); Kurt Burch and Robert Denemark (eds), *Constituting International Political Economy* (Lynne Rienner, 1997); *New Political Economy*; Barry Gills (ed.), *Globalization and the Politics of Resistance* (St. Martin's, 1999); and *Review of International Studies*. I am grateful to the editors of these publications for their feedback, and to the publishers for permission to reproduce various excerpts herein.

Most importantly, I am grateful for the love and support of my family, Margaret Clark and Anna Elise Clark Rupert. Margaret, who is a librarian and an accomplished indexer, constructed the index for this book. Anna provided love, inspiration, and hope. This book is dedicated to her.

Acknowledgements

The authors and publishers would like to thank the following for granting permission to reproduce material in this work. All previously published material appears here in a revised and updated form:

Cambridge University Press for material from "(Re)Engaging Gramsci: A Reply to Germain and Kenny," *Review of International Studies,* 24(3) (July 1998), adapted for use in Chapter 1.

Cambridge University Press for material from "Globalization and the Reconstruction of Popular Common Sense in the US," in Stephen Gill and James H. Mittelman (eds), *Innovation and Transformation in International Studies* (1997), adapted for use in Chapter 5.

Lynne Rienner Publishers, Inc., for material from "Contesting Hegemony: Americanism and Far-Right Ideologies of Globalization," in Kurt Burch and Robert Denemark (eds), *Constituting International Political Economy* (1997), adapted for use in Chapter 5.

Taylor and Francis Ltd, PO Box 25, Abingdon, Oxon, for material from "Globalization and American Common Sense: Struggling to Make Sense of a Post-Hegemonic World," *New Political Economy,* 2(1) (1997), adapted for use in Chapters 6 and 7.

Taylor and Francis Ltd, PO Box 25, Abingdon, Oxon, for material from "Policizing the Global Economy: Liberal Common Sense and Ideological Struggle in the US NAFTA Debate," *Review of International Political Economy,* 2(4) (1995), adapted for use in Chapters 2, 3, and 4.

Every effort has been made to contact copyright holders for their permission to reprint material in this book. The publishers would be grateful to hear from any copyright holder who is not here acknowledged, and will undertake to rectify any errors or omissions in future editions of this book.

1 Introduction

Something extraordinary happened at the end of November, 1999: a conclave of trade ministers, international bureaucrats and diplomats—meeting to discuss the arcane rules and regulations governing international trade and related matters—was met with a mass popular mobilization numbering in the tens of thousands. Marches, rallies, and coordinated acts of civil disobedience in the streets of Seattle disrupted the ministerial meetings of the World Trade Organization (WTO). Acting together in opposition to neoliberal globalization were coalitions of non-governmental organizations (NGOs) and activist groups who came from many countries to denounce the WTO as undemocratic in both the process and the substance of its governance (Economist, 1999; Henwood, 1999; Longworth, 1999; Members of International Civil Society, 1999; Moberg, 1999). While the sort of coordinated mass opposition evident in Seattle was unprecedented, and to much of the mainstream media seemed suddenly to burst forth out of nowhere, it was in fact the product of historical-structural transformations and political struggles which have been unfolding for years. This book is the product of my attempts to understand these struggles, especially as they have unfolded in the nexus between the political economy of the US and the global economy.

I must underscore for the reader that I do not intend this to be anything like a synoptic overview of the politics of globalization. For me, globalization is shorthand for a process of re-articulating relations between local sites and the world economy. I presume that this global–local dialectic cannot be mapped whole, but must be examined as it unfolds through the social struggles and contested representations of concretely situated social agents. Accordingly, this study represents a particular—historically and socially situated—perspective on these processes. My claim is no more than to have examined one of the sites in which the global–local interface is undergoing reconstruction, and moreover to have done so from the perspective of a particular social situation (i.e., "middle-class" socialist, white, male, relatively privileged along a number of dimensions). While I cannot presume to speak for those differently located in social space, I do hold out the hope that despite myriad significant differences, a common structural situation—especially in relation to globalizing capital—will create the potential for relations of solidarity and mutual support. The realization of any such potential will require the negotiation of common political horizons across meaningful social differences.

Social critique and democratizing projects

I will try to make sense of political contests over the meaning of globalization in terms of a particular reading of historical materialism, the intellectual tradition associated with Karl Marx and his various interpreters. Historical materialism is not univocal and is itself continuously contested and redefined. But for me the core insight of this rich and varied tradition can be summarized by Marx's famous aphorism:

> Men [sic] make their own history, but they do not make it just as they please; they do not make it under circumstances chosen by themselves, but under circumstances directly encountered, given, and transmitted from the past. The tradition of all the dead generations weighs like a nightmare on the brains of the living.
>
> (Marx, 1997b: 300)

In this statement, Marx acknowledges the powers of human social agents to (re)construct their world, but suggests that these agents and their powers must be understood in terms of their specific historical and social circumstances. Among these circumstances are the social organization of production and the ways in which this social organization has been articulated with social self-understandings (which are not themselves reducible to production relations). For Marx, the capitalist organization of production—premised upon social relations of class and the commodification of labor-power along with its concomitant understanding of social agents as abstract individuals, primordial monads whose contractual interactions create social relations to serve their wants and needs—is neither natural nor necessary. Rather, these are *historical social products* and, as such, may be reconstructed or transformed by historically situated social agents. To treat historically specific social relations and social self-understandings as if they were natural or necessary is to abstract them from the social and historical processes which produced them, and then to reify this abstraction, to treat it as if it were itself an objective reality, a given constraint upon all of social life.

To me, then, the primary significance of historical materialism is that it offers critical resources for questioning and de-reifying capitalism and its various forms of appearance (Rupert, 1995: ch. 2). On this view, commodification of social life, and especially commodification of labor, are not natural, necessary, universal, or absolute; nor, therefore, is the separation of the political from the economic which is entailed in the capitalist wage relation. Ellen Meiksins Wood describes in the following terms the structural differentiation of the economic sphere from the political in capitalism:

> the social functions of production and distribution, surplus extraction and appropriation, and the allocation of social labor are, so to speak, privatized and they are achieved by non-authoritative, non-political means. In other words, the social allocation of resources and labor does not, on the whole, take place by means of political direction, communal deliberation, . . . [etc.], but rather through the mechanisms of commodity exchange . . . based on a contractual relationship between "free" producers—juridically free and free from the means of production—and an appropriator who has absolute private property in the means of production.
>
> (Wood, 1995: 29)

Capitalism's structural separation of the "economic" from the "political" may have crucial ideological effects: for it enables the wage relation to take on the appearance of a voluntary exchange between abstract individuals in the market; while, at the same time, the state may appear as a class-neutral public sphere in which abstract individuals may interact as formally equal citizens pursuing an instrumental politics of self-interest.[1]

> The political sphere in capitalism has a special character because the coercive power supporting capitalist exploitation is not wielded directly by the appropriator and is not based on the producer's political or juridical subordination to an appropriating master. . . . This is the significance of the division of labor in which the two moments of capitalist exploitation—appropriation and coercion—are allocated separately to a private appropriating class and a specialized public coercive institution, the state: on the one hand, the "relatively autonomous" state has a monopoly of coercive force; on the other hand, that force sustains a private "economic" power which invests capitalist property with an authority to organize production itself—an authority probably unprecedented in its degree of control over productive activity and the human beings who engage in it.
>
> (Wood, 1995: 29–30)

Although grounded in the social organization of production, this authority, and these "private" powers, are understood in terms of ownership and control of property, and hence are *not democratically accountable*. Paul Thomas argues that the complex of social relations associated with capitalism—including the modern state—entails an "alien politics" which profoundly limits possibilities for communal self-determination: "The thoroughgoing denial of democracy in civil society, where the chief activities of daily life most immediately take place, is the ongoing, institutionalized counterpart to the concentration, distillation and fusion of all features of common action and collective concern within the state" (Thomas, 1994: xii; see also Wood, 1995).

Marx was scathingly critical of abstract individualism as the ideology of the capitalist market, a social self-understanding which submerged and hid from view the relations of power and exploitation which reside in the capitalist organization of production. In volume I of *Capital*, Marx famously explained how this individualistic vision of social reality is instantiated in and reproduced by the (very real, if also one-sided and self-limiting) appearances of market relations, which abstract politics from the economy and obscure the relations of class power underlying capitalist production relations:

> The sphere of circulation or commodity exchange, within whose boundaries the sale and purchase of labor-power goes on, is in fact a very Eden of the innate rights of man. It is the exclusive realm of Freedom, Equality, Property and Bentham. Freedom, because both buyer and seller of a commodity, let us say labor-power, are determined only by their own free will. They contract as free persons who are equal before the law. Their contract is the final result in which their joint will finds a common legal expression. Equality, because each enters into relation with the other, as with a simple owner of commodities, and they exchange equivalent for equivalent. Property, because each disposes only of what is his own. And Bentham, because each looks only to his own advantage. The only force bringing them together, and putting them into relation with each other, is the selfishness, the gain and the private interest of each. Each pays heed to himself only, and no one worries about the others. And precisely for that reason, either in accordance with the pre-established harmony of things, or under the auspices of an omniscient providence, they all work together to their mutual advantage, for the common weal, and in the common interest.
>
> (Marx, 1977a: 280)

Inhabitants of the capitalist market, the subjects of capitalist modernity, are then abstract individuals who, as such, are largely unable to discern— much less communally to govern—the social division of labor in which they are embedded. As Derek Sayer interprets Marx's theory of the modern subject: "People appear to be independent of one another because their mutual dependence assumes the unrecognizable form of relations between commodities" (Sayer, 1991: 64).[2] On this view, the rise of capitalism and the commodification of labor (the rise of abstract labor, qualitatively undifferentiated labor-power) made it possible to conceive of the individual independent of social context, the individual as such, the individual for whom all social bonds are external; and it is precisely this (implicitly male) autonomous individual who is the presupposition and centerpiece of liberal theories of politics and economics.

> It is this solitary individual—"the individual" in the abstract, without any distinction of, or reference to the "accidental" peculiarities of concrete circumstance—who is the moral subject of the modern world. He [sic] is sanctified as such in the Rights of Man.
>
> (Sayer, 1991: 58)

This line of analysis is similar to John Dryzek's critique of "democracy in capitalist times" as "a minimally authentic liberal democracy, which may be defined in terms of competitive parties, limited opportunities for public participation through voting and organized groups, constitutional constraints on government activity, the insulation of the economic sphere from democratic control, and a politics that mostly involves the pursuit and reconciliation of interests defined in private life" (Dryzek, 1996: 9).

In short, the historical structures of capitalism effect a formal separation of politics from economics and in so doing privilege the putatively private powers exercised by capital in the economy, at the same time that they individuate political subjects and evacuate from the explicitly political sphere any real capacity for democratic deliberation and communal self-determination in and through social relations, particularly the social organization of production. "It is capitalism that makes possible a form of democracy in which formal equality of political rights has a minimal effect on inequalities or relations of domination and exploitation in other spheres" (Wood, 1995: 224). On this view, then, *democracy is an unfulfilled promise of liberal capitalism*—a promise which could not be fulfilled without calling into question the privileged status of private property, the powers of the class which owns it, the apparently apolitical economy within which it is ensconced, and the social self-understandings of abstract individualism which are attendant upon all of these.

Feminist critiques extend the horizon of this democratizing project into the "private" sphere of the household, family life, and sexuality. Feminists have argued persuasively that the abstract individual of capitalist modernity is implicitly gendered as well as classed, with the construction of a male-dominated public sphere of state and market being parasitic upon the concomitant creation of a feminized domestic sphere and a domesticated femininity (Pettman, 1996: 7–24; Peterson, 1997). And socialist feminists have pointed out that Marx's analyses of the material reproduction of society tends uncritically to presume as a relatively unproblematic given the reproductive activity which takes place within the household. As Susan Himmelweit explains, "Marx's account, although it analyzes in great depth how use values are produced, fails to explain the equally important social fact that people also have to be produced if capitalism, or any other social system, is to continue" (Himmelweit, 1991: 202). This omission is a serious one, both analytically and politically. Analytically, it weakens Marx's own account of the material reproduction of capitalist society insofar as labor-power is central to the account. We may then fairly ask: how is it that the (re-)production of labor-power is itself socially organized? And, by opening the door to the domestic sphere, this raises further questions about the (unpaid) work within the family which makes possible both the reproduction of wage labor and the family as a unit of consumption. As Himmelweit points out, such questions are politically significant for Marx's project:

> The omission of relations of human reproduction has an important political effect, for it means that Marx's and Engels' analysis does not come to grips with gender differences among the working class. It is by their potential roles in human reproduction that the sexual difference between males and females is defined, and it is by the actual place of human reproduction in our society that the lives of men and women are largely structured. Without taking account of these, Marxist analysis has to be largely silent on the reasons that working-class women suffer a double oppression, as members of the working class and as potential reproducers.
>
> (Himmelweit, 1991: 220–1)

Even on its own terms, then, a Marxian account of capitalism is radically incomplete without a critical analysis of gender relations and the structuration of the household (Sayer, 1991: 31–2, 36–7). But how can such an articulation be effected?

In a classic manifesto of socialist feminism, Michelle Barrett challenged those who would reify gender relations by deploying a transhistorical notion of patriarchy as near-universal male domination, as well as those who would subsume gender relations as but one of the areas where capitalism secures its functional reproduction. Prior to her conversion to more postmodern forms of thought, Barrett championed a Marxian feminism in which gender and capitalism were understood to be mutually irreducible but historically intertwined. "No one would want to deny that there are physiological differences between the sexes, but what is at issue is how these differences are constructed as divisions by human social agency" (Barrett, 1988: 250). The social construction of gender difference did not begin with capitalism, but capitalist relations of production emerged from (conflictual and open-ended) historical processes which included the re-working of socially constructed gender relations, such that they became interwoven with the social fabric of capitalism. Barrett's formulation merits quotation at length:

> It is clear that on the one hand the wage relation characteristic of capitalism, and the accompanying separation of home and workplace,

have historically made a substantial contribution to the formation of the present sexual division of labor in which women's position is located principally in relation to responsibility for domestic labor and dependence upon a male wage-earner. On the other hand, some elements of this sexual division undoubtedly existed prior to the development of capitalism; they have not been totally constructed by capitalism. In addition to this historically prior sexual division of labor, upon which capitalism has built a more rigidly segregated division, we can isolate many points of struggle in which the eventual outcome is not pre-given in terms of the requirements of capital.

A model of women's dependence has become entrenched in the relations of production of capitalism, in the divisions of labor in wage work and between wage labor and domestic labor. As such, an oppression of women that is not in any essentialist sense pre-given by the logic of capitalist development has become necessary for the ongoing reproduction of the mode of production in its present form. Hence, the oppression of women, although not a functional pre-requisite of capitalism, has acquired a material basis in the relations of production and reproduction of capitalism today.

(Barrett, 1988: 137, 249)

Under capitalist relations of production, women are seen to have a "dual relationship" to class structure: they may be wage laborers themselves, directly exploited through the sale of their own labor-power, and/or they may be involved in a mediated relationship of exploitation through their dependence upon a male wage-earner and their responsibility for domestic labor and child care (Barrett, 1988: 139, 151). The dependent position of women in the context of modern capitalism is thus produced both in the workplace and in the family.

In the workplace, women are subject to a "vertical" division of labor in which they are subordinated to men in terms of power and remuneration, and a "horizontal" division of labor in which women are overrepresented in some types of work and underrepresented in others. Evidence from the US political economy strongly supports the existence of these divisions: at every level of education, women are paid substantially less than men; and women tend to be concentrated in clerical and service jobs, and in the relatively lower-status and lower-paid professions such as nursing and teaching (Albelda and Tilly, 1997: 4–6, 46–7). Both the "vertical" and "horizontal" divisions of labor are related to women's positioning with the family. Insofar as women are assigned primary responsibility for child rearing and domestic labor, they may be more likely to work part time or to leave the workforce altogether for extended periods, and correspondingly they may be less powerful and more insecure at work, less able to develop and defend job skills, to form ties of solidarity and bargain from a position of (relative) strength, to accumulate seniority and to be promoted along a career track parallel to that traveled by many men. "Furthermore, the construction of a family form in which the male head of household is supposedly responsible for the financial support of a dependent wife and children has militated against demands for equal pay and an equal 'right to work' by women" (Barrett, 1988: 157). According to Albelda and Tilly (1997: 4–5), women in the US make about two-thirds of men's hourly wage, but women tend to work fewer hours a year than men, primarily because of their domestic burdens, which means that women's average annual earnings are about one-half those of men. The ideology of domesticity also affects the "horizontally" gendered division of labor, insofar as women may be disproportionately assigned to areas of work which involve service or caring, and hence are understood in terms of this ideology as quintessentially "feminine."

Barrett points toward the "family-household system" (uniting kinship with cohabitation and, under capitalism, separating residence and consumption from waged work) as the primary historical locus of women's oppression, for it is here that the material relations of dependence upon male wage-earners, and the ideological construction of women as domestics and caregivers, have been situated. Women have been enveloped in a privatized domestic sphere which is culturally defined as the home of all that is feminine, at the same time that they have been effectively blocked from equal participation in the labor force and thus rendered economically dependent. "The family-household system has resulted in the 'double shift' of wage labor and domestic labor for many working class women, and the assumption of their household dependence has left many 'unsupported' women in a very vulnerable position" (Barrett, 1988: 219). This division of the labor force by gender has been politically consequential not just for the disempowerment of women but for the working class as a whole. Gendering the division of labor in these ways has meant the relative privileging of male workers and the concomitant assignment of women disproportionately to the ranks of the poorly paid and the insecure. This gendered division, which produces predominantly female "cheap labor" and intensifies competitive pressures among working people, makes it more difficult to realize possibilities for a politics of solidarity. The real, if also partial, gains which organized (mostly male) workers have won are made vulnerable under conditions in which a feminized "reserve army of labor" can be employed by capital to undercut the power of the labor movement (Barrett, 1988: 171, 218, 258).

Overturning this situation requires de-reification and restructuring of the family-household system such that domestic and childcare responsibilities are no longer gendered in the same way that they have been. This, in turn, implies massive changes in the gendered divisions of labor in the workplace and in the public policies which support them; in short, a gendered emancipatory project entails transforming much of the contemporary political economy of capitalism, as well as "domestic" life. This creates considerable potential, Barrett argued, for the confluence of feminist and socialist political projects.

Likewise, it might be argued that racialized social identities were not created by capitalism and are not essential to it, but that racism has been powerfully articulated with the particular historical structures of modern capitalism in ways which have been politically consequential. Michael Goldfield has argued in his historical analysis of the politics of race and class in America: "Race has been the central ingredient, not merely in undermining solidarity when broad struggles have erupted, not merely in dividing workers, but also in providing an alternative white male nonclass worldview and structure of identity that have exerted their force during both stable and confrontational times" (Goldfield, 1997: 30). Effectively dividing American working people against one another, this ideological formation of white supremacy has also served to rationalize imperial expansion and the domination and hyper-exploitation of people of color around the world. Historian Michael Hunt describes a vision of racial hierarchy which has served as a crucial ideological support not only for the subjection of African-Americans, but for American continental expansionism and subsequent imperial projects:

> They [white Americans] drew distinctions among the various peoples of the world on the basis of physical features, above all skin color . . . and guided by those distinctions they ranked the various types of peoples in the world. Those with the lightest skin were positioned on the highest rung of the hierarchy, and those with the darkest skin were relegated to the lowest . . . Each color implied a level of physical, mental, and moral development, with white Americans setting themselves up as the unquestioned standard of measurement. "Superior peoples" thus spoke English or some language akin to it, responsibly exercised democratic rights, embraced the uplifting influence of Protestant Christianity, and thanks to their industry enjoyed material abundance. Those at the bottom were woefully deficient in each of these areas.
>
> (Hunt, 1987: 48)

In such terms were rationalized the displacement and destruction of Native Americans; aggressive territorial acquisition from Mexico; the conquest of Puerto Rico, Cuba, and the Philippines (and the bloody colonial war waged there); the virtual theft of Hawaii and of the Panama canal zone; and innumerable imperial interventions in Latin America, Asia, and elsewhere. With the expansion of American power and influence (by whatever means) the virtues and progressive energies imputed to (implicitly male) white Americans were seen to be reinforced at home and exemplified to putatively lesser peoples in other lands.

Ideologies of white supremacy are closely linked to gender domination as well, since they generate a phobia of miscegenation and thus authorize strict control over the bodies, sexuality, and reproductive activities of white women. Further, as feminist scholars have argued, masculinist ideologies which domesticate women by representing them as closer to nature than men, more emotional and less rational, passive rather than active, and so on, are readily extended to peoples of color such that their domination by white men may be rationalized through representations which, in effect, feminize non-white peoples (Pettman, 1996: ch 2; Hunt, 1987: 59–61). All of this suggests that the projects of resistance to racism and imperialism are historically intertwined with those seeking to oppose relations of gender or class-based domination, creating conditions of possibility (necessary if not sufficient) for a broad-based politics of solidarity.

Toward transformative politics

Critiques such as these imply that the abstraction of politics from the economy and the naturalization of a civil society of (implicitly white, male, and propertied) abstract individuals are historical conditions which are open to question and hence potentially to transformation. This transformation would necessarily entail (but not necessarily be limited to) the re-politicization and democratization of the economy, civil society, and the family, such that they cease to be pseudo-objective and apparently natural conditions which confront isolated individuals as an ineluctable external "reality." Rather, they would become sites for—and objects of—reflective dialogue and contestation, mutable aspects of a broad process of social self-determination, explicitly political.

Marx suggested that socialist transformation might emerge out of the confluence of capitalism's endemic crisis tendencies, the polarization of its class structure, and the relative immiseration of the proletariat; and, most importantly, the emergence of the latter as a collective agent through the realization of its socially productive power, heretofore developed in distorted and self-limiting form under the conditions of concentrated capitalist production (Marx, 1977a). The Italian political theorist and communist leader Antonio Gramsci accepted in broad outline Marx's analysis of the structure and dynamics of capitalism (Gramsci, 1971: 201–2), but was unwilling to embrace the more mechanical and economistic interpretations of Marx circulating in the international socialist movement.

> It may be ruled out that immediate economic crises of themselves produce fundamental historical events; they can simply create a terrain more favorable to the dissemination of certain modes of thought, and certain ways of posing and resolving questions involving the entire subsequent development of national [and transnational—MR] life.
>
> (Gramsci, 1971: 184)

Progressive social change would not automatically follow in train behind economic developments, but must instead be produced by historically situated social agents whose actions are enabled and constrained by their social self-understandings (1971: 164–5, 326, 375–7, 420). How, indeed whether, such change occurs depends upon struggles to delimit or expand the horizons of these social self-understandings. Thus, for Gramsci, popular "common sense" becomes a critical terrain of political struggle (1971: 323–34, 419–25). His theorization of a social politics of ideological struggle—which he called a "war of position," to distinguish it from a Bolshevik strategy of frontal assault on the state (1971: 229–39, 242–3)—contributed to the historical materialist project of de-reifying capitalist social relations (including narrowly state-based conceptions of politics) and constructing an alternative—more enabling, participatory, democratic—social order out of the historical conditions of capitalism.[3]

For Gramsci, popular common sense could become a ground of struggle because it is not univocal and coherent, but an amalgam of historically effective ideologies, scientific doctrines, and social mythologies. This historical "sedimentation" of popular common sense "is not something rigid and immobile, but is continually transforming itself, enriching itself with scientific ideas and with philosophical opinions which have entered ordinary life. [It] is the folklore of philosophy . . ." (1971: 326). As such, it is "fragmentary, incoherent and inconsequential, in conformity with the social and cultural position of those masses whose philosophy it is" (1971: 419). On my reading, then, Gramsci understood popular common sense not to be monolithic or univocal, nor was hegemony an unproblematically dominant ideology which simply shut out all alternative visions or political projects. Rather, common sense was understood to be a syncretic historical residue, fragmentary and contradictory, open to multiple interpretations and potentially supportive of very different kinds of social visions and political projects. And hegemony was understood as the unstable product of a continuous process of struggle, a "war of position," a "reciprocal siege," hardly a foreclosure of the horizons of meaningful political contestation (1971: 182, 210, 239, 323–34, 350, 419–25). Gramsci's project thus entailed addressing popular common sense, making explicit the tensions and contradictions within it as well as the socio-political consequences of these, in order to enable critical social analysis and transformative political practice. "First of all," Gramsci says of the philosophy of praxis, "it must be a criticism of 'common sense,' basing itself initially, however, on common sense in order to demonstrate that 'everyone' is a philosopher and that it is not a question of introducing from scratch a scientific form of thought into everyone's individual life, but of renovating and making 'critical' an already existing activity" (1971: 330–1). At the core of Gramsci's project, then, was a critical pedagogy which took as its starting point the tensions and possibilities latent within popular common sense, and which sought to build out of the materials of popular common sense an emancipatory political culture and a social movement to enact it—a counter-hegemony.

Randy Germain and Michael Kenny (1998) have usefully highlighted the ambiguities which must be faced in any attempt to use Gramsci to interpret contemporary social reality. They are, I believe, quite correct to point out that Gramsci's legacy is fragmentary, and fraught with analytical and political tensions. Gramsci's relationship with the Marxian tradition—with its problems of base and superstructure, structural determination, and potentially transformative agency, its dialectical openness and its teleology of proletarian revolution, its explicit Eurocentrism and its implicit masculinism—is one source of such tensions (Sayer, 1991: 14–17, 31–2, 36–7).

However, there are viable interpretations of Gramscian historical materialism which, while not escaping altogether the tensions to which sympathetic critics call attention, provide conceptual tools for negotiating them. In particular, I have found Stuart Hall's non-teleological conception of a "marxism without guarantees" especially helpful in thinking about this set of issues (Hall, 1996a). Hall frankly acknowledges the drawbacks inherent in many interpretations of classical Marxist theory, and seeks to address them through a sophisticated combination of discourse analysis and Gramscian historical materialism (Hall, 1988a, 1988b, 1996b, 1997):[4]

> the class/ideology identity marxism *assumes* in the beginning is, for me, the end result, the product of politics. Politics must always construct meanings and deliver the group to the slogans, not assume that the group always "really" knew the slogans and always believed in them.... It's quite possible for a class to be mobilized behind other slogans ... That is what gives political practice a certain necessary openness. Somebody else might have a more effective politics and organize the class around some other slogan; then the connections get forged in a different way.[5]
>
> (Hall, 1988a: 60)

Hall borrows from Laclau the notion that there is no necessary correspondence between class position and ideology, no fixed set of social self-understandings with which a particular group must identify by virtue of its relation to the means of production.[6] And from Volosinov he takes the insight that language is "multi-accentual," implying that there are multiple possible meanings which might be associated with any particular sign, and that these associations may be objects of social struggle. "This approach replaces the notion of fixed meanings and class-ascribed ideologies with the concepts of ideological terrains of struggle and the task of ideological transformation" (Hall, 1996a: 41). Such transformations may be accomplished through practices of "articulation," the forging of contingent discursive linkages between symbols and social systems of meaning, and between these ideologies and particular social subjects. According to Hall, this conception "enables us to think how an ideology empowers people, enabling them to begin to make some sense . . . of their historical situation, without reducing those forms of intelligibility to their socio-economic or class location or social position" (Hall, 1996b: 142).

This should not be understood as an abandonment of historical materialism or of an identifiable socialist project. Rather, Hall is seeking to understand the conditions and processes through which ideological self-understandings are formed and reformed within particular historical circumstances.

> Ideologies may not be affixed, as organic entities, to their appropriate classes, but this does not mean that the production and transformation of ideology in society could proceed free of or outside the structuring lines of power and class.
>   . . . class interest, class position, and material factors are useful, even necessary, starting points in the analysis of any ideological formation. But they are *not sufficient*—because they are not sufficiently determinate—to account for the actual empirical disposition and movement of ideas in real historical societies.
>
> (Hall, 1988a: 45)

"It is therefore possible," Hall tells us, "to hold both the proposition that material interests help to structure ideas and the proposition that position in the social structure has the tendency to influence the direction of social thought, without also arguing that material factors univocally determine ideology or that class position represents a guarantee that a class will have the appropriate forms of consciousness" (Hall, 1988a: 45). And here we arrive at Hall's appropriation of Gramsci as the theorist of open-ended ideological struggle, the "war of position" waged across various social sites:

> Where Gramsci departs from classical versions of Marxism is that he does not think that politics is an arena which simply reflects already unified collective political identities, already constituted forms of struggle. Politics for him is not a dependent sphere. It is where forces and relations, in the economy, in society, in culture, have to be actively worked on to produce particular forms of power, forms of domination. This is the production of politics—politics as a production. This conception of politics is fundamentally contingent, fundamentally open-ended.
>
> (Hall, 1988b: 169)

While there are many Gramscis for which textual warrants may be produced, Hall's Gramsci is one which sees history as a complex and contradictory story of social self-production under specific social circumstances; it is, in Gramsci's words, a process of "becoming which . . . does not start from unity, but contains in itself the reasons for a possible unity" (Gramsci, 1971: 355–6). I understand this to mean that the class-based relations of production under capitalism create the *possibility* of particular kinds of agency, but this potential can only be realized through the political practices of concretely situated social actors, practices which must negotiate the tensions and possibilities—the multiple social identities, powers, and forms of agency—resident within popular common sense. In Hall's appealing formulation, social relations of production may be understood as having some determining effects in the first instance, rather than the last (Hall, 1996a: 45). I believe Hall's concept of "articulation" can open the way to constructive engagements of historical materialist theories and political projects with those centrally concerned with challenging oppressions of race and gender. Further, it seems to offer a language which might enable discussions of the complex intersection of hegemonic forces, resistances, and counter-hegemonies across cultures, without foreclosing this reciprocally educative relationship by imposing upon it an implicitly gendered or Eurocentric teleology.

For me, then, chief among the lessons of Marx and of Gramsci is the importance of understanding the world as a human social product, constructed through broadly productive practices shaped by the social relations and self-understandings prevalent in particular historical times and places. This implies a stance of critical questioning which refuses to accept the simple presumption that things are as they are because they could not be otherwise, that the way things are now somehow must reflect "human nature" or some other ineluctable condition of existence. Any such presumption takes for granted as fixed parameters of social life our institutionalized ways of knowing and doing; that is, the social relations, self-understandings, and practices of the present. This kind of presumption naturalizes and legitimizes the relations of power and domination which reside in contemporary society, and suppresses questions about the terms on which these social forms were produced and potential alternatives which might be constructed out of the social relations of the present. I believe that Marx and Gramsci would have us ask by what means and under what specific historical circumstances—through what kinds of social conflicts and struggles—present social relations and self-understandings have been produced, and what possibilities for progressive change reside within the contemporary social forms which emerged out of these struggles. If it is to be emancipatory and empowering such change must reopen our institutionalized ways of knowing and doing, entailing the simultaneous reconstruction of social relations, self-understandings, and practices. The horizons of progressive change cannot be contained within the historically specific categories of contemporary social forms, but must transgress conventional boundaries to encompass what we now understand as the spheres of "economics," "politics," "culture," and the articulations of class with race and gender-based oppressions.

If this is the critical impulse which animates this project, then I cannot accept (as so many writers do) "globalization" as ineluctable or immutable, simply "the way the world is." Rather, I must inquire into its production through historically specific social relations, self-understandings and practices which interweave the economy, politics, and culture. And I must look at the ways in which the specific historical forms of liberal capitalism have shaped this process, not by predetermining its outcome, but by providing the historical terrain on which are waged struggles over the meaning of globalization and the social relations and practices bound up with it. In short, I must look at "globalization" as a product of historically situated social agents, struggling over alternative possible worlds. Globalization, then, should be seen not as a condition, but as an open-ended process, the content and direction of which are being actively contested.

Plan of the book

My purpose in this book is to argue that the dominant liberal narrative of globalization is being contested within the US from at least two distinct positions.[7] One of these might be described as the cosmopolitan and democratically-oriented left, and I will refer to it as the progressive position. The other I will refer to as the nationalistic far right. I will outline what I take to be the defining features of each of these perspectives, and draw out the different possible worlds toward which each points. I will argue that the contests being waged over popular common sense by these social forces have potentially important implications for the nexus of relations linking the US with the global political economy.

In Chapter 2, I will sketch the historical structural context in which these debates are unfolding. I will pay particular attention to the hegemonic ideology of postwar liberal anti-communism and the processes by which it became effectively anchored in popular common sense. I will argue that the institutionalization of Fordism was crucial to the incorporation of large segments of the industrial working class (especially, but not exclusively, white males) into the historic bloc which constructed the postwar world order. I will then survey the changing conditions which, I believe, make the ideology and political project of liberal globalization increasingly problematic.

The contested meanings of globalization in the US have surfaced most explicitly in the intense public discussions surrounding recent agreements fostering further international liberalization, especially the North American Free Trade Agreement (NAFTA) and, to a lesser extent, the Uruguay Round of the General Agreement on Tariffs and Trade (GATT) which created the World Trade Organization (WTO). Globalization then reemerged as an important focus of public deliberation during Congressional debates over whether to give the President Fast Track authority to conduct further trade negotiations. The anti-WTO demonstrations in Seattle articulated many of the critical themes developed in these earlier struggles. NAFTA, GATT, and Fast Track are important not only as policy instruments aimed at facilitating the long-term growth of international trade and investment, but also as occasions for political argument in which latent tensions of liberal democratic capitalism—especially the ambivalence between private property on the one hand and social self-determination on the other—were once again represented in public discourse as open questions, a terrain of active socio-political struggle.

A powerful phalanx of social forces has arrayed itself behind the agenda of intensified market-led globalization. In Chapter 3 I will review some of the evidence suggesting that, although it is possible to exaggerate the extent and significance of globalization, there are real material processes underlying the increasing salience of this term.[8] I will represent liberal globalization as a confluence of two related historical processes: most fundamentally, it is the product of capitalism's expansive dynamic and its drive for limitless accumulation; in a more proximate sense, globalization is the ongoing project of a particular constellation of dominant social forces seeking to institutionalize their power in historical structures which will facilitate the transnational expansion of capitalism. I will show that major corporations, corporate associations such as the Business Roundtable, academic economists, and the mainstream press all vigorously supported NAFTA, GATT, and Fast Track as part of a larger project of continuing global liberalization. There were two primary themes which consistently emerged from their pro-liberalization representations. First, they claimed that liberalization would encourage greater specialization according to comparative advantage. This specialization, coupled with intensified international competition and greater economies of scale, would result in significant efficiency gains. Thus liberalization would produce on a transnational scale lower prices for consumers and, in the long-run, more jobs and higher incomes. Second, the social forces pressing for liberalization argued that failure to enact these measures would represent not just lost economic opportunities but also a potentially catastrophic US abdication of its historic role as promoter of international liberalization, peace, and prosperity, a giant step backward into the era of isolationism and protectionism. Generally portrayed as promising economic benefits to the American public and serving the national interest by sustaining a more open and liberal world, liberalization received predominantly favorable press coverage and was editorially endorsed by numerous papers large and small. This perspective was aggressively promoted to the public and to Congress by major corporate supporters and lobbies such as the Business Roundtable, USA*NAFTA, and America Leads on Trade.

The agenda of increasing liberalization of trade and investment and the global integration of the US economy has not gone unopposed. NAFTA, GATT, and Fast Track prompted vigorous opposition from a constellation of labor unions, consumer groups, environmentalists, feminists, and citizen activists, as I will show in Chapter 4. They represented the trade pact as augmenting the power of multinational capital relative to workers, unions, local communities, women, and citizens. Beginning to frame an alternative vision of global political economy based on democratic self-determination and transnational linkages among working people, consumers, and citizens —rather than allowing unfettered markets and the criterion of private profit to determine social outcomes—these progressive forces emphasized the common sense value of "democracy" over liberalism's more traditional valorization of private property.

Opposition to liberalization has not been univocal, however. There are sectors of the anti-liberalization movement which explicitly rejected free trade in favor of a more assertive nationalism, and which continue to organize against globalization in any form. These far-right groups, who sometimes identify themselves as "Patriots," are often portrayed as misfits, intellectually limited or emotionally unstable, their political motivations capable of being encapsulated in the diagnosis "paranoid." On the contrary, I will suggest in Chapter 5 that far-right resistance to globalization is understandable as a response to changing socio-political circumstances, a response which draws upon the cognitive resources available in popular common sense to understand a complex and changing world in a way which maintains a stable identity. Far-right anti-globalists tap deeply entrenched strains of American common sense, articulating in varying degrees liberal individualism with masculinist, religious, and racial identities in order to construct an image of American exceptionalism as a bastion of white, male, Christian privilege. This faith has led a segment of the American public to interpret globalization as an alien tyranny engulfing the US through a treacherous conspiracy, breaching the citadel of American exceptionalism and relentlessly destroying its special qualities. In a historical-structural context of fluidity and uncertainty, in which formerly hegemonic ideologies may be losing their power over popular imagination and chronic socio-economic degradation faces large segments of what used to be thought of as the "middle class," we would be unwise simply to dismiss or ridicule ideologies of a conspiratorial New World Order. To the extent such ideologies are able to address the real concerns and fears of these people, to make some kind of sense of what is happening in their world, and to mobilize them behind political projects of cultural, ethnic or racial nationalism, they are a potentially serious threat to democracy, diversity, and transnational solidarity. In Chapter 6, I will tell the story of the rise, fall, and rise of populist radio talk-show host Chuck Harder, whose *For the People* radio show reflects many of the crucial ambiguities of popular common sense in the era of neoliberal globalization. Finally, in my concluding chapter, I will discuss the ways in which the social forces pressing for liberal globalization have responded to the populist backlash, and have sought to co-opt some of its power into a new hegemonic vision, "globalization with a human face." I will interpret the events in Seattle in terms of these struggles. As I write these words, and as you read them, the "war of position"—which will ultimately determine the political significance of globalization—is ongoing.

2 Americanism, Fordism, and hegemony

Americanism and world order ideology

In darkened auditoriums crowded with military trainees soon to be sent into combat, and in hometown theaters throughout the country, US citizens were watching *Why We Fight: Prelude to War*. Directed by famed Hollywood movie-maker Frank Capra, *Why We Fight* was a masterpiece of political propaganda as well as the film-maker's craft, and won the Academy Award for best documentary film of 1942. Originally produced as a training film for the US War Department and shown to as many as nine million servicemen during the war, it was released for general public viewing in 1943 (Manvell, 1974: 168; see also Steele, 1979). As audiences watched *Why We Fight*, they were being addressed by their government, situated in terms of an ideology of world order, ascribed with a common identity and sense of collective purpose as "Americans."

As the lights dim, the official seal of the US War Department appears on the screen and the audience is called to attention by the sound of a bugle. Capra's film opens with images of massed American troops marching in unison across the screen. How, the narrator asks, did so pacific and individualistic a people as we (Americans) become united in a mass mobilization for total war? From the outset, Capra addresses his audience as members of the great American "we," and proceeds to answer the question of "our" involvement in the war by constructing a series of stark contrasts between "us" and "them," between our world and theirs. In terms of these contrasts, the audience is brought into an image of "Americanism," a world-view and self-understanding which powerfully combines elements of liberalism, masculinism, Christianity, nativism, and racism long present in the popular common sense of US citizens.

Capra's two worlds

I will argue that the representation of *two worlds* around which Capra constructed his masterful film was a central element of the dominant ideology of world order which began to anchor itself in US popular common sense during World War II, and by the early Cold War was effectively setting the terms by which crucial segments of the American public and policy-makers alike understood "the way the world is," determining the horizons of political action and defining the limits of the possible. Later in this chapter I will argue that one of the defining characteristics of late twentieth-century world politics—at least as it is understood and practiced by Americans—is the unraveling of this stark vision of two worlds and the political practices it supported. As increasing numbers of Americans cast about for the cultural and intellectual resources with which to understand this apparently new and unfamiliar world, ideological struggles over dominant meanings of "globalization" within popular common sense are intensifying. More than at any time in the last fifty years, I want to argue, the substance of world order politics in the nexus of relations linking the US into the global political economy is now being contested.

Sitting in the dark watching Capra's film, however, the world must have seemed anything but ambiguous or open-ended. The universe of Capra's film is instead characterized by a sharp division between two worlds—the "world of light" and the "world of darkness," the world of liberty, democracy, and progress on the one side, and the world of tyranny, regimentation, and militarism on the other. Through animated maps produced by the Disney studios (Manvel, 1974: 175), these two worlds were represented as locked in mortal combat; only one way of life, the audience was warned, can survive the struggle.

Americans in Capra's audience would instantly recognize themselves as inhabitants of the "world of light." Here, it is presumed in accordance with the political culture of liberal individualism, government serves the people and the essential rights and liberties of individuals are protected from the exercise of arbitrary (governmental) power. Americans are represented to themselves as individuals "free" to live their private lives, worship their god and raise their children in whatever way they deem appropriate. A peaceful and a generous people, preoccupied with work and family, the film suggests that Americans have so little interest in conquest that they are prone to avoid power politics altogether, thereby submerging themselves in isolationist sentiment and refusing to recognize the looming menace.

Not all peoples of the earth, "we" are told, are so dedicated to liberty and peace as Americans. In its representations of the "world of darkness," Capra's film interweaves the liberal individualism of American common sense with its longstanding strains of nativism and racism. For not only are the people of the Axis powers—Germans, Italians, and Japanese—without the basic liberties which Americans take for granted, but they are also predisposed toward authoritarianism and militarism by their cultural traditions and ethnic or racial identities.

Long sequences which Capra excerpted from Nazi propaganda films show seemingly endless ranks of Germans marching in lockstep to the accompaniment of highly repetitive martial music. Capra's narrator attributes this kind of collective behavior to the Germans' "inborn national love of regimentation and harsh discipline," and then the audience is left for several long minutes to observe. As the sense of monotony grew, viewers may have begun to feel confined in their theater seats; increasingly aware of the boredom and discomfort induced by having to sit through this relentlessly invariant military ritual. In this way, American audiences might have been led to wonder what discomfort they might feel if their entire lives were so regimented.

In another scene from "that other world," a German labor battalion is shown digging a canal with picks and shovels. An officer appears, calls them to attention, and in unison they shout "heil Hitler." Then they are curtly commanded to resume their back-breaking work and, without hesitation, they do. The narrator notes the contrast with American workers, who are said to be free to organize for purposes of collective bargaining and to enjoy the rights of citizens even in their work life.[1] The world of light, it seems, offers respect, dignity, and legal protection for working class men; should the world of darkness triumph, these rights and privileges would not long survive.

Still more alarming, viewers are shown uniformed German, Italian, and Japanese children marching, saluting, participating in military exercises. In a matched pair of scenes from Italy and Japan we watch armed military units—comprised of young boys—practicing infantry assaults. In the world of darkness, we are led to believe, children are socialized into submission and conformity by state-run schools, and male children are rigorously prepared from an early age for military service and conquest.[2] The film attributes to Hitler a statement expressing a longing "to see in the eyes of youth the gleam of the beast of prey." With its special effects the film underscores this theme: as we watch, images of marching boys metamorphose into ranks of disciplined, goose-stepping troops. All of this is contrasted with the joyous innocence and natural liberty of American children seen boisterously at play.

In keeping with these representations of child-rearing in a regimented and militarized society, women of "that other world" are depicted as the fatherland's breeders, duty-bound to reproduce and honored by the state for their feats of fecundity. The film suggests that in the world of darkness the state's claim to women's bodies might be institutionalized, and makes explicit reference to one Nazi's fantasy in which a system of camps would be created where racially pure SS men would dedicate themselves to impregnating multiple Aryan women—in effect, mass producing the master race. Capra would have his audience believe that one of the main reasons "why we fight" is to maintain the insulation from state power of a private sphere of home and family.[3]

Capra's audience witnesses dramatized representations of the suppression of freedoms of speech and religion in the axis countries, intermixed with documentary and newsreel footage. Great pyres mount as books are burned, while the political leadership exercises comprehensive control over all channels of public information, turning them into conduits for "propaganda" and "lies, lies, lies." Capra shows his audience newspaper headlines (in English, and thus presumptively free of the propaganda so pervasive in the other world) reporting the repression of dissident religious leaders in Germany. The audience sees church windows smashed as the Fuhrer's image looms up behind the shattered stained glass: a statement equating Hitler's pronouncements with religious revelation is attributed to Nazi propaganda chief Joseph Goebbels. A Japanese military assassination team is depicted breaking into the office of a political opponent: the camera focuses closely on their gun barrels as they fire repeatedly at their unarmed victim. In a scene depicting the fate of political dissidents in Mussolini's Italy, a large 1930s-vintage automobile careens around a corner, the car door flies open, and a body rolls out into the dust. The ethnic stereotyping implied in such imagery, which would instantly recall hundreds of Hollywood gangster movies, would not have been lost on American film audiences in the 1940s.

As a people, the Japanese are represented as virtual automatons, motivated by "fanatical worship of their god-emperor," eager to sacrifice their lives for his glory and entirely indifferent to the suffering of others. We witness frighteningly vivid scenes of the Japanese conquest of China and the brutalization of its people: a woman sobs over the corpse of an infant killed by Japanese bombardment; images of Japanese aircraft, artillery, and combat infantry are juxtaposed—repeatedly and at length—with scenes of civilian bodies littering the streets of Shanghai. The Japanese are, in the narrator's words, Hitler's "buck-toothed pals," attacking the world of light from the Pacific while the Germans seek to dominate Eurasia and complete the encirclement of North America. In what must have been, for its day, a spectacular and shocking special effect, the audience is invited to imagine legions of conquering Japanese troops marching down Pennsylvania Avenue with the Capitol dome behind them. In the end, the film asserts, the denizens of the world of darkness are coming for us, and when they get here they will take "our" liberties, "our" families, "our" lives.[4]

This kind of dualistic world-view has been influential—if also contested—among American leaders and in public political rhetoric since before the revolution, when Tom Paine's *Common Sense* depicted the New World as "the asylum for the persecuted lovers of civil and religious liberty" in contrast to the monarchical and aristocratic abuses of liberty characteristic of the Old World (quoted in Hunt, 1987: 20). Arguably its most articulate modern spokesman was Woodrow Wilson. In a classic statement of the doctrine—now once again fashionable among mainstream American international relations scholars—that democratic polities are naturally pacific, Wilson addressed a joint session of both houses of Congress on 2 April, 1917, asking for a declaration of war against Germany: "The menace to . . . peace and freedom lies in the existence of autocratic governments backed by organized force which is controlled wholly by their will, not by the will of the people" (quoted in Commager, 1958: 310). This world-view presupposes that the natural condition of civilized man is "peace and freedom," and that this condition is violated by the predations of tyrannical aggressor states. Accordingly, the horizons of political action are defined in terms of making the world "safe for democracy" through a system of collective security. Explaining his interpretation of US war aims, Wilson declared:

> Our object is to vindicate the principles of peace and justice in the life of the world as against selfish and autocratic power and to set up amongst the really free and self-governed peoples of the world such a concert of purpose and of action as will henceforth insure the observance of those principles.
>
> (Wilson, quoted in Commager, 1958: 310)

While a wartime propaganda campaign of historically unprecedented proportions attempted to anchor this vision in the common sense of Americans, and thus to mobilize them behind a project of global order, Wilson's project was finally scuttled by the forces of a resurgent nationalism. It was not until the socio-political transformations wrought by Fordism and the world order struggles of the mid–twentieth-century (World War II and the Cold War) that this world-view—and its corresponding self-understanding of Americans as "champions of the rights of mankind"—became deeply rooted in popular imagination. By the time it emerged from these social transformations, the dualistic world-view had come to associate liberty with prosperity and a world order supportive of American-style "Fordist" capitalism.

Fordism and hegemony

The social institutions of mass production—collectively referred to as Fordism—began to emerge in the US early in the twentieth century and were at the center of a decades-long process of social struggle which extended into the immediate post–World War II era (Rupert, 1995). Cold War ideology played a crucial role in the political stabilization of Fordist institutions in the US, providing the common ground on which de-radicalized industrial labor unions could be incorporated as junior partners in a coalition of globally-oriented social forces which worked together to rebuild the "free world" along liberal capitalist lines, and to resist the encroachment of a presumed communist menace globally and at home. Institutionalized Fordism, in turn, enabled the US to contribute almost half of world industrial production in the immediate postwar years, and thus provided the economic dynamism necessary to spark reconstruction of the major capitalist countries, and to support the emergence of both the consumer society and the military–industrial complex in the postwar US.

Fordism has often been understood in terms of an institutionalized macroeconomic balance between mass production and mass consumption (following Aglietta, 1979, but compare Brenner and Glick, 1991). Following Gramsci, however, I understand Fordism in terms of a socio-political regime, a set of institutionalized relationships between the social organization of production on the one hand, and social self-understandings and political organizations on the other. Antonio Gramsci, the Italian communist imprisoned by the fascists during the 1920s, was among the first to recognize the potential political and cultural significance of "an ultra-modern form of production and of working methods—such as is offered by the most advanced American variety, the industry of Henry Ford" (Gramsci, 1971: 280–1). Through heightened managerial control over the organization and performance of work, the system of Fordist mass production might intensify exploitation of labor and thereby counter capitalism's endemic tendency toward a falling rate of profit. However, thought Gramsci, the institutionalization of such a system of production required a combination of force and persuasion: a political regime in which trade unions would be subdued, workers might be offered a higher real standard of living, and the ideological legitimation of this new kind of capitalism would be embodied in cultural practices and social relations extending far beyond the workplace. Gramsci called attention to the "long process" of socio-political change through which a Fordist capitalism might achieve some measure of institutional stability.

Henry Ford is conventionally credited with synthesizing the various elements constituting the modern model of mass production which bears his name, and which is often said to date from the development of the first moving assembly lines, put into operation at Ford's Highland Park, Michigan, plant in 1913–14 (Meyer, 1981; Rupert, 1995). Displacing predominantly craft-based production in which skilled laborers exercised substantial control over their conditions of work, Fordist production entailed an intensified industrial division of labor: it required increased mechanization and coordination of large scale manufacturing processes (e.g., sequential machining operations and converging assembly lines) to achieve a steady flow of production; a shift toward the use of less skilled labor performing, *ad infinitum*, tasks minutely specified by management; and the potential for heightened capitalist control over the pace and intensity of work. In the mid-1920s, one production worker described as follows the relentless and strenuous effort which his job required, and the consequences of failing to meet that standard on a daily basis: "You've got to work like hell in Ford's. From the time you become a number in the morning until the bell rings for quitting time you have to keep at it. You can't let up. You've got to get out the production . . . and if you can't get it out, you get out" (quoted in Rupert, 1995: 111). At the core of the Fordist reorganization of production, then, was the construction of new relations of power in the workplace; to the extent that these relations of power could become established parameters of the work process, capital would reap the gains of manifold increases in output per hour of waged labor.[5] The promise of massive increases in productivity led to the widespread imitation and adaptation of Ford's basic model of production through the industrial core of the US economy, and in other industrial capitalist countries.

Yet, while the system of mass production generated the potential for capital and its managerial agents to exert greater control over the performance of work, it did not guarantee the realization of that potential. In the forty years following the first experiments in line assembly at Highland Park, industrial struggles focusing on issues of unionization and the politics of production waxed and waned throughout the industrial sector of the US economy. This process entailed bouts of explicit class conflict during which the socio-political conditions of liberal capitalism were opened to potential challenge. Especially during the 1930s and 40s, industrial workers vigorously contested liberal capitalism's valorization of private property rights, and counterposed conceptions of "industrial democracy" and collective participation in work life—grounded in the more democratic aspects of popular common sense—in order to legitimate their new and embattled industrial unions. The relationship of industrial workers to the corporate giants which dominated the manufacturing heart of the US economy was not effectively stabilized until the militant industrial unions which arose in the 1930s were de-radicalized, incorporated into the social infrastructure of the American economy, and assigned a place in the ideology of liberal capitalism, becoming junior partners in the coalition which established American global hegemony in the postwar world. The relationship of industrial labor and American global power was consummated during the early years of the Cold War when the Congress of Industrial Organizations (CIO) purged its leadership of radicals and expelled entire unions which were perceived to be under communist leadership or influence, for example, because they criticized America's emerging global role and opposed the Marshall Plan. The CIO then embarked on a long period of active support for US global anti-communism (Sims, 1992; Rupert, 1995: 173–4).

In the context of rising Cold War fears and access to an unprecedented affluence (through pattern bargaining, rising real wages secured for unionized industrial workers, the linking of wages to productivity growth, Cost of Living Adjustments (COLAs), insurance, and pension plans, and so on), the challenge of industrial labor was contained within the bounds of a vision of liberal capitalism as the social system best able to secure—on a global basis, and with the active collaboration of "free trade unions"—individual rights and liberties and a more generalized prosperity. On the basis of union participation in this hegemonic world-vision, and their acceptance of its implied commitment to the priority of individual rights over collective self-determination, the state and capital accepted industrial unions as junior partners in the postwar project of reconstructing a liberal capitalist world order (Rupert, 1995: chs 4–7).

Liberal anti-communism was the ideological cement which bound industrial labor together with internationally-oriented segments of corporate capital in the project of reconstructing the postwar world economy along liberal capitalist lines. By 1950, Walter Reuther, the president of one of the most militant and progressive industrial unions in America, and Ford Motor Company, formerly one of the most violently intransigent anti-labor firms in America, had constructed political common ground on the basis of an ideology of global anti-communism, individual freedom, and prosperity secured through a modified capitalism in which corporations and unions would cooperate to increase productivity and deliver rising real standards of living for American workers and other peoples who would follow the American model of Fordism. Reuther delivered to President Truman an ambitious plan for a liberal capitalist world order, highlighting the importance of "free trade unions" for a successful Cold War strategy:

> We must meet the challenge of Communism, not by pious slogans about democracy's virtues, but by a positive program of social action that can and does win a fuller measure of social justice for people everywhere. . . . Instead of driving their bodies for the Soviet war machine, we propose to assist [those peoples putatively threatened by communist domination] in achieving decent wages, hours, working conditions and the right to collective bargaining.
>
> (Reuther, quoted in Rupert, 1995: 160–1)

Similarly, Ford Motor Company presented to its workers a vision of the Cold War world in which the right to collective bargaining was integral to the American system of liberty and prosperity:

> Right now the peoples of many nations are faced with a choice between Communism and Democracy . . . And they are looking to us for help and leadership. They are looking at the promise of individual reward that has stimulated American invention and business enterprise; at American technical progress which has performed miracles of mass production; at American workers free to organize, to bargain collectively with their employers . . . and constantly increasing real wages for shorter working hours.
>
> (Ford Motor Company, quoted in Rupert, 1995: 160–1)

These dualistic representations of world order struggles, and of the identity and role of "Americans," partake of the world-views which animated much of US postwar foreign policy, the unifying ideology of the postwar historic bloc. These statements and the ideology they reflect share the vision of "two worlds" articulated by Wilson and popularized by Capra, but they have updated this vision through the identification of the "world of light" and its liberties with liberal capitalism and the potential for a more widespread prosperity. Explicitly or implicitly, industrial workers and their unions are assigned a place (if only a subordinate one) in this world.

In a pivotal statement of US postwar policy, Harry Truman declared that the nations of the world confronted a choice "between alternative ways of life." One way he characterized in terms of popular sovereignty and the consent of the governed, protections of individual rights and liberties, and representative democracy; the other was totalitarian, coercive, and aggressive, "based upon the will of the minority forcibly imposed upon the majority." Echoing Wilson, Truman declared that "totalitarian regimes imposed on free peoples . . . undermine the foundations of international peace and hence the security of the United States." However, for Truman as for Reuther and Ford, the antidote to the perceived threat of (communist) tyranny and aggression entailed a more generalized prosperity made possible by American-style Fordist capitalism: "The seeds of totalitarian regimes are nurtured by misery and want. They spread and grow in the evil soil of poverty and strife. They reach their full growth when the hope of people for a better life has died. We must keep that hope alive" (Truman, quoted in Commager, 1958: 704–6). The Marshall Plan was the major policy initiative designed to foster (capitalist) prosperity within the "free world," and thus to secure its political stability, unity, and integration into the (capitalist) world order sponsored by the United States. Secretary of State George Marshall was explicit about the linkage of renewed capital accumulation, more widespread prosperity, and a reconstructed world order hospitable to American values and forms of social organization:

> The United States should do whatever it is able to do to assist in the return of normal economic health in the world, without which there can be no stability and no assured peace. . . . [Our goal] should be the revival of a working economy in the world so as to permit the emergence of political and social conditions in which free institutions can exist.
>
> (Marshall, quoted in Commager, 1958: 711–12)

In the hegemonic ideology of Cold War liberalism, liberty and prosperity were so closely identified that it became relatively easy to conflate capitalism and democracy, and thus to obscure, for a time, the deep-seated tensions between them.

The political ambiguities of Fordism in America

The political institutions of Fordism were profoundly ambiguous. On the one hand, they did enable working people to have some collective voice in the conditions under which they sold their labor-power, and they did provide organized labor with some recognition and influence within one of America's major political parties. These are real historical victories, hard won and not to be taken lightly. But the democratizing potential of Fordist political institutions was severely constrained. The collective bargaining which these institutions fostered and channeled was of an economistic nature, for the most part limited to wages, benefits, and working conditions, and was premised upon an acceptance of capitalist control of the labor process (in the form of a "workplace rule of law") and the prioritization of private profits as the primary social value (Rupert, 1995). Whereas the industrial union movement of the 1930s and 40s was a vibrant and polyvocal grassroots movement, central to which were political tendencies which envisioned a broad-based democratization of the capitalist economy under the banner of "industrial democracy," the unionism which was institutionalized under the Fordist regime was a bureaucratic and economically-oriented "business unionism." "This metamorphosis," Kim Moody explains, "involved the suppression of internal political life, the ritualization of the bargaining process, the expansion of the administrative apparatus to unprecedented levels, and the abandonment of the concept of social unionism that had been the public face of the CIO" (Moody, 1988: 41). Tendencies toward this officially sanctioned business unionism dammed and diverted the more solidaristic currents within the early industrial union movement, and in the early postwar years the CIO's Operation Dixie failed utterly to organize working people on a transracial basis in the American south. According to Michael Goldfield, this was a crucial strategic defeat, for it further solidified the power of business unionism within the CIO, left intact the system of racial supremacy in America, and undercut the possibilities for a broad-based politics of solidarity in the postwar US (Goldfield, 1997: 246–9).

Under the Fordist regime, then, organized labor was both empowered and disempowered. It was empowered to bargain over wages and working conditions, and thus to attempt to secure for its members a larger share of the social surplus which the Fordist organization of production made possible. But the condition of this empowerment of industrial unions was the disempowerment of their rank and file on the shop floor and within the increasingly hierarchic unions themselves, and the exclusion and repression of more broadly-based, explicitly political, transformative visions of what the union movement could be. Industrial unionism was empowered to cast its organized support behind the Democratic party and its modest agenda of social reform. But it was disempowered insofar as, for labor, there was no real political alternative to the Democratic party; the Democrats were well aware that they could afford to take organized labor's support for granted without major or sustained exertions on labor's behalf, and organized labor became politically dependent upon a Democratic party which was not prepared to challenge business hegemony in America or promote an agenda of transformative democratization.

The politics of Fordism were also ambiguous insofar as even its limited forms of empowerment were unevenly distributed across the working class, made available to some workers while excluding many others. These processes of inclusion/exclusion have not been race or gender-neutral, and this segmentation of the working class has been politically consequential. Gordon, Edwards, and Reich (1982: 192–210) document the emergence within the postwar US industrial economy of a sectoral division between an industrial "core" and an industrial "periphery." In the core, large and concentrated manufacturing firms enjoyed a growing productivity advantage over smaller manufacturing firms in the more hardscrabble peripheral sector. Core firms tended to be more densely unionized than the periphery, paid significantly higher wages (further, the core/periphery wage gap grew wider between 1958 and 1973–5), and offered somewhat greater job security. These latter tendencies are likely to have been mutually reinforcing for core firms, since unionization and higher wage rates create incentives for firms to invest in productivity-enhancing technology even as higher productivity enables these firms to purchase labor peace through collective bargaining with industrial unions.

As women and African-Americans entered the industrial labor force in greater numbers, segregation by race and gender interacted with labor market segmentation. Women and African-Americans were disproportionately represented in peripheral sector employment, and while they were also present in the core industries, they tended to be concentrated in the least rewarding and secure activities. According to Gordon et al. (1982: 210), 60 percent of Black workers were employed in secondary jobs (peripheral manufacturing or low-paid service sector) in 1970. Still more extreme was gendered division: "Four categories of female workers—those in the peripheral manufacturing industries, in retail trade, in clerical occupations, and in the health and educational sectors—accounted for 95 percent of all female employment in 1970" (Gordon et al., 1982: 206). Because women have been concentrated in less unionized industries—and have been subjected by the union movement itself to a long history of exclusionary gender discrimination—female workers have been less well represented within unions even though they have been more likely than men to want unionization (Freeman and Medoff, 1984; Nussbaum, 1998; AFL–CIO, 1999).

Nonetheless, it is too simple to claim that Fordist unions have been a white man's preserve or that their overall effect has been to increase inequality by creating a privileged industrial aristocracy. "Non-white" workers, for example, have been more likely than "whites" to belong to industrial unions (Freeman and Medoff, 1984: 27–30). And belonging to a union has tended to shield those workers, as well as unionized female workers, from the full effects of labor market discrimination: using Labor Department data for 1999, the AFL–CIO[6] reports that the union wage benefit (the difference between union and non-union wages) is 30 percent for all workers, 35 percent for women, 39 percent for African-Americans, and 55 percent for Latino workers (AFL–CIO, 2000). These data also reveal, however, that even *within the unionized workforce* the median weekly earnings of male workers are substantially higher than the overall median ($711 vs. $672), that this median male wage is higher than the median for women ($608), and that median wages for African-American ($575) and Latino ($561) workers are lower still. Despite these ambiguities, the authoritative study by Freeman and Medoff argues against the labor aristocracy thesis. Rather, they argue that three effects attributable to unions contribute to overall income equalization: "union wage policies lower inequality of wages *within* establishments; union wage policies favor equal pay for equal work *across* establishments; and union wage gains for blue-collar labor reduce inequality between white-collar and blue-collar workers" (Freeman and Medoff, 1984: 78). My own conclusion is more ambiguous: it seems to me that the unions of the Fordist regime have lessened, but also at the same time failed to eliminate—and to that extent may be said to have institutionalized—inequalities based on race and gender.

Finally, the politics of Fordism were ambiguous insofar as securing a livable wage for working class families came at the expense of women. Fordism reinforced the ideology of female domesticity by emphasizing a "family wage" sufficient to support the dependents of the breadwinner. In this way was normalized an understanding of "the family" as comprising dependent women and children as well as a male breadwinner. In the words of Martha May, "the family 'living wage' for male workers assumed that all women would, sooner or later, become wives, and thus it was legitimate to argue for the exclusion of women from the labor force. Working women were believed to devalue wages, making a 'living wage' difficult to achieve and upsetting a natural sexual order" (May, 1990: 277). Thus the family wage ideology implied the norm of a privatized life of domestic dependency for women, while it justified paying female workers lower wages since the implicit norm suggested that women either were, or should be, provided for by the family wage earned by a husband or father.

In all of these ways, then, the politics of Fordism were deeply ambiguous—progressive and enabling of democratic self-determination in some ways while divisive and disempowering in others. But the historical structures underpinning such politics were not to last.

Restructuring capitalism; contesting hegemony

In the first decade of the twenty-first century the Fordist world order is under great strain. Following on the disintegration of the "Evil Empire," the Cold War has been officially pronounced to be over: anti-communism can no longer serve as a crucial ingredient in the ideological cement binding together the postwar historic bloc. The vision of "two worlds," which helped Americans to make sense of their place in the postwar world order, seems no longer to have a clear referent. Further, the postwar prosperity which US industrial labor had enjoyed as a result of its participation in the hegemonic bloc is evaporating.

After the mid-1960s, the remarkable productivity growth which Fordism had generated began to slow down; perhaps because, among other factors, the institutional framework of Fordism along with relatively full employment had the effect of sheltering core workers from the potential violence of the labor market and lessened the disciplinary power of capital in the workplace (see Moody, 1988: ch. 4; Bowles et al., 1990, ch. 7).[7] As productivity growth slowed, profit rates declined (for evidence, see Harvey, 1989: 143; Bowles et al., 1990: 79). Capital and the state responded harshly. Beginning in the late 1970s, the Federal Reserve enacted austere monetary policies designed to "squeeze inflation out of the economy" by maintaining relatively higher levels of interest rates, unemployment, and insecurity among people who must work for a living. Unions—the central institutions of "industrial democracy" in Fordist America—were subjected to intensified attacks by the state and capital, union memberships continued their long-term decline, and real wages were effectively reduced even as productivity growth rebounded somewhat during the 1980s (Goldfield, 1987; Moody, 1988, 1997a; Gordon, 1996; Mishel et al., 1997: 131–5, 166–8). With the mutation of the postwar historic bloc such that transnational financial and industrial capital are increasingly predominant and industrial labor within the US is no longer a relatively privileged junior partner, socio-political relations and popular ideologies which once seemed firmly grounded are now increasingly up for grabs.

In sharp contrast to the central presuppositions of Fordist hegemony, working Americans increasingly realize that they live in an environment where corporate profits need not correspond to rising standards of living or improved quality of life for themselves and their co-workers, and that their ability to exercise any control at all over their economic futures is, under current institutional arrangements, quite limited. Long-term tendencies toward transnational production, corporate "restructuring," subcontracting and outsourcing, plant closings and layoffs, concessionary bargaining and union-busting, increasing exploitation of part-time and contingent workers, declining real wages, widening and deepening poverty, and economic uncertainty among average Americans has in the past decade been juxtaposed to news of resurgent corporate profits, happy days on Wall Street, and breathtaking inequalities of income and wealth. In this context, the liberal vision of a transnational order institutionalizing the values of freedom and prosperity—most firmly embedded in popular common sense during the postwar decades—may begin to seem bitterly ironic to growing numbers of Americans.

Once solidly hegemonic, the liberal narrative of globalization is now increasingly vulnerable to challenge. The liberal narrative associates capitalism and globally competitive markets with prosperity and liberty (understood in terms of individual choice). In the socio-political circumstances of the century's beginning, however, average Americans might be more likely to find some plausibility in narratives which claim that global capitalism can be relied upon to deliver neither prosperity nor liberty; rather, that it delivers these to socially privileged groups at the expense of the majority.

A constellation of factors (including surplus capacity and de-industrialization, the shift toward service employment, de-unionization, and increasing vulnerability to trade and the transnational mobility of capital) have all contributed to a palpable shift in social power in favor of capital and capitalists and to the disadvantage of workers, communities, and unions. Indicators of this shift are not hard to find. After rising steadily through the postwar decades, the real wages of production and non-supervisory workers have been declining more-or-less steadily since 1972–3. Further, after dramatic reduction between 1964 and 1974, the proportion of workers earning wages insufficient to support a family of four above the official poverty level increased by 50 percent between 1974 and 1990. By the latter year, according to more conservative estimates, almost one in five year-round full-time workers was earning below-poverty wages (US Census Bureau, 1996a: 3; compare Mishel et al., 1997: 149–56).

The proportion of the workforce engaged in provision of services has increased from around 50 percent in 1950 to about 75 percent in 1990; there has also been a decline in manufacturing employment from around 35 percent to about 22 percent of the labor force. This is significant because the service sector is typically less productive and pays substantially lower wages than manufacturing. In 1993, average hourly compensation (wages + benefits) in services was $15.51, compared with $20.22 in goods production (Folbre, 1995: 2.2–2.3). So a shift in the composition of the economy away from manufacturing and toward services would tend to lower overall productivity and overall wages.

However, declining overall rates of productivity growth resulting from an increasingly service-based economy cannot explain why compensation has lagged behind productivity since the mid-1960s. During the "golden years" of postwar Fordism, real wages rose steadily along with productivity (Rupert, 1995: 179). That relationship has since been severed: productivity continues to rise (albeit more slowly than during the "golden age"), while real wages have generally been declining and total compensation (wages + benefits) has not done much better (Mishel et al., 1997: 131–8).[8]

Accounting for over 80 percent of total employment in the US, according to David Gordon, production and non-supervisory workers "represent that group in the labor force that is most clearly dependent on wage and salary income. They include both blue collar and white collar workers, both unskilled and skilled. They cover not only laborers and machinists, but also secretaries, programmers and teachers" (Gordon, 1996: 18). To approximate take-home pay, Gordon estimated real spendable hourly earnings for these workers, and then calculated the average annual rates of growth (from business cycle peak to peak): real take-home pay grew by about 2.1 percent yearly from 1948–66; slowed to a 1.4 percent growth rate from 1966–73; then declined by almost 1 percent a year from 1973–89; and continued to shrink by about 0.6 percent annually from 1989–94 (1996: 18–20; see also Mishel et al., 1997: 140). Gordon concludes that a "wage collapse" has occurred:

> By 1994 . . . real hourly take-home pay had dropped by 10.4 percent since its postwar peak in 1972. More dramatically still, *real spendable hourly earnings had fallen back below the level they had last reached in 1967*. Growing massively over those nearly three decades, the economy's real gross output per capita in 1994 was 53 percent larger than it had been in 1967, but real hourly take-home pay was four cents lower.
>
> (Gordon, 1996: 20, emphasis in original)

Moreover, evidence suggests that this "wage collapse" for production and non-supervisory workers is not ameliorated even if non-wage benefits are included in measures of real hourly compensation (Gordon, 1996: 31; Mishel et al., 1997: 135–8).

Contrary to the claims of many mainstream economists (e.g., Burtless et al., 1998: 63), Doug Henwood, editor of *Left Business Observer*, explains that sluggish productivity growth is an inadequate explanation for the wage collapse:

> We're constantly told by economists and pundits that the key to getting wages up again is raising productivity. But over the last several decades, productivity—the inflation-adjusted value of output per hour of work—has risen much faster than real compensation (wages plus fringe benefits adjusted for inflation) . . . Here's another way to think about the growing gap between productivity and wages. According to the World Bank, in 1966, U.S. manufacturing wages were equal to 46% of the value added in production (value-added is the difference between selling price and the costs of raw material and other inputs). In 1990, that figure had fallen to 36%.
>
> (Henwood, 1997a)

Academic economists have not rushed to embrace this thesis of intensified exploitation. For example, Gary Burtless and his co-authors claim that if real wages and total compensation are measured in such a way as to reflect faster productivity growth in the producer goods sector (machinery, equipment, computers)—that is, if wages are corrected for inflation in investment goods as well as in consumer goods—then overall inflation appears to be lower and real compensation appears not to have lagged behind overall productivity at all. By this statistical legerdemain, they suggest that compensation and productivity have actually moved in tandem, and that compensation is growing more slowly simply because of slower productivity growth (Burtless et al., 1998: 60, 63–4). This analytical maneuver would make sense only if workers used their pay to purchase means of production; but, of course, they do not. Despite the liberal triumphalism of recent years, the classical Marxian concept of class based upon relationship to the means of production surely has some purchase in the contemporary American political economy. Ownership of the means of production is concentrated within the wealthiest 10 percent of American families: according to Federal Reserve data for 1995, this top decile owned 84 percent of the stock and 90 percent of the bonds owned by individuals (including indirect ownership through mutual funds), as well as 92 percent of business assets. And ownership of these financial and business assets is even more highly concentrated in the upper reaches of the top decile: the richest 1 percent of the population owned over 42 percent of stocks, almost 56 percent of bonds, and more than 71 percent of business assets (Federal Reserve data reported in Henwood, 1997d). On the classical Marxian view, the private ownership of the means of production (and appropriation of its product by the owning class) presupposes the existence of a class of people who are, from day to day, dependent upon the sale of their labor-power to secure the necessities of life. Bowles and Edwards report that in 1988, the richest 1 percent of US families (enjoying annual incomes of more than $1 million) received almost three-quarters of their income from property ownership in the form of profit, interest, capital gain, rents, and royalties. This contrasts markedly with the great majority of families who are primarily dependent upon wage labor to enable them to meet their needs and who are, therefore, more or less fully subject to the manifold relations of power and domination which inhere in the capitalist wage relation. In 1988, the 46 million families whose incomes fell between $20,000 and $75,000 dollars received almost 84 percent of their income from labor (Bowles and Edwards, 1993: 105). With a seemingly prosaic technical "correction," Burtless and his co-authors would mask these relations of class in the US political economy: presuming, in effect, that there is no such thing as class, they are then able to argue that no class-based effects of globalization are apparent. Given the premises, the conclusion is not altogether surprising.

The vigorous evasive action of mainstream economists notwithstanding, it seems to me difficult to escape the conclusion that working people in

post-Fordist America are less able to lay claim to the fruits of their growing productivity. This intensified exploitation of workers is a large part of
the explanation for higher corporate profits, a roaring stock market, and
growth in executive compensation so extravagant that even the business
press seems embarrassed.

The labor-oriented Economic Policy Institute concurs that a significant
power shift in favor of capital has occurred. According to EPI economist
Lawrence Mishel (1997), whereas "labor's share of corporate sector income rose from 79.2 percent in 1959 to 83.9 percent in 1979," it had
declined to about 81 percent by 1996. In the manufacturing sector, the
reversal has been sharper still (Mishel, 1997). Correspondingly, EPI reported that over the last business cycle corporate profit rates have hit
peaks substantially higher than the profit peak of the rabidly pro-business
Reagan–Bush years, despite the fact that levels of investment are propor-
tionally similar:

> Corporate profits have risen by approximately 62 percent in real
> terms over the last five years, an average rate of more than 10 percent
> annually. No period in the postwar era has seen such rapid profit
> growth. This growth is even more striking in light of the fact that
> the economy was actually growing relatively slowly over this period.
> The average rate of economic growth from 1992 to 1997 was just 2.9
> percent. . . . Since economic growth has been comparatively slow dur-
> ing this upturn, the main factor pushing up profits has been redistribu-
> tion from wages. The capital share of net corporate income was 21.7
> percent in 1997; the previous business cycle saw [capital's share] peak
> at 18.7 percent in 1988. There is no precedent in the postwar period
> for this sort of upward redistribution.
>
> (Baker, 1998: 1; see also Baker and Mishel, 1995)

Conditions favoring extraordinary levels of corporate profitability have
translated into rich rewards for investors. According to Henwood, recent
record highs on Wall Street (the Dow first surging past 7,000, and then 8,
9, 10, and 11,000) represent the crest of a wave which has been building
for years: "Over the last 15 years, the real (inflation-adjusted) Standard &
Poor's 500 index, a proxy for blue-chip corporate America, is up 574%,
by far the biggest 15 year real rise since good statistics start in 1886; in
1964, it was 434%; in 1929, 205%. By most conventional measures of
whether stocks are reasonably priced, the market is at or near historic
extremes." Not only have investors made out like bandits on the apprecia-
tion of their assets, but they have also been receiving generous dividends:
"firms are paying out near-record shares of their profits to their stock-
holders—70% of after-tax profits since 1982, [almost] twice historical
averages." Henwood suggests that, Alan Greenspan notwithstanding,
this "exuberance" in the markets is not altogether "irrational," but rather

"stock markets are celebrating the political triumph of capital worldwide" (Henwood, 1997b: 1). It is increasingly common now to encounter claims that growing participation in mutual funds and pension plans has "democratized" the ownership of capital, implying (among other things) that the benefits of a booming stock market are widely shared. For example, Thomas Friedman, global affairs columnist of the *New York Times*, baldly declares: "For the first time in American history both Joe Six-pack and Billionaire Bob are watching CNBC to see how their shares in the market are faring" (Friedman, 1999a: 105). It is important, however, to remember that ownership of financial and business assets remains highly concentrated among the very rich (Henwood, 1997d), and the great bulk of the gains from the stock market boom have accrued to the top 10 percent of US households (see Mishel et al., 1997: 287–92).

If the 1990s have been good to members of the investor class who derive the bulk of their income from the ownership of financial and business assets, they have also been happy times for corporate executives (who, as recipients of large stock options, are also members of the investor class). In 1978, the average American corporate CEO earned about 60 times as much as the average worker; by 1995 the average CEO was pulling down 172 times as much as his workers. The compensation of the average CEO grew by 152 percent between 1978 and 1995, rising to more than $4.3 million annually (Mishel et al., 1997: 226). Even *Business Week* allowed as how executive compensation was "out of control" (Reingold, 1997).

In an environment where the rewards to corporate managers and investors have far outstripped the wages of working people, it should not be surprising to discover that inequalities of income and wealth are at historically high levels. According to the US Census Bureau, income inequality increased markedly between 1968 and 1994, such that the income gap between rich and poor was wider in 1994 than at any time since 1947, when they began collecting such data (US Census Bureau, 1996b). By 1997, the top 5 percent of families received 20.7 percent of aggregate income, a postwar record and substantially more than the share of the bottom 40 percent of families who together received only 14.1 percent (Economic Policy Institute, 1999). Inequality of wealth is even more stark than the income gap. The top 1 percent now control more wealth than the bottom 90 percent of the population (Henwood 1997d; see also Wolff, 1995: 7; and Mishel et al., 1997: 278–81).

Working people have not shared in this bounty, in fact it has been predicated upon their re-subjection to more direct forms of class-based power. Formerly privileged as junior partners in the postwar hegemonic bloc, unions have been the object of a sustained assault in recent decades (Moody, 1988), and union membership has been declining since the 1950s (Goldfield, 1987). Recent figures show the continuing decline of the union movement from over 20 percent of wage and salary workers in 1983 to

14.5 percent in 1996. This is directly related to declining real wages since unionized workers enjoy a substantial pay advantage over the non-unionized (as well as creating significant "spillover" effects into non-unionized workplaces): in 1996, median weekly earnings for unionized workers were $615, compared to $462 for workers without union representation (US Bureau of Labor Statistics, 1997). But even unionized workers have been on the defensive since the early 1980s, negotiating dramatically smaller pay increases and ever more reluctant to invoke the strike weapon (Rupert, 1995: 183–7). This decline of union power translates into a lessened ability for working people to bargain collectively and thereby to have a voice in determining the conditions of their labor (for further evidence, see Mishel et al., 1997: 198–203).

The Economic Policy Institute claims that increasing trade, especially imports of manufactured goods from developing countries, has contributed to de-industrialization and job losses in the US, and has put downward pressure on the wages of industrial workers (Mishel et al., 1997: 190–7). But the effects of globalization go far beyond the relatively small (if also growing) proportion of the US economy affected by imported goods. Employers throughout the economy are fully aware of the fearful dependence of working people upon their jobs, and in an era of transnationalized production they are prepared to exploit this economic insecurity as a source of workplace power. This is clearly demonstrated by the fact that employers now commonly threaten to close plants and eliminate jobs when they are faced with unionization drives or new collective bargaining situations. According to one of the most comprehensive and systematic studies of unionization campaigns in the post-NAFTA period (Bronfenbrenner, 1997), this type of workplace extortion has taken a variety of forms: "specific unambiguous threats ranged from attaching shipping labels to equipment throughout the plant with a Mexican address, to posting maps of North America with an arrow pointing from the current plant site to Mexico, to a letter directly stating that the company will have to shut down if the union wins the election." One firm shut down a production line without warning and "parked thirteen flat-bed tractor-trailers loaded with shrink-wrapped production equipment in front of the plant for the duration" of the unionization campaign, marked with large hot pink signs reading "Mexico Transfer Job." Between 1993 and 1995, such threats accompanied at least half of all union certification elections (Bronfenbrenner, 1997: 8–9). In the words of one auto worker contemplating his future in a transnationalized economy, the threat of runaway jobs "puts the fear in you" (quoted in Rupert, 1995: 195); and, indeed, it is intended to do so. For it is the threat of transnational capital mobility and job loss, combined with the ideologies of "global competitiveness" and "workplace cooperation," which represent the articulation of coercion and consent in the post-Fordist workplace (Moody, 1997a).[9]

The restructuring of Fordist historical structures has had important gendered dimensions. Linda McDowell (1991) has argued that the restructuring of Fordist political economy in Britain has entailed a dismantling of a corresponding set of historical structures to which she refers as the Fordist gender order: "That old order, based on a stable working class, on the nuclear family supported by a male breadwinner and by women's domestic labor underpinned by Keynesian economic and welfare policies that ensured the reproduction of the working class, is passing from view" (McDowell, 1991: 403). The classic conceptualization of patriarchy, wherein men appropriate the unpaid domestic labor of women—the product of which is the labor-power sold by male workers as if it were entirely their own—may have been most appropriate to the Fordist form of capitalism with its institutionalized norm of the family wage. In recent decades, restructuring of capitalist enterprise has undermined the family wage and women have entered the labor market in growing numbers, especially among the ranks of part-time and contingent workers. At the same time, the neoliberalism of Thatcher and Reagan resulted in abandonment of the Keynesian policies which supported the regime of the family wage, and reductions in the social services and benefits which contributed to the reproduction of working class families. The gendered effects of these transformations thus include a heightening of the double burden upon women, a condition which might be described as a sort of "social speed-up" (1991: 416).

> During the 1980s, for the many working class women propelled into the labor market by economic necessity, as well as a desire for greater independence, two incomes were essential to maintain their previous standard of living. This means that these families are now doing three jobs for the price of one previously: two in the paid labor force and one unpaid at home—the labor of household work and child rearing—if it is accepted that previously the male "family wage" reflected some contribution towards the unpaid domestic labor of female partners.
>
> (McDowell, 1991: 415)

These burdens have not been equally distributed among all women: rather, it is working class women who bear the brunt of the social speed-up, while those middle class women who are able to gain access to core labor markets and professional occupations may be able to purchase on the market commodities and services formerly produced within the household (perhaps ironically, by employing working class women relegated to the lowest-paying segments of the service sector). These processes of restructuring, then, have included the degradation of the labor market position of many working class men, the social speed-up for working class women, and labor market progress for middle class women, all of which adds up to "a widening of class divisions and a narrowing of gender divisions in the labor market" (1991: 411). McDowell suggests that this points toward a possible convergence of class and gender politics: "In this latest round in the continuous struggle over the control of women's labor, the majority of women *and* men are losing. Capital is the beneficiary" (1991: 416).

Evidence suggests that tendencies similar to those described by McDowell are at work in the US. It remains true that women are more likely than men to earn low wages: "In 1995, 36.8 percent of women earned poverty-level wages or less, significantly more than the share of men (23.3 percent). Women are also much less likely to earn very high wages. In 1995, only 6.1 percent of women, but 13.5 percent of men, earned at least three times the poverty level wage" (Mishel et al., 1997: 151). However, the wages of formerly privileged male workers have been under nearly relentless pressure for twenty years, driving the wages of most male workers closer to those of women: "from 1979 to 1989, the median hourly wage fell $1.25 for men and rose $0.49 for women. These moves led to a growth in the hourly wage ratio between men and women by 10.6 percentage points, from 62.8 percent in 1979 to 73.1 percent in 1989, representing a sizable reduction in gender wage inequality" (Mishel et al., 1997: 147). Since 1989, the median wage for both male and female workers has been falling, but female wages have fallen more slowly, leading the gender wage ratio to rise still further to 76.7 percent. While the gender gap has been compressed by the de-privileging of all but the most highly paid male workers, inequality has increased among women working outside the home. In the period 1979–89, the bottom 20 percent of female wage earners lost ground, the middle deciles gained modestly, and the wages of the top 20 percent of women workers grew rapidly. Between 1989–95, on the other hand, only the top 20 percent of female wage workers experienced any growth at all (with the exception of the very bottom 10 percent, which may have benefited from minimum-wage legislation). So there has been a marked dispersion among female wage earners since 1979, with the top 20 percent pulling away from the rest (Mishel et al., 1997: 145–7). Economic restructuring has had the effect of reducing, if hardly eliminating, gender divisions within the waged workforce, while heightening the class-based oppression of both men and women workers.

That something profound was happening to Fordism's version of "the American Dream" was brought home to many people by waves of corporate "restructuring," often involving massive layoffs of blue-collar workers and middle managers. The Institute for Policy Studies released a report showing that CEOs who engineered major layoffs received higher than average pay raises (including stock options), that Wall Street tended to reward layoffs by bidding up the stock prices of these firms when layoffs were announced, and that CEOs and investors together enjoyed windfalls from these bouts of job destruction (Anderson and Cavanagh, 1996). For a time, this theme received intense media attention. Major journalistic interpretations of the end of the Dream were serialized in the *Philadelphia*

Inquirer and the *New York Times*, and were subsequently republished in book form (Barlett and Steele, 1992, 1996; New York Times, 1996). These were narratives of the profit motive run amok, of corporate power and arrogance overriding the simple decency of average working people. Media attention to these issues seemed to reach a crescendo in early 1996, when the *New York Times* published its "Downsizing of America" series, and Pat Buchanan made the plight of American working people one of the primary themes of his right-populist Presidential campaign. During this period, stories about corporate downsizing were commonplace in the mainstream media, sometimes coming close to questioning the presumptive priority of profit maximization as a social norm. *Newsweek* ran a controversial cover story on the architects of major corporate restructuring plans whom it identified as "the Hit Men": the story highlighted the tens of thousands of jobs recently liquidated by top corporate CEOs and juxtaposed these figures with their million-dollar salaries (26 February, 1996).

There is some evidence that these experiences and their interpretation in terms of arrogant and unresponsive corporate power have begun to effect changes in popular common sense, changes which may not bode well for the hegemonic ideology of liberal capitalism. The 1997 strike of package handlers and drivers at United Parcel Service (UPS) evoked much greater sympathy from the public at large than other major industrial actions of recent decades. In its representations of strike issues, the Teamsters' union highlighted the usage of lower-paid part-time workers by UPS to create a two-tiered wage system, and this issue appears to have resonated with people attempting to make a living in a post-Fordist America where many fear being relegated to the growing sector of part-time, temporary, or contingent workers, earning substantially lower hourly wages and more meager benefits than full-time "core" employees (Mishel et al., 1997: 257–61, 265–71; Uchitelle, 1997; Carre and Tilly, 1998). Survey data suggest that a majority of the public claimed to support the striking Teamsters' union while just over one-quarter voiced support for UPS management. This reflects what may be a longer-term weakening of a core element of Fordist hegemony: the presumptive identification of American working people with the interests and profits of employers. In 1984, 34 percent of the public claimed generally to support labor in industrial disputes, while 45 percent said they favored management; in 1996 responses to a similar survey question suggested that 44 percent favored workers while only 24 percent were predisposed toward management. John J. Sweeney, president of the AFL–CIO, explained how the expansion of corporate profits at the expense of the American Dream has made working people more responsive to the union's message: "People understand when you talk to them about the transition from full-time, middle-income jobs to part-time, low-income jobs" (Greenhouse, 1997a). When you speak to people now about the death of the American Dream as they had come to know it during the postwar decades, they may be more ready to listen.

Much celebrated have been recent wage gains which, between 1996–8, reached down to even low-income workers and which seem to have lent renewed credibility to the capitalist-friendly metaphor that a rising tide floats all boats. However, the Economic Policy Institute puts this wage growth in perspective: "Historically, increases in productivity have meant growth in real compensation for much of the workforce. . . . however, the gap between productivity and the median wages of both males and females grew through the 1989–96 period, and, despite the stronger wage growth since 1996, this gap between the economy's growth and the growth of workers' wages remains significant. Even with the recent growth spurt in wages, the economic fortunes of the median worker continue to diverge from the overall growth in the economy" (Bernstein and Mishel, 1999: 3). Moreover, recent wage gains are largely attributable to a conjuncture of tight labor markets at the peak of a long business cycle upswing, low inflation, and the federally mandated minimum-wage increase. These conjunctural gains do not portend a significant shift in what we might call the "underlying fundamentals" of the US political economy: the relative disempowerment of people who depend upon wages to live.

This, then, is the historical-structural context in which battles over the meaning of "globalization" are being waged. The hegemonic bloc of the Fordist period is being restructured, and organized labor in the US finds itself shut out of its once privileged position, denied access to the affluence it took for granted during the postwar "golden years," and deprived of a meaningful voice in the conventional political process. The agenda of capital accumulation dominates both major parties just as capital itself dominates the economy. Ordinary Americans find themselves struggling with social power relations obscured from, and by, the hegemonic ideology of liberal capitalism. Under these circumstances, it seems to me unwise to presume that the formerly dominant ideology will continue to define the ways in which "globalization" will be interpreted and acted upon. Rather, the meanings assigned to globalization, and the kinds of political projects enabled by these world-views, will be determined by struggles waged on the terrain of popular common sense.

3 The hegemonic project of liberal globalization

There is no reason to believe that liberal globalization is ineluctable. Contrary to much of the evolutionary imagery or technological determinism which is often invoked to explain it (for example Friedman, 1999a: 7–8, 18, 285), globalization has been neither spontaneous nor inevitable; it has been the political project of an identifiable constellation of dominant social forces and it has been, and continues to be, politically problematic and contestable. Indeed, the very idea that there have been significant tendencies in the world political economy which might usefully be described as "globalization" is vigorously contested. This chapter will sketch out a case claiming that although it may be possible to exaggerate the extent and significance of globalization, real material processes are underway which are creating new possibilities for meaningful transnational social relations. How, or indeed whether, these possibilities are realized will depend upon the outcomes of current social struggles, struggles in which the meanings assigned to "globalization" are central.[1]

In the first part of the chapter, I will provide a brief historical account of the social power bloc whose hegemonic project has been to construct a liberalized transnational order. Then I will survey some of the more salient evidence to support my claim that globalization is a real material process pregnant with potential political significance. Finally, I will show how this bloc has publicly justified its project of liberal globalization in the context of US debates over the North American Free Trade Agreement (NAFTA) and the Uruguay Round of the General Agreement on Tariffs and Trade (GATT). In particular, I will examine the pro-NAFTA–GATT representations of academic economists, business people, lobbyists, and newspaper reporters and commentators in the mainstream press. I will argue that these representations partake of a hegemonic ideology, that they presuppose and thereby naturalize an image of social life framed in terms of abstract individuals interacting freely in an apolitical market, and that their political project entails the projection of this image on a global scale. Then, in subsequent chapters, the basic terms of these representations will be contrasted with those of critics of globalization situated both to the left and the right of the hegemonic liberal internationalist position.

Globalization in question?

The very idea of "globalization" is the object of controversy. Some of the more dramatic and simplistic versions of the globalization thesis have been challenged by scholars and journalists who are skeptical about the actual extent of transnationalized economic activity, and about the social and political effects which are frequently imputed to it (Gordon, 1988, 1996: 187–97; Hirst and Thompson, 1996; Henwood, 1997c). Common to these critics is a reluctance to embrace facile claims that the universal is negating the particular; that globalized economic relations are supplanting more familiar social relations, cultural identities, and political forms; and that we have therefore entered a qualitatively new era of human social history. Rather than rehearse these debates, I will stake out a position rejecting dichotomized views of globalization as either a wholly new world, or as nothing more than old wine in a new, spherical bottle. I will instead acknowledge the need for a more nuanced vision of globalization as a historical process which is not altogether novel or unprecedented; which is incomplete and uneven, ambiguous and often contradictory in its effects; and which is integrally related—if not entirely reducible—to the historical process of capitalist social development.[2]

Capitalism is a social order which is premised upon accumulation for its own sake, endless accumulation; and, as such, it recognizes neither spatial nor social boundaries. Anticipating a process of capitalist globalization with broad social implications, Marx and Engels famously declared in 1848: "The bourgeoisie cannot exist without constantly revolutionizing the instruments of production, and thereby the relations of production, and with them the whole relations of society. . . . The need of a constantly expanding market for its products chases the bourgeoisie over the whole surface of the globe. It must nestle everywhere, settle everywhere, establish connections everywhere" (Marx and Engels, 1977: 224). On this view, globalization is not so much a break with the past as its continuation; it represents the ongoing, if episodic, development of the capitalist organization of production and its historically associated social forms. These historical structures—the particular economic, political, and cultural forms with which capitalism is articulated in particular times and places—are sites of social power relations and objects of struggle among social agents positioned within these structures. As such, their reproduction is problematic, and contingent upon the outcomes of various historically specific struggles.

Capitalism's globalizing tendencies have been substantially realized in a particular historical context, and this has been the political project of a transnational historic bloc comprised of particular fractions of the capitalist class, state managers and international bureaucrats, journalists, and mainstream labor leaders (van der Pijl, 1984, 1997, 1998: ch. 4; Cox, 1987; Gill, 1990; Rupert, 1995; Sklair, 1997). In a classic work of modern

Marxist scholarship, Kees van der Pijl mapped the decades-long process of formation of a transatlantic ruling class in the early–mid-twentieth century: "In this era, the specific form and content of the internationalization of capital allowed the bourgeoisie in the North Atlantic area to regroup and develop a series of *comprehensive concepts of control* by which it could reinforce its hegemonial position both nationally and . . . internationally" (van der Pijl, 1984: xiii).

Around the turn of the last century, transatlantic finance was the predominant form of the internationalization of capital. Huge volumes of European, and especially British, portfolio investment had poured into North America to finance economic development in the late nineteenth and early twentieth centuries. By the end of World War I, the allies had borrowed such vast sums from American bankers that Wall Street had become the world's financial center. The class fractions most closely associated with this "Atlantic circuit of money capital" represented a liberal-internationalist concept of control, a frame of reference "in which the free flow of . . . merchandise, dividends, or cash crops is guaranteed by a set of conditions including free trade, unhampered competition, and cosmopolitanism" (van der Pijl, 1984: 10). These laissez-faire fundamentalists were predominantly international bankers, but also included merchants and agricultural interests engaged in transatlantic trade, as well as some allies among relatively labor-intensive manufacturers who were financially tied to the bankers. However, as mass production industry emerged in the US, large American manufacturing firms penetrated foreign markets, reshaped the global division of labor, and set new standards of productivity and competitiveness worldwide (Rupert, 1995: 67–78). The predominance of money capital and its liberal-internationalist world-view were increasingly challenged by the rising class fraction representing large-scale, Fordist industrial capital and its associated "productive capital concept," which tended to be more critical of "unproductive" and volatile money capital and its reign through unregulated markets. This emerging intra-class critique took on added force in the wake of financial collapse and global crisis in the interwar years. As fascism and then war engulfed continental Europe, a new ruling class strategy was emerging in the US which would form the basis for a hegemonic vision of transnational capitalist order—"the synthesis between the original laissez-faire liberalism of the liberal-internationalist fraction . . . and the state intervention elicited by the requirements of large-scale industry and organized labor, which in the period between the wars accompanied various forms of class conciliation generally referred to as corporatism" (van der Pijl, 1984: xiv–xv):

> Eventually, a synthetic concept, *corporate liberalism*, would crystallize in the United States in the context of American control of the Atlantic circuit of money capital and the generalization of Fordism as a productivist class compromise. This corporate–liberal synthesis between

internationalism, a flexible format of labor relations, and state intervention was eventually extrapolated to Western Europe where it served as the vantage point from which successive concepts of Atlantic unity were developed, and to which the entire Atlantic ruling class would in due course adhere.

(van der Pijl, 1984: 10)

It was this proto-hegemonic world-view—along with the common ground provided by postwar anti-communism—which enabled something of an uneasy alliance between Keynesian planners (committed to national economic policies directed toward steady economic growth and full employment) and liberal internationalists (committed to financial stability and multilateral free trade). Although these groups of state managers and the associated class fractions continued to struggle over issues of relative emphasis, the reconstruction of the liberal capitalist world economy after World War II was shaped by the interaction of their visions (Block, 1977b; Aaronson, 1996).

Constructing the institutional infrastructure of international trade and finance, this historic bloc fostered the growth of international trade and investment through the postwar decades, especially within and between the so-called "triad" regions. Successive rounds of the multilateral GATT regime reduced tariff barriers "so that by the end of the Tokyo Round in 1979 they were lower among OECD countries than during the classical Gold Standard era, and reductions agreed during the Uruguay round reduced them still further" (Held et al., 1999: 164). In this context, trade led the postwar boom, with trade in manufactured goods expanding most dramatically (Dicken, 1992: 18; World Trade Organization, 1998: 8). Held and his co-authors summarize in the following terms the development of a global trading regime:

> By the 1970s a largely free trade order had been established among all the OECD countries and since the 1980s this has been extended to developing countries and countries formerly closed to trade under communism, with the result that a global trading system now exists. Historically, protection levels are lower than in previous eras while trade liberalization is likely to continue. Trade levels are higher, both absolutely and in relation to output, than ever before.
>
> (Held et al., 1999: 167)

Moreover, with the founding of the World Trade Organization in 1995, the infrastructure of liberalization has been substantially strengthened and extended. The WTO wields unprecedented powers of surveillance and enforcement, and has extended its ambit to include trade in services as well as trade-related investment and intellectual property issues (World Trade Organization, 1998). This reflects a broadening of the agenda of liberalization beyond tariff reduction to encompass "harmonization" of (formerly "domestic") rules and regulations governing business insofar as these appear, from the liberal perspective, as potential non-tariff barriers to trade.

Liberal globalization has not been limited to trade, however. In the realm of finance, excess liquidity from consistent US balance of payments deficits, the collapse of the Bretton Woods fixed rate regime and its associated capital controls, the recycling of petrodollars, and the emergence of offshore xenocurrency markets, together resulted in astonishing volumes of foreign exchange trading and speculative international investment which now dwarf the currency reserves of governments and can readily swamp, or leave high and dry, the financial markets of particular nations (Wachtel, 1990; Agnew and Corbridge, 1995: 171–8; Held et al., 1999: 199–235). Citing data from the Bank of International Settlements, Held and his co-authors indicate the unprecedented magnitudes of these flows:

> The annual turnover of foreign exchange has grown astronomically from an already huge $17.5 trillion in 1979 to over $300 trillion today; this is a working daily turnover of over $1.4 trillion. Although international trade has always been a key source of demand for foreign exchange, the latter has grown from over ten times world trade flows in 1979 to over fifty times today. Official foreign exchange reserves for all countries combined represent about one day's trading volume on these markets.
>
> (Held et al., 1999: 209)

Responding to short-term differences in perceived conditions of profitability and variations in business confidence between one place and another, these enormous speculative flows are highly volatile. Massive amounts can be shifted from one currency (or assets denominated in one currency) to another literally at the speed of light via the computer modems and fiber optic cables which link together the world's financial markets and enable round-the-clock trading. These changes have been consequential, for the new historical structures embody an enhancement of the social powers of capital, and especially finance capital, which can effectively pre-empt expansionary macro-policies aimed at increasing employment or wage levels. "Financial globalization increases the incentives for governments to pursue national macroeconomic strategies which seek low and stable rates of inflation, through fiscal discipline and a tight monetary policy, since these appeal to global financial markets" (Held et al., 1999: 230). Accordingly, the globalization of finance has been accompanied by a resurgence of laissez-faire fundamentalism since the late 1970s, as neoliberal austerity has largely eclipsed the growth-oriented ideology which originally underpinned the postwar world economy (Gill, 1990: ch. 5; Wachtel, 1990; Agnew and Corbridge, 1995: ch. 7).

A third important aspect of postwar processes of globalization has been the emergence of multinational firms and the transnational organization of production. One indicator of this development is the dramatic growth in direct foreign investment (DFI), reflecting increases in the magnitude of transnational enterprise: "for most of the postwar period stocks and flows of [DFI] have grown faster than world income, and sometimes trade, particularly during the 1960s and since the mid-1980s" (Held et al., 1999: 242). However, as Held and his co-authors point out, relying on DFI as an index of the globalization of production probably understates its magnitude significantly, both because multinational firms finance their activities in a variety of ways, of which DFI is only one, and global production networks are organized and coordinated not only through the ownership and control implied by DFI but also through various forms of contracting relationship or strategic alliance between different firms. Nonetheless, multinational firms, transnational production, and intra-firm trade have emerged as important forms of global economic linkage (Dicken, 1992: 47–88; Agnew and Corbridge, 1995: 166–71; Held et al., 1999: 171–5, 236–7, 242–82). According to UNCTAD estimates reported by Held and his co-authors, "Sales of foreign affiliates have grown faster than world exports: in the 1970s and 1980s they had achieved levels comparable with world export levels but in the late 1990s they were around 30 percent higher. Foreign affiliates sales as a percentage of world GDP has risen from 10–15 percent in the 1970s to around 25 percent today" (Held et al., 1999: 246). Somewhere between one-quarter and one-third of world trade now consists of intra-firm trade: that is, transactions among different branches of a multinational firm (Held et al., 1999: 175). While the great bulk of DFI and multinational corporate activity remains concentrated in the advanced capitalist core, developing countries have been increasingly, if unevenly, incorporated into these global production networks (Dicken, 1992: 54–6, 64–7, 73–4; Held et al., 1999: 243–5, 248–50, 253–5). As production has been rationalized on a transnational scale, the traditional global division of labor—in which manufacturing activities were concentrated in the advanced capitalist "core" areas, while "peripheral" areas were limited to primary production—has been breached and newly industrializing countries (NICs) have emerged as significant producers of manufactured goods for the world economy (Dicken, 1992: 24–7, 33–40; Held et al., 1999: 171–5; but compare Gordon, 1988). According to the World Bank, "in 1990, 17 percent of the labor force in developing and formerly centrally planned economies worked directly or indirectly in the export sector, with exports to the richer countries accounting for two-thirds of this employment effect. [Further,] . . . the share of manufactures in developing countries' exports tripled between 1970 and 1990, from 20 percent to 60 percent" (World Bank, 1995: 51). Agnew and Corbridge explain that this is partly understandable in terms of the complex economic and political calculations of transnational corporations (TNCs):

TNCs have been attracted to developing countries that are reasonably
well managed and that show signs of economic growth and development. TNCs do not generally set up shop in countries like Bangladesh
or Sudan, no matter how low unit labor costs might be in such countries. They prefer to locate in countries where labor is cheap by the
standards of the high-income economies, but which is also skilled or
semi-skilled and disciplined in the ways of the market and time-
management.

(Agnew and Corbridge, 1995: 169)

They summarize the implications of these developments in terms of the
tendential de-territorialization of economic activity: "the internationalization of production capital has been significant for the way that it has
helped to explode the unity so often assumed to exist between a given
country's 'economic interests' and the interests of a particular territorial
economy" (Agnew and Corbridge, 1995: 170).

This restructuring of the global division of labor has significant implications for the US political economy, and for the socio-political regime of
Fordist hegemony. As I argued in an earlier work, "Whereas the whole
ideological thrust of Taylorism and Fordism had been an identification of
the interests of workers with productivity and the profitability of their
employer . . . this identification has become problematic as US-based multinational firms have pursued global profits at the expense of American
workers, and as the consequences for Fordist mass consumption in America
have become more painfully apparent" (Rupert, 1995: 192). Data generated by Kravis and Lipsey (1992) suggest that even while the US (as a
territorial entity) lost around one-third of its share of world exports of
manufactures between 1966 and 1986–8, US-based multinationals maintained their global share by shifting their production for world export
markets toward majority-owned foreign affiliates (MOFAs), whose export
share increased over this period. "In 1986–88, US multinationals were
exporting more from their overseas affiliates than they were from the
United States" (Kravis and Lipsey, 1992: 194). Evidence such as this seems
to suggest that over the last several decades transnational production for
world markets has to a significant degree displaced export production
from within the territorial US. Nominally American multinational firms
have maintained their global competitive position, but their US workers
now produce less for world markets while workers employed by their
foreign affiliates produce more. Further indicative of this tendency, employment in the manufacturing MOFAs of US-based firms grew from 2.4
million in 1966 to almost 4.1 million in 1987, an increase of about 70
percent. Although direct foreign investment by US-based firms has re-
mained heavily concentrated in the developed market economies, after
1966 employment by US multinational corporations (MNCs) engaged in
manufacturing in the newly industrializing countries—especially in Brazil,

Mexico, and Asia—grew almost five times as rapidly as did such employ-ment in the developed countries. This suggests that US-based MNCs may have sought to transfer some of their more labor-intensive manufacturing activities to these areas (Dicken, 1992: 51–3, 59–67). Further, internation-alized production has dramatically affected manufacturing within the US: the import content of US finished manufactures has increased eightfold—from 3 percent throughout most of the twentieth century and as late as 1963, to 24 percent in 1985 (Held et al., 1999: 174). Reflecting the in-creased significance of multinational firms as mediators between the US and the world economy, Dicken claims that intra-firm trade now consti-tutes more than half of all US trade (Dicken, 1992: 48–9; but compare Henwood, 1997c).

Perhaps ironically, then, neoliberalism's resurrection of laissez-faire fun-damentalism has been attendant upon the increasing extensity and inten-sity of transnational relations. Even as people in locations around the globe are increasingly integrated into—and affected by—transnational so-cial relations, neoliberalism seeks to remove these relations from the public sphere—where they might be subjected to norms of democratic govern-ance—and subject them to the power of capital as expressed through the discipline of the market. As van der Pijl puts it, "The core of the new concept of control which expressed the restored discipline of capital, neoliberalism, resides in raising micro-economic rationality to the validat-ing criterion for all aspects of social life" (van der Pijl, 1998: 129). If globalization poses profound challenges of global governance (Held, 1995; Held et al., 1999), then this is all the more true of neoliberal globalization which subjects people to social power relations of transnational scope even as its relentlessly individualist discourse implicitly denies the existence of structured dominance relations rooted in the capitalist organization of production (or anything else, for that matter).

The ideology of liberal globalization: displacing politics from the economy

Although it has turned on its erstwhile junior partners in organized indus-trial labor, and turned away from the "productive capital concept" toward the laissez-faire fundamentalism characteristic of finance capital, the his-toric bloc pushing contemporary transnational liberalism nonetheless retains a fundamental continuity with the political project of the postwar hegemonic bloc. While the growth-oriented "corporate liberalism" of the postwar decades and the hard-edged neoliberalism of more recent times may disagree on the terms of international openness, both share an under-lying commitment to a more open world economy based on private owner-ship of the means of production and generalized commodity exchange.

The ideological justification for this ongoing project of liberal capitalist globalization is found in the orthodox theory of international trade. Quoting the renowned international economist Paul Krugman, the authors of one trade text note that:

> the advocacy of free trade is "as close to a sacred tenet as any idea in economics." In deference to most economists' strong views on this subject, political scientists, legal scholars, and editorial writers often take it on faith that free trade is the best policy for the nation and the world and view any departures from free trade as capitulations to interest group politics or nationalistic sentiments.
>
> (Cohen et al., 1996: 55)

The world-historical influence of free trade doctrine is attributable not just to "deference" paid to a strongly articulated view, but rather constitutes the core of a world order ideology embodied in the political project of a constellation of dominant social forces, as we have seen above. Nor is this to deny that there is a powerful intellectual rationale for free trade to be found in mainstream economic theory; indeed, its rhetorical force registers strongly within the individualistic frame of a liberal world-view: "Instead of highlighting the dull compulsions of the market to which many critics of 'market idolatry' are keen to draw attention, proponents of neoliberalism see in the market a site of empowerment that provides for equality of opportunity and that maximizes a local comparative advantage" (Agnew and Corbridge, 1995: 201; for an example of this kind of rhetoric see Friedman, 1999a).

What then is the force of this doctrine? According to mainstream economists, what should citizens in a putatively democratic republic[3] know about international trade? Paul Krugman has done as much as anyone within the profession of economics to shake up the received wisdom of trade theory (for example, by including imperfect competition, scale economies, and externalities in its analyses, thus creating openings for those who wish to argue that there may be particularly desirable comparative advantages which can be created by effective state policy). Yet, Krugman concludes that, for practical purposes and in the context of education for sound economic citizenship, the traditional bases of international trade theory retain their validity: "In the last decade of the twentieth century, the essential things to teach students are still the insights of Hume and Ricardo. That is, we need to teach them that trade deficits are self-correcting and that the benefits of trade do not depend on a country having an absolute advantage over its rivals" (Krugman, 1993b: 26).

Absolute advantage refers to a situation in which one country is more productive in a particular industry than other countries; but in Ricardian theory comparative advantage may obtain and provide for mutual benefits from trade, even when one trading partner has no absolute advantage whatever. This is so because comparative advantage is primarily concerned with the opportunity costs of producing one good rather than another. As

Russell Roberts explains in his popularized account, "The 'comparative' in the title doesn't mean compared to other nations. It means compared to other products" (Roberts, 1994: 11). Every nation has a comparative advantage in something, since it will have one good which it can produce more efficiently, and at lower relative cost, than other possible goods it might produce. These advantages are likely to differ across countries, creating the possibility for mutual gains from specialization and trade. The payoff from trade occurs when a country opens itself to the world market and is able to use its exports (embodying its comparative advantage) to acquire imports (embodying somebody else's comparative advantage) which would be more costly if produced domestically. Emphasizing the enhanced consumption possibilities which are indirectly accessible through specialization and exchange, Roberts calls this "the Roundabout Way to Wealth." On this view, the opportunity costs of forgoing trade—and domestically producing all goods, regardless of comparative advantage—are significant; and it is this comparison between consumption possibilities under openness and under autarky which underpins the traditional case for free trade. As Caves and Jones put it in their international economics text, "To be self-sufficient in every item is to throw away the benefits that are associated with international trade" (Caves and Jones, 1981: 29). There are other benefits to be had from openness, including access to lower cost inputs for one's own industries, enhanced competition as a spur to innovation, access to larger markets creating possibilities for economies of scale, and so forth; but the fundamental case for freer trade rests on the bedrock of comparative advantage.

Economists recognize that free trade is not without its costs, and that these costs are not distributed evenly. In particular, those industries embodying the comparative advantage will benefit from the export opportunities of openness, while other industries may face stiffer competition from imports and could be substantially harmed. As a consequence, economists worry that there is likely to be vocal opposition to policies of increased openness. Yet, they maintain that freer trade will yield a net gain for the overall economy, as the gains made available by exploiting comparative advantage will outweigh the losses to less efficient domestic industries, and consumers will enjoy enhanced consumption possibilities. The great fear of economists is that vociferous "special interests" harmed by openness will take advantage of any political opportunity for departure from free trade and will use specious economic claims about lost jobs and trade balances to justify appeals for protection, which can be purchased only at the expense of aggregate efficiency and overall consumption possibilities. Thus a firm commitment to free trade can act as a prophylactic against an otherwise potentially virulent infection of protectionism. Lacking such prophylaxis, the politics of special interest may result in a kind of "prisoner's dilemma" outcome wherein pursuit of a strategy of defection, rather than cooperation for the common good, makes everyone worse off. "In a country in which each interest group gets the protection it wants, the net effect may be to make even the interest groups themselves worse off than if there had been a prior commitment to free trade" (Krugman, 1993c: 365; see also Low, 1993: 147). Recognizing that his own work demonstrating some of the weaknesses of traditional trade theory might be appropriated by those seeking a rationale for departures from openness, Krugman writes: "The broad argument for free trade, to which many economists implicitly subscribe, is essentially political: free trade is a pretty good if not perfect policy, while an effort to deviate from it in a sophisticated way will probably end up doing more harm than good" (Krugman, 1993c: 364).

Notwithstanding Krugman's lamentations that mainstream economists cannot find an audience, that no one aside from economics students seems willing to sit still for the theory of comparative advantage (Krugman, 1996), this doctrine continues to be integral to the core ideology of postwar world order institutions such as the World Bank and the General Agreement on Tariffs and Trade, the latter since 1995 subsumed within the World Trade Organization. Both institutions promote liberalization, and fear the politicization of trade as a slippery slope toward closure, as one interest group after another demands protection.

In a special edition of its annual *World Development Report* (1995), The World Bank directly addressed the concerns of "Workers in an Integrating World." As the Bank would have it, "fears that increased international trade and investment and less state intervention will hurt employment are mainly without basis. Workers have made great advances in many countries, especially those that have embraced these global trends, effectively engaging in international markets and avoiding excessive state intervention" (World Bank, 1995: 2). On this view, the best way to improve the situation of the world's working people is increasing openness to the opportunities of the world economy, combined with "sound" government policies. As far as the Bank is concerned, "sound" policies must be fundamentally market-friendly, but need not entail the strictest possible interpretation of laissez-faire. The state may have an important role to play in creating the conditions for market-led development, especially in educating and enhancing the skills of its workers, protecting the most vulnerable, combating discrimination and perhaps even recognizing basic worker rights such as the right to "join the union of their choice or not to join any union" (1995: 82). However, the Bank is quite clear about its priorities. Such policies are to be subordinated to the overriding goal of greater liberalization: "The real danger of using trade sanctions as an instrument for promoting basic rights is that the trade–standards link could become hijacked by protectionist interests attempting to preserve activities rendered uncompetitive by cheaper imports" (1995: 79; see also 58). Access to the global trading system, then, is not to be made conditional upon respect for common labor standards. And, while the Bank is willing now to entertain the notion that trade unions may have a legitimate role to play in the world economy, the Bank cautions against collective bargaining at the national, sectoral, or industrial level. Rather, enterprise-level bargaining should be the norm since, under those circumstances, "the union's ability to effect monopolistic wage increases is tempered by the strong competitive pressures on the firm from the product market" (1995: 83). Insofar as the basic rationale of trade unionism is to take wages out of competition, the Bank's insistence on enterprise level bargaining and on the right of workers *not* to join any union (a situation euphemistically referred to as the "right to work" in the notoriously anti-union states of the US South) implicitly undermine the World Bank's putative commitment to labor rights as a norm of the emerging global economy.

The World Trade Organization also represents itself to the world in terms of this ideology of liberal globalization. In order to promote "predictable and growing access" to the world's markets, the GATT–WTO regime has sought to institutionalize on a multilateral basis international norms of non-discrimination (between domestically produced and imported goods) through such legal means as "most favored nation" and "national treatment" provisions. "In almost every policy area which impinges on trading conditions, the scope of members to pursue capricious, discriminatory and protectionist policies is constrained by WTO commitments" (World Trade Organization, 1995: 6). As of October, 1997, over 150 countries were either members of the WTO or were in the process of negotiating for entry. The WTO defends its mission by starkly contrasting a world of multilateral openness and market-led growth with one of closure and stagnation:

> The alternative [to openness] is protection against competition from imports, and perpetual government subsidies. That leads to bloated, inefficient companies supplying consumers with outdated, unattractive products. Ultimately, factories close and jobs are lost despite the protection and subsidies. If other governments around the world pursue the same policies, markets contract and world economic activity is reduced. One of the objectives of the WTO is to prevent such a self-defeating and destructive drift into protectionism.
>
> (World Trade Organization, 1998: 8)

Accordingly, the WTO eschewed any attempt to link its trading norms and opportunities with respect for internationally recognized core labor standards, disingenuously endorsing these standards while deferring responsibility for their enactment to the relatively toothless International Labor Organization. The official declaration of the 1996 ministerial-level meetings of the WTO clarified the organization's basic commitments: "We believe that economic growth and development fostered by increased trade and further trade liberalization contribute to the promotion of these [core labor] standards. We reject the use of labor standards for protectionist purposes, and agree that the comparative advantage of countries, particularly low-wage developing countries, must in no way be put into question." Accordingly, the WTO relates, it has "no committees or working parties dealing with the issue" (World Trade Organization, 1998: 51).

In summary, then, it seems fair to say that Professor Krugman, his colleagues, and their doctrines have been very much more influential than they sometimes wish to let on. The mainstream theory of international trade, and the liberal world-view in which it is embedded, constitute the governing ideology of the world economy and its central institutions. Moreover, as we shall now see, this ideology is vigorously propagated by a constellation of dominant social forces in the nexus between the US and the global political economy.

NAFTA and the politics of a depoliticized world economy

In the first major US public debates explicitly addressing issues related to liberal globalization, proponents of the North American Free Trade Agreement presented it to the general public as the product of enlightened public policy, guided by generally recognized and scientifically established principles of economics, extending and enhancing the freedom and efficiency of the market on a continental scale. Writing for the *New York Times*, Sylvia Nasar suggested that among academic economists there was a remarkable degree of unanimity in support of NAFTA:

> When economists of every stripe agree on anything, it is noteworthy. So it is a sign of unusual accord that 300 economists, ranging from conservatives like James M. Buchanan and Milton Friedman to liberals including Paul A. Samuelson and James Tobin, recently signed a letter to President Clinton supporting the North American Free Trade Agreement.
>
> (Nasar, 1993a)

This impression of unanimity was reinforced by University of Chicago Nobel laureate Merton Miller, who told another *Times* reporter: "I don't know of any serious economist who doesn't support NAFTA" (Johnson, 1993). This apparent consensus among (presumably otherwise contentious) economists was presented as "unusual" and "noteworthy," implying that it reflects the extraordinary merits of NAFTA and the overwhelmingly compelling intellectual weight of the case for the agreement. However, it may have reflected nothing more remarkable than the fundamental congruence of the case for free trade with the paradigmatic presuppositions of the world-view held in common by mainstream (that is, "serious") economists who, after all, are largely responsible for framing, legitimating, and promoting such arguments.[4] The case for NAFTA as presented by academic economists—and echoed in the mainstream press, in business-oriented publications, in pro-NAFTA lobbying materials and propaganda—rests upon the case for free trade in general, which in turn rests upon a world-view of abstract individualism.

Referring to Samuelson's classic textbook, the *Times'* Sylvia Nasar finds a quote from John Stuart Mill which explains that the classic rationale of trade theory is simply "a more efficient employment of the productive forces of the world." Nasar explains for the benefit of the *Times'* mass audience the basic principles of trade theory to be found in any introductory economics textbook: given two individuals with differing skills and abilities, both will be better off if they eschew autarky and instead specialize in the one thing each does best, and then exchange with each other. Even if one party is better than the other at both activities, the result of specialization and trade according to comparative advantage is "greater total productivity and incomes." Nasar summarizes the lesson in the following terms: "while razing trade barriers may hurt some businesses and some workers, it generally raises the incomes of all countries." Nasar (1993a) explains to the *Times'* readers that although US–Mexico trade is somewhat more complicated than the two-person model of the textbooks, the same basic principles apply, and this is what accounts for the widespread support for NAFTA among professional economists.

Indeed, the authors of widely cited and very influential studies of NAFTA, Gary Clyde Hufbauer and Jeffrey Schott, envisioned the primary benefits of the agreement in precisely these terms:

> Over the long term, the main impact of larger US–Mexican trade will be higher incomes made possible by greater efficiency and faster growth. Efficiency in both economies will be boosted by the tendency of each country to export those goods and services in which it has a comparative advantage. Faster growth will result from more intense competition among a larger number of firms in each segment of the market and from an expanded North American market that will enable each firm to realize economies of scale. In turn this could result in an improved trade balance for North America with the rest of the world or better terms of trade for North America.[5]
>
> (Hufbauer and Schott, 1993: 22)

Due to the asymmetry of size between the US and Mexican economies, economists argued, integration would have relatively less impact upon the (larger) American economy and relatively more upon the (smaller) Mexican. Yet, insofar as Mexicans have a relatively high propensity to import products from the US, an agreement which makes Mexicans better off should have some positive effects on American export industries as well. Further, Mexican tariffs were relatively higher than American, so the agreement should enhance access to the Mexican market for American producers.

US financial service firms would also enjoy greater access to the Mexican market, and NAFTA commits Mexico to treat American and Canadian investors as well as Mexican firms and to protect intellectual property rights (Dornbusch, 1991: 74; Hufbauer and Schott, 1993a: 107, 110–12).

In sum, mainstream economists argued that NAFTA is likely to have modest positive effects on the US economy, and somewhat larger positive effects upon the Mexican. Realizing these potential benefits is not without cost, since some workers in some industries will be displaced as specialization according to comparative advantage unfolds through the operation of market forces, but this is the price which must be paid to achieve the efficiency gains which trade makes possible. According to the letter addressed to President Clinton and signed by a phalanx of professional economists, the bottom line should be "a net positive for the United States, both in terms of employment creation and overall economic growth. . . . Moreover, beyond employment gains, an open trade relationship directly benefits all consumers."[6]

While mainstream economists have discussed the implications of NAFTA for the US largely in terms of the operation of seemingly apolitical market forces, they have been less circumspect in assessing the political stakes of the NAFTA debate for Mexico. In concluding their cases in favor of NAFTA, Hufbauer and Schott (1993a: 113–14), Dornbusch (1991: 74–6), and Krugman (1993a: 18–19) all are direct and explicit in arguing that support for NAFTA has the important political consequence of ratifying, supporting, and extending the market-oriented reforms enacted by the Salinas regime. Further, these authors variously claim that such support could result in gradual reform of the (admittedly imperfect) Mexican political system, help to extend pro-market and pro-democracy reforms throughout the hemisphere, and generally advance the global order agenda of multilateral openness. It would seem, then, that when it comes to Latin America or to the world as a whole these economists have a fairly acute sense of the importance of political struggle in achieving the kind of world they are envisioning; yet this sense is largely lacking in their arguments about the domestic implications of NAFTA, which are understood in more narrowly economic terms. This contrast is illuminating. The predominance of market forces abroad represents a political achievement not yet won, a goal to be striven toward through explicitly political strategies; while at home these same market forces are represented as natural, objectively necessary, beyond (any but the most irrational) politics. This naturalization of the market economy in the US, and the abstraction of politics from the domestic economy despite the recognition of the political preconditions of market relations elsewhere, reflects the hegemony of abstract individualism among American economists and those under their intellectual influence.[7]

Much of the mainstream press reproduced this line of argument and, both implicitly and explicitly, endorsed the agreement. In the news coverage of two leading papers, the *New York Times* and the *Washington Post*, pro-NAFTA perspectives tended to predominate (Cohen and Solomon, 1993). Both papers ran special multi-page supplements in which advertisers touted the agreement (see, for example, *New York Times*, 19 October, 1993; *Washington Post National Weekly Edition*, 1–7 November, 1993). And editorial statements in these papers were strongly supportive of the agreement. The *Times* (17 November, 1993) suggested that "As a trade pact, NAFTA helps the economy modestly" by promoting the exports of some industries and generally lowering consumer prices. But the paper stressed that the domestic economic implications of the agreement were small potatoes compared to the global political stakes. "That is what the NAFTA vote is ultimately about: whether the country is willing to move forward or retreat into economic isolation. . . . NAFTA's most important job is buttressing the historic US role in promoting freer trade, a policy that has done more to nurture worldwide [economic] growth since World War II than any other." The *Washington Post* similarly placed NAFTA's relatively small economic benefits in the context of larger issues of regional and global liberalization, casting it as "an enormous opportunity not only to promote economic prosperity but democracy, freedom and political stability" (*Washington Post National Weekly Edition*, 8–14 November, 1993). Generally portrayed as promising economic benefits to the American public and serving the national interest by sustaining a more open and liberal world, NAFTA received editorial endorsements from the *Boston Globe, Atlanta Constitution, Chicago Tribune, Chicago Sun-Times, St. Louis Post-Dispatch, Houston Chronicle, San Francisco Chronicle*, and numerous other papers, large and small.[8]

Not surprisingly, the perspective articulated by professional economists and represented in the mainstream press resonated with the pro-NAFTA representations of the American corporate community. Sandra Masur, Director of Public Policy Analysis for Eastman Kodak and a leading spokesperson for the Business Roundtable's efforts in support of the agreement, argued that there were four major reasons why US business should support it (Masur, 1991: 99–103). She stressed Mexico's growing importance as a market for American exports, explaining that Roundtable members (executives of the 200 largest American corporations) had done particularly well in Mexico since the Salinas liberalization policy went into effect, and expected to do even better there after NAFTA. She further argued that NAFTA is politically important in order to "expand and lock in" the Salinas reforms, making it more difficult for future Mexican regimes to reverse them and thus boosting the confidence of potential American business partners in the long-term profitability of their Mexican ventures. Third, Masur argued that a corporate strategy of "co-production" in Mexico could "keep costs down" and thus boost the global competitiveness of US-based firms. Insofar as this headed off the dilemma of shutting down production operations or relocating them in their entirety, Masur argued that this was actually a boon for US manufacturing employment. Finally, she suggested that NAFTA could be useful as a model for hemispheric liberalization, a model which might then be extended to other regions of the world. In a programmatic statement of the global political agenda of US-based corporations, she asserted that "The companies of the Roundtable are seeking across-the-board liberalization of trade in goods, services and investment" (Masur, 1991: 102; see also Business Roundtable, 1991). Although Masur acknowledged that American business faces a political battle at home in which it must "go head to head with organized labor" in order to win approval of NAFTA, the socio-political roots of this conflict were nowhere explored and did not enter into her analysis of the merits of the pact. As in the analyses of the mainstream economists, the explicitly political stakes of NAFTA were displaced onto Mexico, Latin America, and the outside world more generally. Once these realms were liberalized, politics might then be (ideologically) displaced from the world economy altogether.

Meanwhile in the battle for Congressional approval of the agreement, USA*NAFTA—the organization described by the *Washington Post* as "big business's lobbying arm"—mounted a multi-million dollar campaign to influence the vote. USA*NAFTA ran television and newspaper advertisements in the Washington area promoting the agreement as "Good for jobs. Good for US." On Capitol Hill, corporate lobbyists made business's support for the agreement crystal clear to all, while major employers from each state and district were mobilized to put pressure on their particular representatives. In materials obtained as part of USA*NAFTA's lobbying packet, the organization presented a state-by-state and industry-by-industry breakdown of the importance of trade with Mexico and the economic benefits expected to flow from the agreement. In its statement of purpose, USA*NAFTA explained that the agreement "offers the US greater market access for goods, services and agricultural products, improved protection of intellectual property and elimination of most restrictions on investment." USA*NAFTA emphasized that this will boost US exports and thus contribute to employment in the US. Further, "NAFTA locks in economic reforms in Mexico and provides a model for trade agreements with other countries." Should the agreement fail, USA*NAFTA warned, Mexico's liberalization and its friendlier tone toward the US could be reversed, "severely damaging US business prospects." In a clear attempt to counter the arguments of the agreement's critics, USA*NAFTA touted the environmental and labor side agreements negotiated by the Clinton administration, and included in its lobbying packet a copy of the economists' letter endorsing the agreement, along with official statements from the office of the US Trade Representative explicitly countering the claims made by Ross Perot and Pat Choate in their anti-NAFTA book.[9]

In the months and days before the final Congressional votes on NAFTA, academic, corporate, political, and media supporters of the agreement used a number of rhetorical strategies to bolster their own position and to marginalize NAFTA's opponents. In particular, liberal understandings of "politics" and "economics" were deployed in ways which obscured the organic tension between private property and democracy and thus rendered the positions of NAFTA critics, when viewed from this liberal perspective, unintelligible. Seeking to depoliticize the economy and to transform NAFTA into a technical issue, the weight and status of "science" could then be invoked to reinforce the credibility of pro-NAFTA representations: to emphasize this, USA*NAFTA included in its lobbying packet the pro-NAFTA letter bearing the signatures of almost 300 economists. In further efforts to appropriate the mantle of scientific truth, USA*NAFTA asserted that the "economic studies" which promised material benefits from NAFTA were "nonpartisan," "rigorous," and "highly respected" (USA*NAFTA, 1993c: 8). Implied or explicit was the converse, that anti-NAFTA arguments were unscientific, the product of delusional thinking and irrational fears. Moreover, according to these representations, the consequences of giving in to such irrational forces would include a setback for the general interest in free trade and investment, with narrow special interests instead leading the country, the continent, and perhaps the world toward isolationism and protectionism. Finally, proponents of the agreement sought to associate its critics with Ross Perot, who in turn was readily portrayed as a "crank," and as someone whose business interests revealed him to be a hypocrite.

Viewed from within the parameters of the predominant economistic vision of a depoliticized world of individual market actors, the arguments and positions of more progressive NAFTA opponents—which make sense within a very different world-view, one which presupposes a structure of power relations between multinational corporate capital, workers, and communities—could be condescendingly cast as the common sense of the simple, those uninitiated into the more sophisticated and scientifically valid truths of liberal economics. And, to the extent that NAFTA critics refused to be persuaded by economistic arguments, they could be cast as unreasonable. In the pages of *Foreign Affairs*, perhaps the leading American journal of commentary on matters international, Paul Krugman suggested that opponents of NAFTA were open to persuasion by neither reason nor evidence, and were polluting popular discourse with "simplistic but politically effective rhetoric" (Krugman, 1993a: 14). And, in the same issue of *Foreign Affairs*, William Orme affected the classic stance of journalistic objectivity, taxing both sides of the debate with mythologizing the agreement's effects and counterposing to these myths his own battery of "facts." Orme's bottom line, however, was the economists' axiom that freer trade is generally beneficial and that critics were propagating a retrograde zero-sum world-view: "Through the efforts of NAFTA opponents, millions of Americans have been persuaded that a prosperous Mexico would be a direct threat to their jobs and incomes" (Orme, 1993: 3). Bob Davis of the *Wall Street Journal* described opposition to free trade in terms of a newly popular "demonizing myth" in which trade is blamed for the country's various ills, a peculiar "psychodrama" in which foreigners are perceived as using low wages or high technology to undermine American economic health and US jobs. NAFTA opponents were portrayed as "shrill," holding "an elevated standard of 'social justice'" which they (unrealistically, it is implied) expect the agreement to meet (Davis, 1993). In the *New York Times*, economist Gary Hufbauer characterized labor's opposition to NAFTA as "foolish," "misguided," "a huge mistake" based on "a grave misunderstanding of how businesses operate." He suggested that labor's opposition pointed inevitably toward "new barriers against trade" and "isolation from the booming markets of Latin America and Asia" (Hufbauer 1993). Hufbauer and Schott asserted in *Foreign Policy* (1993a: 104–5, 110) that the arguments against NAFTA were "myths . . . propounded by Ross Perot and his congressional and labor allies." The agreement's critics were suffering from "emporiophobia," an irrational fear of trade which led them to accept "major delusions" such as the arguments that NAFTA could depress employment and wages in the US, or that it might shift investment from the US to Mexico. "What NAFTA opponents . . . really want," they asserted, "is new protection against producers in Mexico (and other developing countries)." From the perspective of liberal economic theory, the universe of possibilities is defined in terms of a continuum stretching between the poles of free trade (individual liberty within a market context) or protectionism (external constraint hampering individuals in the market). Insofar as critics were opposed to NAFTA's definition of free trade, they must therefore be protectionists; and in light of the (putatively self-evident) lessons of Smoot–Hawley, that could hardly be a respectable position.[10]

When viewed from the perspective of a liberal vision of "politics" in which electoral competition is paramount and the economy is not seen as intrinsically political, opposition to the agreement also could be made to appear irrational insofar as it challenged the position of the first Democratic President in twelve years. Labor's apparently inexplicable opposition to a "friendly" administration which had so much riding on this issue was criticized in the press as being clumsily self-defeating, "as rational as a wounded bear crashing through the forest" (Hall, 1993). Labor's opposition was portrayed as disrupting the Democratic coalition in order to protect its own narrowly selfish interests. Writing for the Progressive Policy Institute—the think tank of the Clintonite "New Democrats"—Paula Stern asserted that "Support for free trade constitutes one of the [Democratic] party's most venerable and progressive principles. . . . Today, however, organized labor and other party constituency groups are demanding that Democrats junk that principle and instead seek to protect specific jobs rather than the interest of American workers in general." This remark was quoted by Hobart Rowen of the *Washington Post*, adding that it was "bravely, directly, and accurately put" (Rowen, 1993a). While multimillion dollar pro-NAFTA lobbying campaigns were orchestrated by US-based corporate groups and by the Mexican government (Lewis and Ebrahim, 1993; Weisskopf, 1993), the attempts of organized labor to exercise its comparatively modest political clout by promising to withhold its support from legislators who voted for the agreement were portrayed in terms of the anti-labor stereotype of ignorant and inarticulate strong-arm thugs with underworld connections. On national television, President Clinton denounced labor's "roughshod," "musclebound" tactics and the theme was picked up in the press and even found its way into a widely syndicated political cartoon by Oliphant in which Clinton was portrayed man-handling a pair of poorly spoken labor goons along the road to NAFTA (Friedman, 1993; Rowen, 1993b).[11] The very idea that NAFTA could be understood in terms of its implications for class relations in the US was ridiculed by Hobart Rowen (1993c), who criticized Ralph Nader for "try[ing] to make a class issue out of the trade agreement: He peddled the notion that if NAFTA is good for American business it must be bad for working Americans. This is false. But the glib suggestion has worked its way into unfocused dialogue on radio and TV talk shows, and, as the polls show, there are a lot of believers out there."

The press and the Clinton administration elevated Ross Perot to the status of unofficial spokesman for the anti-NAFTA forces and subjected him to blistering criticism. Perot's opposition to NAFTA was represented as something other than a principled stand: the Perot family was exposed as having business interests in a Texas free trade zone (Moffett and Opdyke, 1993) and Perot's co-author, Pat Choate, was accused of fronting for Roger Milliken and protectionist textile interests (Gigot, 1993). After the release of his anti-NAFTA book, the *New York Times'* Michael Weinstein (1993) characterized his case against the agreement as "an inept diatribe that mistates facts, misleads readers and misunderstands trade." J. W. Anderson (1993) of the *Washington Post* labeled Perot's position as "non-sense" and suggested that Perot's opposition might actually help NAFTA insofar as "Perot, Buchanan and company have increased the aura of kookiness and unreliability that surrounds the opposition to NAFTA." Eight days before the House of Representatives was to vote on the agree-ment, the administration skillfully emphasized Perot's idiosyncrasies and inconsistencies by presenting him in contrast to the extremely low-key, matter-of-fact Gore in a nationally televised "debate" from which Perot was widely seen as having emerged the "loser." Testifying before Con-gress, Mickey Kantor, the US Trade Representative, played up this increas-ingly unpopular image by referring to Perot as "chairman of the board at the Mad Hatter's tea party" (quoted in Ifill, 1993a). The day before the House vote, an editorialist for the *Atlanta Constitution* (16 November, 1993) pronounced the bankruptcy of NAFTA opposition: "There is simply no legitimate argument that the North American Free Trade Agreement would not be good for the people of the United States as a whole. The opposition has been reduced to the rantings of Ross Perot, the ravings of eco-radicals, and the blatant self-interest of labor unionists."

Just prior to the Congressional vote, the American public was roughly split on the issue of NAFTA—with the division breaking along lines of class—but survey results suggested that most people were willing to shift their position on the agreement depending upon whether it was cast as a job creator or a job destroyer (Ifill, 1993b). The decisive issue in the minds of the public, then, appeared to be defined on the economistic terrain where NAFTA proponents had constructed their arguments. Rhetorically marginalized and unable to counter an administration which showered favors and dispensations upon those willing to vote for the agreement, the anti-NAFTA forces failed to stop Congressional approval of NAFTA in the fall of 1993. The legacy of this struggle is, however, an ambiguous one. While the hegemonic ideology was not overturned, the contradictions of global liberalism were more explicitly defined in the common sense of unionists, environmentalists, and citizen activists, and these social forces began to articulate a vision of a more participatory transnational political economy—as we shall see in the following chapter.

Round Two: GATT–WTO

In December, 1993—before the dust had settled from the NAFTA fight —117 nations successfully concluded the Uruguay Round of GATT negotiations providing for the creation of the WTO—a new international organization to oversee further liberalization, to review the trade-related policies of member states, and to settle disputes among them. Patrick Low, an economist who worked for the GATT and then the World Bank, summarized in quite orthodox terms the central rationale of the agreement: "if one were to try to identify the theoretical underpinning of the GATT, it would certainly be articulated around the theory of comparative advantage, relying on the existence of welfare gains from specialization through unrestricted trade." In a book published by the Twentieth Century Fund prior to the conclusion of the Uruguay Round, Low argued that "Renewed commitment to a rules-based set of multilateral trading arrangements, founded on nondiscrimination, is the surest way of reducing the risk that the system will degenerate into a web of special case deals, choking off the benefits of specialization through trade, stifling change, and accelerating economic decline" (Low, 1993: 146, 251).

The public debate in the US over GATT was noticeably less intense than the NAFTA debate had been, perhaps because the issues were more arcane, because the structure of the global trading system seemed less immediate to US citizens than economic integration with Mexico, or because some key elements of the opposition—especially the AFL–CIO and the Perot forces—were less vigorous than they had been in the NAFTA debate (Grier, 1993; Bradsher, 1994).

Ratification of GATT was advocated by the same coalition of social forces which had successfully promoted NAFTA in the US, and in substantially similar terms. Proponents in the private sector formed the Alliance for GATT NOW to evangelize newspaper editorial boards around the country, and to lobby Congress directly in favor of the Uruguay Round. According to Susan Aaronson, "the Alliance eventually had a membership of more than 200,000 small and large businesses" and their allies, but community and labor groups were conspicuously absent. The Alliance issued pro-GATT fact sheets, and placed advocacy ads in key newspapers and on national television. Seeking the mantles of scientific authority and enlightened statesmanship, its materials noted that "former trade officials, forty governors, former presidents, and 450 leading economists endorsed the Uruguay Round." The Alliance called GATT "A Home Run for America," claiming it would enhance US exports and economic growth, create a million US jobs, protect US intellectual property, and insure that international competitors "play by the same rules we do." In lobbying materials featuring a photo of Senators Smoot and Hawley, the Alliance advised Congressional representatives that "History has not been kind to those in Congress who embrace protectionism" and asked them to "Remember these fellas when you vote on GATT" (Aaronson, 1996: 150, 157–8, 160; see also Behr, 1994; Myerson, 1994).

Once again, in the mainstream media liberalized trade was repeatedly linked to both increased export opportunities and enhanced consumption possibilities in a world of increasing efficiency and growth—the roundabout way to wealth which underlies orthodox trade theory. As in the NAFTA debate, Sylvia Nasar ably undertook the challenge of explaining the economists' reasoning to *New York Times* readers (Nasar, 1993b). Nasar reported on her discussions with three economists (Krugman of MIT, Sherman Robinson of Berkeley, and Gary Hufbauer of the Institute for International Economics), and was able readily to synthesize their arguments into a single coherent narrative on the virtues of openness and the positive-sum world it is said to bring in train. While hers was perhaps the most directly pedagogical contribution, it was not difficult to find news reports and commentaries explaining in terms of the economists' tale what was at stake in the GATT debates (for example Thomas, 1993; New York Times, 1994; Samuelson, 1994). Aaronson reports that "some fifty newspapers endorsed the GATT–WTO, including all of the nationwide papers (*USA Today, Wall Street Journal, Journal of Commerce, Washington Post,* and *New York Times*)" (Aaronson, 1996: 157). In the *New York Times*, special supplements appeared in which advertisers underwrote pro-GATT commentaries by administration officials (R. Brown, 1994; Kantor, 1994), international bureaucrats (Sutherland, 1994), manufacturers and consumer groups (D. Brown, 1994; Jasinowski, 1994a), all stressing the benefits of freer trade, greater efficiency, and a virtuous cycle of worldwide economic growth. In an article highly critical of media coverage of trade issues, progressive economist Dean Baker noted with some amazement that a front-page news story in the *New York Times* had actually opened with the following mantra: "Free trade means growth. Free trade means growth. Free trade means growth. Just say it fifty more times and all doubts will melt away." Reflecting on the general tone of mainstream news reporting, Baker suggested that this kind of cheerleading "is somewhat more concise, but not significantly more biased, than the bulk of the media's coverage of trade issues" (Baker, 1994: 9).

As with NAFTA, the icing on the cake was the case for continuing US global leadership and the danger that the liberal world order—with its imputed virtues of prosperity, peace, and democracy—might be supplanted by the "law of the jungle" should the US abdicate its global responsibilities (Jasinowski, 1994b; Lewis, 1994; New York Times, 1994; Sanger, 1994a). President Clinton set the tone here, arguing that while more open trade would have significant implications for the US economy, the political stakes were still higher: "this new fabric of commerce will also shape global prosperity or the lack of it, and with it the prospects of people around the world for democracy, freedom and peace" (quoted in Aaronson, 1996: 145).

By 1 December, 1994, the proponents of GATT–WTO had carried the day in the US Congress, and by a wider margin than they had in the case of NAFTA (Sanger, 1994b, 1994c). I would suggest that this outcome reflects the continuing hegemony of liberal doctrines among the most influential social forces in the US political economy, and the successful furtherance of their project of neoliberal globalization. Liberal economists, and those under their ideological influence, sought NAFTA and GATT–WTO as vehicles for the progressive depoliticization of the global economy, casting their opponents as narrowly self-interested, and globally dangerous, protectionists in order to legitimize the exclusion of explicitly political concerns from the realm of world trade. They feared that politicization of trade could only lead to distributive struggle, in large part because the philosophy of abstract individualism which underlies their world-view can admit of no politics other than that of distributive struggle among preconstituted individuals and the groups they form in order to further their interests. As we will see in the next chapter, however, this was not the only possible view of politics at play in the globalization debates. A deeper understanding of politics—one which understands it in terms of a process of social self-construction—casts the restructuring of the global economy as an opportunity for deepening and broadening the democratic institutions and practices through which meaningful self-determination can be achieved.

4 From liberal globalization to global democratization

In the last decade of the twentieth century, the historical structure of liberal capitalist hegemony is transforming itself. This chapter will argue that the public debate in the US over the North American Free Trade Agreement (NAFTA) and, to a lesser extent, the Uruguay Round of the General Agreement on Tariffs and Trade (GATT), reflected these socio-political changes and the possibility of renewed challenges to the hegemony of liberal capitalism and the predominant transnational capitalist bloc. I want to suggest that NAFTA and GATT were (and are) important, not just as international agreements to encourage trade and investment, but as occasions for political debate in which central tensions of liberal capitalism—long dormant within the terms of the postwar hegemonic order—were once again represented in public discourse as open questions, terrains of active socio-political struggle.[1]

I will try to show that there was a clash of world-views implicit in the debate over NAFTA and GATT, and that the long hegemonic vision based upon abstract individualism—sanctioning private profit as the criterion of social good and presuming that generalized benefits flow from expanded trade, intensified competition, enhanced productivity, and aggregate growth—was challenged by potentially counter-hegemonic visions, at least some of which recognized class differences and upheld democracy—understood in terms of communal self-determination—as a value to be defended against globalizing market forces and the criterion of private profit. Then I will argue that this progressive politicization of the economy—pointing toward transformative possibilities rather than distributive struggle within established social positions—converges with gendered critiques of liberal globalization, creating possibilities for creative syntheses of class-based and gender-based political projects.

(Re)politicizing the global economy: NAFTA

Prior to the Congressional vote on NAFTA, journalists and commentators remarked upon the extent to which differing orientations toward the agreement were associated with the different class positions of their informants.

Noting that the Chicago stock brokers and lawyers with whom he spoke seemed generally to favor the agreement, while blue collar workers were almost invariably opposed, Dirk Johnson (1993) wrote in the *New York Times*: "As much as any issue in generations, the trade accord has prompted sentiments that seem to break along economic class lines throughout the country." Johnson's inference was supported by a *New York Times*–CBS News poll conducted just before the first Congressional vote in November, 1993. The poll found support for NAFTA concentrated among college graduates and those with household incomes of $75,000 or more. Those with a high school education or less, adults under 30, blue collar workers, and those with union members in their households tended to oppose the agreement (Ifill, 1993b; see also Aaronson, 1996: 135, 225, n.3).

There was among commentators and pundits a great deal of condescension and sneering toward those who opposed the agreement—implying or asserting that they were illogical, misguided, mistaken, or mendacious, at best ignorant of the most elementary principles of economics, at worst backward protectionists, selfish special interests standing in the way of the greater good which must inevitably flow from freer trade and investment. On the contrary, my argument will be that many of those who opposed the agreement did so on the basis of a very different reading of its significance, and that this significance was directly tied to the politics of class in post-Fordist and post-Reagan America.

The ideological identification which had been at the heart of the postwar hegemonic regime has been opened to question by the anti-labor offensives of the 1980s, but also by long-term tendencies fostered by the liberal world order: in particular, the rise of multinational corporations and transnational production networks in the decades after World War II. Whereas the whole ideological thrust of Fordism had been an identification of the interests of workers with productivity and the profitability of their employer—and, with the assistance of industrial unions, the linking of this identity with a conception of "Americanism" which validated liberal capitalism as a universal model of individual opportunity and freedom—this identification has become problematic as US-based multinational firms have pursued global profits at the expense of American workers, and as the consequences for Fordist living standards in America have become more painfully apparent.[2] While the process of shifting world market production overseas from the US appears to have slowed down somewhat relative to earlier decades, its tangible effects upon American workers have been magnified by the crisis of Fordism in the industrial core and the intensified anti-labor climate established in the 1980s and 1990s.

It was from the perspective of this socio-political context that a cluster of politically progressive NAFTA opponents constructed their arguments. Whereas its supporters tended to cast the agreement (especially in its domestic American ramifications) as politically neutral, a technical instrument enhancing the functioning of international markets and contributing thereby to the general welfare of North American consumers, these NAFTA opponents rejected the economists' homogenizing vision of a world of individual market actors. In a post-Fordist world where global competition turns in significant measure on the reduction of labor costs, this consumer-oriented vision may no longer find an easy resonance with the lives of many Americans fearing wage reductions, benefit cutbacks, downsizing, layoffs, and plant closings. In an attempt to begin to reconstruct popular common sense, and to (re)politicize the linkage between domestic and global economies, these progressive critics envisioned the world as divided by fundamental political-economic inequalities. Accordingly, they represented NAFTA as augmenting the power of multinational capital relative to workers, unions, women, and local communities. Beginning to frame an alternative vision of global political economy based on democratic self-determination and transnational linkages among working people and citizens—rather than allowing markets and the criterion of private profit to determine social outcomes—they counterposed the common sense value of "democracy" to liberalism's traditional valorization of private property. Progressive NAFTA opponents thus aimed at a central tension in liberal common sense in order to attempt to develop an alternative political agenda to that of multinational capital.

I don't want to overstate the coherence or romanticize the radicalness of NAFTA opposition, some of which was indeed nationalistic in its tone. For example, in an article in *Foreign Policy*, Senator Ernest Hollings (Democrat, South Carolina) denounced the agreement in language which resonated with democratic themes, but directed his critical attention entirely at "the ruling oligarchy that thwarts Mexicans' aspirations for representative democracy" (Hollings, 1993–4: 92). Hollings did not link his critique of the PRI regime and the Salinas reforms with an analysis of global liberalization and the power of multinational capital, nor did he relate these themes to the plight of industrial workers after the demise of Fordism. His central point was that unless and until major political reforms are enacted, Mexico's undemocratic regime is not fit for economic union with the United States. Other criticisms of NAFTA were still more overtly nationalist. Ross Perot and Pat Choate claimed that "Mexico had out negotiated the United States," securing favorable provisions in an agreement which "will give away millions of American jobs and radically reduce the sovereignty of the United States" (Perot and Choate, 1993: ii, 1). Although they did express some sympathy for the exploited and downtrodden of Mexico, Perot and Choate's principal goal in rejecting NAFTA appeared to be the renegotiation of a more favorable trade agreement which would be part of "a coherent, long-term US trade strategy" designed to create jobs for Americans, enhance the tax base and reduce the national debt (1993: 103–4). In perhaps the most pernicious criticism of the agreement, Pat Buchanan (1993b) articulated an "America First" perspective in terms of which NAFTA appeared as a diminution of American sovereignty and a dilution of its "unique character" through closer ties with (by implication, culturally inferior) Mexico.

Notwithstanding such highly publicized retrograde arguments against NAFTA and others less commonly represented in the mainstream press—which I will take up in subsequent chapters—I want to suggest now that the positions adopted by the more progressive constellation of agreement critics represented an ideological opening in the postwar consensus, bringing to the surface the contradictions of liberal capitalism such that a counter-hegemonic project—organized around the extension and deepening of democracy—might become thinkable. These anti-NAFTA representations were not free of contradiction and often embraced some liberal norms while rejecting others; however, a recurrent theme was transnational resistance to the prerogatives of private property in the name of collective self-determination.

Despite its basically conservative political commitments and its historic role of upholding the American imperial order (Sims, 1992), the AFL–CIO may have contributed to this questioning by explicitly (if not unambiguously) recognizing the growing tension between American unionism and transnational capitalism, and by backing away from its earlier, less equivocal support of free trade, beginning in the late 1960s and early 1970s. Even those AFL–CIO foreign policy statements of the late 1980s which continued to insist upon the overriding importance of global anti-communism also acknowledged that the world was changing in significant ways, ways which threatened to do further violence to core Fordism and the unions it had supported. In the words of an AFL–CIO foreign policy pamphlet (1987: 1–2), "The exploitation of foreign workers by their employers—often multinational corporations—hurts American workers, too." It hurts them, the AFL–CIO explained, because low-wage foreign workers will not be able to afford to buy their own products, much less American exports. Thus not only is the growth of such employment overseas unlikely to contribute to the prosperity of American labor by extending Fordist affluence on a global scale, but the products of foreign exploitation are likely to be exported to wealthier markets such as the US where they will undercut American wages and endanger union jobs. The American union movement, then, no longer lends its unequivocal support to the liberal agenda of international openness and the expansion of transnational capitalism.

It was on these grounds that the AFL–CIO, along with the United Automobile Workers and other unions, opposed NAFTA as exploitative of Mexican labor, and a threat to American workers and what remains of their Fordist standard of living and institutions of "industrial democracy." An AFL–CIO pamphlet significantly entitled *Exploiting Both Sides* explicitly linked NAFTA to the liberalizing ideology and political agenda of the Reagan–Bush administrations and transnational capital:

The proposed free trade agreement with Mexico is merely the most recent, albeit extreme, manifestation of an ideological world view that believes overall progress can only be achieved if the organization and structure of economic and social affairs is left entirely to private capital. The damage caused by this approach during the past 10 years will be deepened by free trade with Mexico.

(AFL–CIO, 1991: 1)

Unionists argued that the Salinas government was pursuing a strategy of liberalization and low-wage production for export as a way of attracting foreign capital, earning foreign exchange and addressing Mexico's debt crisis, and that these policies and the conditions they supported were the primary attraction for US-based firms seeking "co-production" in Mexico. While acknowledging that closer economic ties with Mexico were likely whether NAFTA was approved or not, AFL–CIO officials argued that it was "neither inevitable nor desirable" that "economic integration [be] based on an international division of labor in which Mexico supplies cheap labor and lax enforcement of health, safety and environmental standards, the United States supplies the consumer market, multinational corporations derive the profit, and US workers face further wage cuts and the loss of their jobs" (Friedman, 1992: 27). The UAW explained how industrial unionists perceived NAFTA and the agenda of hemispheric liberalization as a threat to their already tenuous position in the American political economy: "It will allow employers to take advantage of the poverty and hardship of workers in debt-burdened Latin America to further undermine the wages and working conditions of workers in the United States" (United Automobile Workers, 1992: 2).

Contrary to the way in which their position was represented by pro-NAFTA forces, unions were not simply rejecting free trade in favor of closure. Rather, they argued that the "fast track" negotiating procedures had been substantially undemocratic, and called for a more open and participatory process. Their expressed hope was that such a process would allow for the formulation of an alternative to the corporate market-oriented agenda, one that might more closely resemble the European Community model of a social charter for integration in which "harmonization of workers' rights and labor, health, safety, and environmental standards would be upward, not downward" (AFL–CIO, 1991: 7–8; see also Donahue 1991: 95; Friedman, 1992: 32; United Automobile Workers, 1992: 14–15). The AFL–CIO, whose historic ties to the main government-dominated federation of Mexican labor, CTM (Confederation of Mexican Workers), were strained by divergent positions on NAFTA, initiated contacts with FAT (Authentic Labor Front), Mexico's largest independent labor organization (Hernandez and Sanchez, 1992: 44). While xenophobic, isolationist, and protectionist stances are hardly unheard of in American organized

labor, in the NAFTA debate one strong theme in US union rhetoric advocated a more assertive engagement with conditions in Mexico so that
multinational corporate capital could not use disparities within the continental political economy as a way to perpetuate the exploitation of Mexican
workers and at the same time undermine unionism in America and Canada.[3]
This kind of participatory stance of transnational political engagement—
in opposition to the corporate agenda of global liberalization and the displacement of politics, and thus democratic participation, from the market
—was the thread which tied together many of the groups articulating anti-
NAFTA positions, including activist groups and left-leaning think tanks,
the left press, and political economists who are not identified with the
"serious" mainstream.

The Economic Policy Institute (EPI), often identified as a pro-labor think
tank, saw NAFTA as institutionalizing a low-wage strategy for global
competition, a strategy in which "Mexico's lack of meaningful democratic
institutions and strong and independent labor unions" creates "a long-
term incentive for US producers to respond to global market competition"
by exploiting Mexican workers and the attractive business climate created
by the debt crisis and the Salinas reforms. EPI claimed that this would
result in a diversion of productive investment from the US, the loss of
hundreds of thousands of high-wage jobs, downward pressure on the wages
of less skilled workers, and still further polarization of income distribution
in the US. Instead of this low-wage strategy, EPI called for a two-prong
integration strategy similar to the European Community's, including: 1) a
"Social Charter which establishes the principle that trade should not be
based on 'social dumping', where poorer countries follow low-wage, low
regulation strategies in order to increase exports"; and (2) a mechanism
for addressing the grossest inequalities by redistributing resources toward
the most disadvantaged countries, regions, or groups within the integrated
zone (Faux and Lee, 1992: 20, 22; see also Lee, 1993).

The Labor Education and Research Project—publishers of *Labor Notes*,
a monthly newsletter for labor activists—also strongly opposed NAFTA
on the grounds that it would facilitate the use of transcontinental competition ("whipsawing") between countries, plants, and workers to undermine potential or actual solidarity among workers and intensify their
exploitation in all three countries. *Labor Notes* saw this as the outcome of
a pro-corporate political strategy: the primary significance which these
labor activists assigned to NAFTA was its integral relation to the post-
Fordist corporate agenda of "deregulating a continent."

> The North American Free Trade Agreement is not about the com-
> merce of nations. . . . It is about letting private business reorganize the
> North American economy without the checks and balances once pro-
> vided by unions, social movements, or governments. [NAFTA] would

roll back a hundred years of controls and restrictions that were placed on private business in the interests of the majority of people.

(Moody and McGinn, 1992: 1)

In response to this transnational corporate strategy, *Labor Notes* called for intensive efforts to build labor solidarity across the emerging continental economy. It identified for American unionists potential allies in Canada and Mexico and set out the basic points of a "solidarity strategy." The premise of this strategy was that "Upward harmonization requires a continuous raising of human and labor rights, social welfare, and environmental standards in all of the countries covered by the free trade agreement." To help realize this goal, *Labor Notes* urged unionists to set up local union committees on international solidarity, to participate in an emerging national grassroots labor network on free trade, and to begin to set up industry-wide or corporation-wide transnational labor networks which might ultimately facilitate internationally coordinated collective bargaining. Further, *Labor Notes* has organized an ongoing series of conferences bringing together unionists and activists from throughout North America and elsewhere (Moody and McGinn, 1992: 44, 51–6; see also Moody, 1991; Moody and McGinn, 1991).

Opponents of NAFTA documented governmental and corporate abuses of internationally recognized worker rights in Mexico. A major study entitled *Mask of Democracy*, authored by labor historian and activist Dan La Botz and sponsored by the International Labor Rights Education and Research Fund, showed how the Salinas government's export-oriented development strategy has entailed the suppression of independent unionism and the widespread violation of workers rights. Major Mexican union federations (especially CTM) are dominated by the one-party state and are internally undemocratic. Further, the state is empowered to grant or deny legal recognition to unions and to declare strikes legal or illegal. And the Mexican government has a track record of using police and military forces to suppress independent unionism and keep control of the workplace in the hands of corporate investors (La Botz, 1992). On this view, then, Mexico's comparative advantage and its primary contribution to the free trade area involve the use of state power to prevent workers (and human rights activists and others) from challenging the Salinas economic strategy of low-wage export production. The implication of this line of argument is that NAFTA will amplify the ramifications of Mexican labor policy for the US and Canadian political economies, generating more intense competitive pressures which will make it more difficult to sustain worker rights throughout the continent.

Mexico's repressive political economy has entailed consistent violations of internationally recognized human rights, as documented by such organizations as Amnesty International and Americas Watch. In a letter sent to

President Clinton only weeks before the Congressional vote, Americas Watch lamented that "little has been done to facilitate Mexico's long awaited and much hoped for transition to democracy. The Mexican government remains intolerant of public criticism and determined to suppress—through devious or overtly brutal means—challenges to its policies." While Americas Watch took no position on NAFTA's approval, it noted that neither the NAFTA agreement nor its supplemental agreements addressed these issues, and urged that democracy and human rights be placed on the agenda if a North American, and ultimately perhaps hemispheric, free trade area was to be created:

> As the European Community realized when it began the process of relaxing trade barriers and building a regional economy, the successful integration of their national economies required a shared commitment to democratic practices and respect for fundamental rights. Similarly, respect for democracy and human rights must be the foundation on which integrated North American development is built. If NAFTA becomes the model for expanding free trade with other nations in the hemisphere, it is all the more important that the United States affirm the centrality of human rights and democratic governance to closer economic relations.
>
> (Americas Watch, 1993)

The tensions and possibilities of liberal common sense were clearly evident in the Americas Watch letter, on the one hand supporting protection of individual rights and liberties and "an unfettered civil society" against governmental depredations, while on the other upholding democracy and communal self-determination as norms indivisible from the process of economic integration.

The International Labor Rights Education and Research Fund (ILRERF), in conjunction with the Canadian Center for Policy Alternatives, also published an analysis of the implications of NAFTA for democracy in the hemisphere written by political scientist Ian Robinson. He began by arguing that economic equality and the protection of worker rights are necessary conditions for stable, "high quality" democracy. Viewing NAFTA in the context of changing regional and national political economies, he suggested that it is likely to do substantial harm to the conditions upon which democracy rests:

> the growing income inequality and the erosion of worker rights that characterized the 1980s in these three countries can be traced, to a considerable degree, to the trade liberalization and other market deregulation initiatives of that decade. . . . since the NAFTA will extend the scope and depth of these initiatives, it is likely to intensify the social trends of the last decade. . . . For Mexico, these trends mean

that its chances of becoming a stable democracy are substantially reduced; for the United States and Canada, it means that the quality of democracy has been deteriorating for more than a decade and will continue to do so at an increasing pace.

(Robinson, 1993: 25, 28)

Like other progressive NAFTA critics, Robinson prescribed what he called a "pro-democracy trade policy" which would include a transnational Social Charter to uphold and protect labor rights, enhance economic equality, and promote democracy within the North American Free Trade Area. Both Robinson and the Economic Policy Institute criticized the labor side agreement negotiated by President Clinton as inadequately protecting labor rights and falling well short of the desired Social Charter (Levinson, 1993; Robinson, 1993: 37–46).

Fears of a continental, hemispheric, or global political economy dominated by the institutionalized power of corporate capital, and the desire to construct a more democratic and participatory vision of the world, provided the common ground upon which NAFTA's labor critics could be joined by environmental activists, consumer advocates, and others. Anti-NAFTA coalitions formed which also stressed the potential degradation of environmental, health and safety, and consumer protection standards in the transnational corporate economy, in addition to the agreement's effects upon labor. Critics feared that such protections might be directly attacked as non-tariff barriers to trade. Further, they warned of the indirect effects which the agreement would have upon the ability of communities and political units to maintain regulatory standards. They suggested that the agreement would facilitate capital mobility and enhance the bargaining power of corporations seeking to avoid democratically enacted restrictions or regulations. In the context of a free trade area in which such regulations have been enacted unevenly, the effect would be to subject producers and communities in zones of higher regulation to intensified competitive pressures from producers located in areas of lesser regulation. This dynamic of downward leveling became known among critics as the "race to the bottom." They feared that attempts to shield more highly regulated domestic or local producers from such competitive pressures could be attacked under the terms of the agreement as discriminatory barriers to trade, and rulings by democratically unaccountable tribunals of international trade bureaucrats could effectively deprive citizens of the ability to maintain local or national standards.[4]

Lori Wallach of Public Citizen summarized in the following terms the concerns of environmental and consumer advocates: "Trade agreements are negotiated in secret by governmental representatives working closely with corporate advisors and are enforced by procedures hidden from public scrutiny. Without reforms to trade policy, the 1990s may become a decade of retrenchment, when hard-won environmental and consumer safeguards are preempted or overruled because citizens around the world are being effectively cut out of the decision making process" (Wallach, 1993: 23–4). In full page advertisements which ran in the *New York Times* and the *Washington Post*, a group of 25 environmental and citizen activist groups denounced NAFTA as a scheme to empower and enrich corporate capital at the expense of the masses of citizens and their democratic representation:

> Promoted as a boon to all of us, the true purpose of NAFTA is to help large corporations increase their profits. NAFTA does this by under-mining laws and standards (in the US, Canada and Mexico) that inhibit uncontrolled corporate freedoms. Freedom to circumvent demo-cratically created environmental, health and safety laws. Freedom to set poor working conditions and keep wages low.... NAFTA will seriously stifle representative democracy by making local, state or national laws *subject to an unelected NAFTA bureaucracy that citizens cannot control.*[5]

Overlapping networks of grassroots activist groups coalesced around the issue of free trade agreements. Exemplifying the critical positions reviewed above, a document entitled *US Citizens' Analysis of the North American Free Trade Agreement* was collaboratively produced by representatives of the UAW, ILRERF, EPI, the Institute for Policy Studies, the Institute for Agriculture and Trade Policy, the Development Group for Alternative Policies, the National Lawyers Guild, the Fair Trade Campaign, Public Citizen, the Sierra Club, and Greenpeace (Development GAP, 1992). Action Canada Network—a broad-based coalition long active against North American free trade—similarly denounced NAFTA and its neoliberal market-based agenda as anti-democratic, and proposed an array of alternatives aimed at citizen empowerment (Action Canada Network, n.d.; 1993).

One of the groups which played a leading role in bringing together labor unionists and grassroots activists from the US, Mexico, and Canada, and in providing information and support to anti-NAFTA organizers across North America, was the Minnesota Fair Trade Coalition. As the NAFTA debate was beginning to intensify and to capture public attention, William McGaughey—to whom Gramsci might have referred as an "organic intellectual" of the fair trade movement—published a book in which he laid out the now familiar set of progressive anti-NAFTA criticisms reviewed above (McGaughey, 1992: 1–81). But, still more interesting, McGaughey also offered his readers a fairly explicit theorization of the socio-political context of NAFTA, and a vision of an alternative future in which international organizations such as the International Labor Organization or even GATT could themselves serve as vehicles for the creation of a more equitable and democratic world. McGaughey's political critique of NAFTA was based upon a pluralistic vision of society which he saw being increasingly menaced by the influence of "free market" strains of liberal ideology which serve to disguise the social power of business. To the extent that deregulation and globalization of private business have enhanced its power relative to government, as well as groups and individuals in civil society, it threatens to create a condition McGaughey called "business totalitarianism" (1992: 83–104). He saw the unfolding NAFTA debate as presenting the potential for "the opening shot in the anti-totalitarian battle against business domination of our hemisphere and world" (1992: 105). For this possibility to be realized, he argued that the American labor movement would have to broaden its agenda, seek alliances with other social forces and extend these coalitions on a transnational basis (1992: 108–10). If successful, he suggested, such a transnational political movement could conceivably reshape the content and meaning of major international institutions (1992: 139–76). Viewed in this way, NAFTA appeared as much more than a simple trade agreement, but rather as one aspect of an ongoing political contest with major implications for social power, democracy, and global order.

In addition to grassroots linkages such as those fostered by the Minnesota Fair Trade Coalition, broad networks of various activist groups from across North America came together to formulate a common critique of NAFTA and the agenda of liberal globalization, and to begin to imagine more participatory, egalitarian, democratic, and sustainable alternatives. Between 1993 and 1994, a series of six transnational meetings took place including representatives of labor, environmental, religious, consumer, farm, and women's groups. The product of these meetings was a document entitled *A Just and Sustainable Trade and Development Initiative for the Western Hemisphere* (Alliance for Responsible Trade, 1994).[6] While initially formulated to address the integration of the Western hemisphere, the Initiative explicitly extended its horizons to encompass the negotiation of a new global order. To ensure social responsibility and accountability on the part of private firms, it called for detailed codes of conduct to be binding upon international economic actors, and reform of the multilateral institutions governing international economic relations so as to safeguard and enforce basic human rights—especially those embodied in the various codes of the International Labor Organization and the UN Conventions on the Elimination of Racial Discrimination and Discrimination against Women. And new standards such as "the right to a toxic-free workplace and living environment" would be added to this battery of social protections. As a yardstick for the assessment of globalization, the Initiative promoted the criterion of "social sustainability" encompassing not just environmental safeguards but also "the protection of children's welfare, the welfare of families, women's and men's well being, minority and indigenous rights, and the broad geographic sharing of economic gains" (Alliance for Responsible Trade, 1994: 3–4). As an integral part of this counter-hegemonic vision, it prescribed the reduction of inequalities among nations, within nations, and across social categories of gender and race. The culture and self-determination of indigenous groups were to be respected. Provisions for adequate health care, elder and child care, as well as proscriptions of child labor, violence and discrimination against women, and job stereotyping, would serve to lessen the economic dependence and double-burden experienced by many women. The Initiative called for economic integration to be accompanied by compensatory financing and debt reduction to lessen economic disparities, forestall the race to the bottom and raise the floor under all participants in the transnational economy, at the same time enabling more widespread participation in its governance. "Development should be a process in which, to the fullest extent possible, citizens participate in and local communities control the initiation and implementation of economic decisions that affect their lives. Achieving this goal will require new mechanisms to make governments, legal institutions, and private corporations more accessible and accountable to the public." Accordingly, the Initiative suggested that "new [transnational] institutions should be managed transparently and democratically with broad social, governmental, and private participation" (1994: 5).

These kinds of critical themes were represented in scattered articles in the mainstream press,[7] and a blizzard of articles and editorial statements in the left press.[8] Accessible essays critical of the liberal global agenda were included in an anthology by scholars associated with the Center for Popular Economics (Larudee, 1993; Schor, 1993). Paperback collections of short essays, aimed at a mass popular audience, were published by the Institute for Food and Development Policy (Food First) in collaboration with the Institute for Policy Studies (Cavanagh, 1992b), by a constellation of non-mainstream authors led by Ralph Nader (Nader, 1993a), and by South End Press (Brecher et al., 1993).[9] A common theme of these representations was the need to counter the corporate vision of global liberalization with a vision of a more participatory global order, a transnational democratic impulse which John Brown Childs referred to as "globalization from below" (Brecher et al., 1993: xv). In the words of John Cavanagh of the Institute for Policy Studies, "The key to genuine democracy in this decade will be the struggle by communities and citizens' organizations to control their own destinies, to take control of their own lands and natural resources, to collectively make the decisions that affect their futures. The free trade agreements that are currently on the table appropriate these decisions and toss them to the private sector" (Cavanagh, 1992a: 6–7).

That these sorts of programmatic statements were not simple posturing is attested by the evidence of cross-border organizing activity on the part of labor activists, citizens, and community groups in all three countries. By June, 1992, researchers associated with the Inter-Hemispheric Resource Center had listed at least 12 fair trade networks, 53 labor organizations, 39 environmental groups, and 58 advocacy organizations, all supporting (to one degree or another, and in varying forms) increased grassroots cooperation on a continental basis (Hernandez and Sanchez, 1992).[10] Such transnational activism did not expire with the passage of NAFTA (Alexander and Gilmore, 1994; La Botz, 1994; Kamel and Hoffman, 1999). This seems to me the strongest possible rebuttal to the widespread allegation that NAFTA critics were nothing more than xenophobic protectionists whose horizons extended no further than the border and the customs house.

GATT

Although formally opposed to GATT, America's primary labor federation, the AFL–CIO, was much less vigorous than it had been in the NAFTA debate; and Ross Perot was slow off the mark as well (Grier, 1993; Bradsher, 1994; Moody, 1995). The most vocal opposition to US approval of the Uruguay Round agreements came from Patrick Buchanan and Ralph Nader's group, Public Citizen. Nader and Buchanan joined forces in June, 1994 for a joint press conference attacking GATT and the proposed WTO. While both men focused upon fears that GATT–WTO would weaken US sovereignty, their reasoning was quite different. Buchanan's economic and cultural nationalism will be discussed in the next chapter. Nader and his group emphasized the extent to which WTO membership would constrain democratic self-government by US citizens and their elected representatives: "If Congress votes to join the WTO, trade bureaucrats meeting in Geneva would have power over economic, environmental, food safety, tax and other US domestic policies" (Public Citizen, quoted in Aaronson, 1996: 154). But this power would be largely unaccountable and anti-democratic: "The World Trade Organization has no place for ordinary citizens. Officials of [the WTO] are not elected by citizens. Citizens cannot attend meetings or tribunal hearings. Documents are kept secret and are not subject to the US Freedom of Information Act. Yet, citizens must live with what the World Trade Organization decides" (Public Citizen, 1994). In effect, rule by unelected WTO officials would insulate transnational corporate activity from direct public accountability, facilitating what Nader called "an unprecedented corporate power grab." On this view, the agenda of global liberalization allows multinational corporations "to expand their control over the international economy and to undo vital health, safety and environmental protections won by citizen movements across the globe in recent decades ... Global commerce without commensurate democratic global law may be the dream of corporate chief executive officers, but it would be a disaster for the rest of the world with its ratcheting downwards of workers, consumer, and environmental standards" (Nader, 1993b: 1, 2–3; see also Wallach, 1993).

While Lane Kirkland and the official leadership of the AFL–CIO were largely missing in action during the GATT debates, labor activists who had been mobilized against NAFTA continued their critique of liberal globalization. Addressing the more militant wing of the US labor movement through the pages of the activist journal *Labor Notes*, Kim Moody denounced the GATT–WTO as a blueprint for "market monarchy" in which businesses enjoy enhanced freedom from the constraints of democratically enacted regulation. Noting that citizens, labor unions, and grassroots organizations have no standing within the global trade forum, Moody concluded that in this new world order "Democracy takes a back seat to business, the market, and the WTO" (Moody, 1994).

Democracy and the emerging critique of globalization

As we saw in Chapter 2, the restructuring of capitalist production and exchange relations—partially understandable in terms of "globalization"— is dramatically enhancing the social powers of employers and investors in relation to governments, communities, citizens and workers, women, and people of color. However, viewed from the perspective of liberal capitalism, these powers are understood not in terms of social relations potentially subject to communal governance but as private prerogatives attendant upon the ownership of property. The result is a peculiar form of democracy in which the potential for social self-determination is undermined by democratically unaccountable concentrations of "private" power. As Ellen Meiksins Wood has it, "Liberal democracy leaves untouched the whole [historically specific] sphere of domination and coercion created by capitalism, its relocation of substantial powers from the state to civil society, to private property and the compulsions of the market" (Wood, 1995: 234). Moreover, even the relatively tepid democracy which is thereby enabled to exist in the public, political sphere of liberal capitalist societies is subject to corruptions and structural constraints which dramatically narrow the range of possible outcomes and effectively institutionalize class-based powers and privileges. For class power is not confined within the boundaries of the "economy"; it has broader political manifestations as well. "Even in a society whose government meets the liberal democratic ideal, capital has a kind of veto power over public policy that is quite independent of its ability to intervene directly in elections or in state decision making" (Bowles and Gintis, 1986: 88). If members of the owning class were somehow unable or unwilling to access political influence through massive campaign contributions, private coffees with the President or nights spent in the Lincoln bedroom, they would nonetheless be uniquely privileged by virtue of their structural situation and social powers. Insofar as the state under capitalism depends for its economic viability upon the investment activities of a class of "private" owners of the social means of production, it is effectively subject to their collective blackmail. If a state fails to maintain conditions of "business confidence" (Block, 1977a: 16), or if it enacts policies which appear threatening to the interests of the owning class, investors responsible only to their own pocketbooks may decline to invest there. In effect, they may subject the state to a "capital strike"—driving up interest rates, depressing levels of economic activity, throwing people out of work, exacerbating the fiscal crisis of the state, and endangering the popular legitimacy of the incumbent government. Thus are market values enforced upon governments which claim to be responsive to popular democratic pressures. "The presumed sovereignty of the democratic citizenry fails in the presence of the capital strike" (Bowles and Gintis, 1986: 90).

The power of transnationally mobile capital to override democratic processes and public deliberations has vastly increased, along with the growth of international liquidity and the sophistication and speed of exchange in the world's financial markets. According to Howard Wachtel, "Only about 18 percent [of the enormous volume of foreign exchange transactions] support either international trade or investment . . . The other 82 percent is speculation . . ." (Wachtel, 1995: 36). These huge speculative flows are highly volatile. The volume and speed of this trading has heightened the potential disciplinary effect of a threatened capital strike, and governments are increasingly obliged to weigh carefully their welfare, fiscal, and monetary policies against the interests of investors who may exit *en masse* in response to expectations of lower relative interest rates or higher relative inflation rates. This disciplinary power has the effect of prioritizing the interests of investors, who are as a class effectively able to hold entire states and societies hostage. Moreover, the particular interests of the owning class are represented as if they were the general interests of all: "since profit is the necessary condition of universal expansion, capitalists appear within capitalist societies as bearers of a universal interest" (Przeworski, quoted in Thomas, 1994: 153). In this ideological construction, the social and moral claims of working people and the poor are reduced to the pleadings of "special interests" which must be resisted in order to secure the conditions of stable accumulation. In William Greider's apt summary,

> Like bondholders in general, the new governing consensus explicitly assumed that faster economic growth was dangerous—threatening to the stable financial order—so nations were effectively blocked from measures that might reduce permanent unemployment or ameliorate the decline in wages. . . . Governments were expected to withdraw more and more benefits from dependent classes of citizens—the poor and elderly and unemployed—but also in various ways from the broad middle class, in order to honor their obligations to the creditor class . . .
> (Greider, 1997: 298, 308)

This disciplinary power was reflected in Bill Clinton's speedy transformation from a candidate advocating "putting people first" (through job creation and public investment strategies) to an incumbent deficit hawk whose eyes were glued to the bond markets (Greider, 1997: ch. 13). The ideological equation of the interests of investors with the universal interest is also reflected in the World Bank's declarations that globalization of capital is a positive force, "richly rewarding policy when it is sound but punishing it hard when it is unsound" (World Bank, 1995: 5).

Formidable as this class-based power may be, however, it is neither omnipresent nor omnipotent. As Jeffrey Isaac usefully reminds us, the reproduction of social power relations "is *always* problematic," embedded in relations which are reciprocal if not necessarily symmetrical: "the successful exercise of power is always a contingent and negotiated outcome of interaction. The interpretation of social norms, the struggle over their meaning, is a crucial ambit of this negotiation" (Isaac, 1987: 93, 101). Thus struggles over the meaning of "democracy" may serve to reproduce or contest the relations of power and domination embedded within liberal capitalism. To the extent that the "private" powers of employers and investors are understood to inhibit communal self-determination, popular aspirations for democracy can become a potentially transformative force; and insofar as liberal globalization is implicated in these relations, it too may be subjected to transformative critique. I wish now to argue that the emergence of such democratizing critiques is among the most significant consequences of recent globalization debates.

Ian Robinson, a political scientist associated with the Canadian Center for Policy Alternatives, has been an outspoken critic of the latest rounds of transnational liberal institutionalization, arguing that NAFTA and the WTO empower transnational capital at the expense of democratic self-government at national and local levels. They do this in two ways. First, these "free capital agreements" directly impose legal restrictions upon the policies which governments may enact, for example prohibiting performance requirements which might otherwise be used to impose some measure of social responsibility upon transnational investors, and limiting public provision of goods and services which might circumvent the market imperatives of private profit. Second, by subjecting established political communities to intensified competitive pressure, investors will be able to seek out the most congenial environment in terms of wages, labor and environmental regulations, tax burdens, and so forth. In this way, the imperatives of market competition are focused upon the public sphere, compelling governments to reduce to the world economy's lowest common denominator the burdens and social responsibilities placed upon investors—fostering a race to the bottom. Together, these two effects have a devastating impact on the bargaining power of democratic communities: "The ban on performance requirements protects corporations from competing against one another to give governments concessions in return for the right to invest. There is nothing to prevent governments from competing to offer concessions to corporations in return for their investment, and much that encourages it" (Robinson, 1995: 176; see also Robinson, 1993).

The journalist William Greider has emerged as one of the public intellectuals of the global economy. Greider sees the post–Cold War world as deeply contradictory: "The historic paradox is breathtaking: At the very moment when western democracies and capitalism have triumphed over the communist alternative, their own systems of self-government are being gradually unraveled by the market system" (Greider, 1993: 212). In a highly suggestive formulation, he has argued for a broadening of political horizons in order to combat the rise of "offshore politics" which institutionalizes the power of transnational capital and further distances citizens from possibilities for democratic self-determination:

> For ordinary Americans, traditionally independent and insular, the challenge requires them to think anew their place in the world. The only plausible way that citizens can defend themselves and their nation against the forces of globalization is to link their own interests cooperatively with the interests of other peoples in other nations—that is with the foreigners who are competitors for the jobs and production but who are also victimized by the system. Americans will have to create new democratic alliances across national borders with the less prosperous people caught in the same dilemma. Together, they have to impose new political standards on multinational enterprises and on their own governments. The challenge, in other words, involves taking the meaning of democracy to a higher plane ...
>
> (Greider, 1993: 196)

As I read Greider, he is suggesting that Americans move away from social self-understandings revolving around American liberal exceptionalism and privilege, and begin to see themselves enmeshed in webs of transnational economic and political relationships, webs which are structured around the social powers of capital. A reorientation of this kind is a condition of possibility for the construction of common interests with others similarly (if not identically) subordinated to transnational capital. "Genuine reform will require new and unprecedented forms of cross-border politics in which citizens develop continuing dialogues across national boundaries and learn to speak for their common values. Only by acting together can they hope to end the exploitation ... across the global production system" (Greider, 1993: 203). While not altogether unproblematic, Greider's vision holds enormous appeal for me.[11] In passages such as these, he is imagining the possibility of new kinds of political identity and action emerging from public deliberations among those located in similar structural circumstances in the global economy. This vision implies the de-reification of liberal dichotomies separating economics from politics, society from state, and domestic from international, and a democratic renegotiation of the social relations of capitalist modernity. If democracy is to be understood as a process of deliberative social self-determination (Arblaster, 1987; Dryzek, 1996), then Greider's vision seems to me a major step beyond the procedural democracy of liberal capitalism. It is a step onto a path of popular empowerment which leads toward challenging the institutionalized powers of transnational capital, and in so doing opens up a range of possible futures which are inaccessible from within the fixed horizons of liberal capitalism. For me, it is this democratizing vision which redeems Greider's calls for global Keynesianism and redistribution (see especially Greider, 1997); for that could become little more than a "passive revolution," disempowering popular movements by granting limited concessions which leave intact the political forms of capitalism and the social powers of capital. The project of democratization, it seems to me, provides critical resources with which to put pressure upon any such pre-emptive accommodation.

How might such a democratizing politics be translated into a strategy for attacking the powers of transnational capital? Jeremy Brecher and Tim Costello are also politically engaged public intellectuals who are committed to furthering democratic self-determination in a transnational political economy. They describe their project as "globalization from below" and explain that it rests on "the fundamental premise of democracy, that people should be able to make the decisions that affect their lives." This project then requires "that global institutions be democratic, transparent, accountable, and accessible to the public" (Brecher and Costello, 1994a: 78). Their "Lilliput strategy" seems to me a useful metaphor for imagining such a new global politics:

> Facing powerful global forces and institutions, people need to combine their relatively modest sources of power with often very different sources of power available to participants in other movements and locations. Just as the tiny Lilliputians captured Gulliver by tying him with many small pieces of thread, the Lilliput strategy weaves many particular actions designed to prevent downward leveling into a system of rules and practices that together force upward leveling.
>
> (Brecher and Costello, 1994b: 758)

Brecher and Costello envision "a multilevel system of democratic governance" (Brecher and Costello, 1994a: 79; see also Held, 1995): networks of overlapping grassroots social movements—encompassing "working people, women, marginalized groups and their communities" (Brecher and Costello, 1994b: 758)—which would produce democratically constructed demands for social responsibility in economic life, enacted and institutionalized at multiple levels from local to global. The vehicles for achieving this popular empowerment and upward leveling might include corporate codes of conduct, social charters in international trade agreements, transnational labor rights and environmental campaigns, and they embrace Jorge Casteneda's call for a "grand bargain" between the global North and South whereby citizens of the North would actively support imports from the South so long as these were produced in accordance with democratically determined social, labor, and environmental standards (Brecher and Costello, 1994a: 110–11, 121–40). This vision presupposes "a dia-

logue among First and Third World popular movements and organizations" (1994a: 110). Accordingly, Brecher and Costello acknowledge the
crucial importance of supplanting liberal individualism with a more
contextualized social self-understanding as a basis for political action: "To
link self interest with common *global* interests, the first step is to clarify
the connections between the immediate conditions people face and the
global processes that are affecting them." They call on their readers to
"resist downward leveling where you are and help others resist it where
they are" (Brecher and Costello, 1994b: 758–9). In contrast to the anti-
democratic "corporate agenda," they call for "a virtual democratic revolution" but insist that this cannot be confined within liberal capitalist
understandings of the political sphere: "the movement to expand democracy will mean little to most people unless democracy gives them the
opportunity to reshape the economic, social and environmental conditions
of their daily lives" (1994b: 760). So they too imagine new forms of
boundary-crossing political practice, and new kinds of subjects to enact
them, inconsistent with those of liberal capitalism.

Kim Moody, veteran labor activist and editor of *Labor Notes*, anti-
cipates the emergence of a new international "social movement unionism"
in response to the hardships and rigors imposed transnationally by neoliberal
regimes and lean production systems—"a rebellion against capitalist
globalization" which begins with a rejection of the ideology of cooperation
with employers in the interest of international competitiveness (Moody,
1997b: 53; see also Moody, 1997a). In place of this strategy of capitulation to market forces, Moody envisions "social movement unionism" as
"an active strategic orientation that uses the strongest of society's oppressed and exploited, generally organized workers, to mobilize those who
are less able to sustain self-mobilization: the poor, the unemployed, the
casualized workers, the neighborhood organizations" (Moody, 1997b: 59).
This strategy implies that unions must work toward broader social agendas in which the interests of the "working class public" may be reflected,
and the linkage of these movements across borders. Thus he calls for
transnational campaigns to spread employment by reducing work weeks,
to reduce or forgive Third World debt, and to reestablish social safety nets.
All of these would effectively strengthen the position of working classes by
reducing the vulnerability of those who must sell their labor-power in
order to survive. As important for Moody, such campaigns could themselves foster a self-transformative process as social forces coalesce and
struggle around common agendas and overlapping social visions.

All of this may sound wildly utopian, but such visions continue to
animate transnational grassroots movements formulating more egalitarian,
democratic, and sustainable visions of globalization. For example, the
Peoples Hemispheric Agreement of 1998 was drafted by coalitions from
Canada, Quebec, Chile, Mexico, and the USA, and embodies many of the
social values and commitments expressed in earlier, trinational documents

such as the *Just and Sustainable Trade and Development Initiative* (Kamel and Hoffman, 1999: 114–15; compare Alliance for Responsible Trade, 1994).

In consultation with a number of the activists and non-governmental organizations involved in these multinational dialogues, Congressional progressives led by Bernie Sanders (Independent, Vermont) in 1999 drafted a document envisioning far-reaching reforms of the global economy (Brecher and Smith, 1999; E. Frank, 1999; Sanders, 1999). In its opening pages, *The Global Sustainable Development Resolution* declared as its overriding purpose that "the people of the United States and the people and governments of the other nations of the world should take actions to establish democratic control over the global economy" (Sanders, 1999: 2). The Resolution declared that unregulated economic globalization has produced the following consequences: heightened financial volatility and instability; intensified competitive pressures driving a race to the bottom in labor, environmental, and social standards; tendencies toward inadequate aggregate demand and underemployment; increased poverty; massive increases in economic inequality; intensification of discriminatory burdens born by women, ethnic, and racial minorities and indigenous peoples; and the degradation of democracy. In contrast to this situation, the Resolution envisioned a global economy which would be framed by such principles as "democracy at every level of government from the local to the global," human rights (including "labor, social, environmental, economic and cultural rights") for all people, environmental sustainability, and "economic advancement for the most oppressed and exploited parts of the population, including women, immigrants, racial and ethnic minorities and indigenous peoples" (Sanders, 1999: 9). Sanders and his collaborators propose reforming international economic institutions so that voting rights are based on population rather than wealth, increasing the openness of their decision-making procedures, and explicitly including in their deliberations "labor unions, environmental groups, women's organizations, development organizations, and other major sectors of civil society in each affected country" (Sanders, 1999: 16). Further, the drafters call for the creation of Commissions on the Global Economy at national and transnational levels to encourage broad public debate (explicitly including the various elements of civil society) on globalization and alternative possible futures. The drafters further envision measures to re-regulate capital and tax foreign exchange transactions in order to reduce short-term speculative capital flows and encourage long-term investment in socially accountable and sustainable development. They call for the cancellation of debts owed by the poorest countries, and the reorientation of international financial institutions toward domestic economic growth and full employment rather than domestic austerity and export-led growth. And they propose enforceable codes of conduct designed to "establish public control and citizen sovereignty over global corporations" (Sanders, 1999: 41). Labor, environmental, and social standards would be inscribed in these codes of conduct, as well as in the governing principles of international financial institutions and trade agreements. According to Sanders' office, the Resolution was endorsed by at least 70 non-governmental organizations, including many which have been active in resistance to neoliberal globalization, for example Public Citizen's Global Trade Watch, Campaign for Labor Rights, Fifty Years is Enough, Global Exchange, Interhemispheric Resource Center, International Labor Rights Fund, Institute for Policy Studies, United Electrical Workers, Friends of the Earth, and the Center for International Environmental Law.

There are resources extant within popular common sense, in the US and elsewhere, which will continue to motivate projects for the democratization of the capitalist (world) economy. These themes find their way even into the nooks and crannies of commercial popular culture in the US. Michael Moore—director of the wildly popular documentary film, *Roger and Me*, and erstwhile practitioner of guerrilla television on his national network program *TV Nation*—appeals directly to these critical resources in order to call into question the undemocratic powers resident within the capitalist economy. In his best-selling book entitled *Downsize This!*, Moore writes: "We live in a country that's founded on the basic principle of fairness: that all people should be treated with dignity and should have a say in matters that affect their lives. Why do we abandon this principle when we enter the [workplace]? Isn't this America, too? Or is 'life, liberty, and the pursuit of happiness' not allowed from 9 to 5 (or 6, 7 or 8 PM)?" (Moore, 1997: 145). Moore's critique and others like it lead toward a questioning of the reified boundaries separating the economic and the political and so opens up space for a potential democratization of the capitalist economy. More importantly still, such a critical politics addresses the inhabitants of the world economy not as abstract individuals instrumentally interacting within the horizons of a market, but as members of participatory political communities whose powers of democratic deliberation extend, through various articulations, to permeate the global economy. Once social self-understandings are redefined in such ways, political horizons may be extended and democratizing dynamics unleashed in ways difficult for capitalism, and its masculinist and racist articulations, to contain.

Globalization and the political economy of gender

Emerging feminist critiques of capitalist restructuring and globalization extend the horizon of this democratizing project into the "private" sphere of the household, family life, and sexuality. Johanna Brenner (1993) has provided an analysis of contemporary US feminism which is in many ways complementary to Michelle Barrett's understanding of a socialist-feminist project and Linda McDowell's analysis of the demise of the Fordist gender order. Brenner argues that gendered aspects of the current wave of transnational capitalist restructuring and the retrenchment of the welfare state in the US have combined to place great political economic pressures upon women, especially working class women and women of color.

In this "new gender order," two major tributaries of "second wave" feminism may appear to have run dry. Liberal feminism, with its demands for abstract equality of women and men, has been largely "institutionalized and culturally incorporated as women's right to compete and contract free from limitations imposed on account of our sex" (Brenner, 1993: 102). Enabling women to participate in the market more fully, however, may seem something of a Pyrrhic victory in an era when the conditions surrounding the sale of labor-power are dramatically worsening for all but the most privileged workers. Moreover, "a politics which focuses *exclusively* on discriminatory treatment is inevitably class and race biased because it ignores women's differential resources for competing in the market" (1993: 117). However, "social welfare feminism" which seeks to go beyond abstract equality and more directly address material issues which affect working women—for instance, advocating government assistance in securing paid parental leave, universal healthcare and quality childcare—is hobbled by its strategic dependence upon a Democratic Party whose concern for working people (much less working women) is ambiguous at best and duplicitous at worst.

Brenner concludes that these two wings of "second wave" feminism should be supplanted by a new, more broadly-based strategy, "a serious and disruptive challenge to capital, a broad and militant 'rainbow movement', including new, more social and political forms of trade union struggle and national political organization independent of the Democratic Party" (Brenner, 1993: 103). She envisions the development of a "third wave" politics that "combines the liberatory moments (the demand for individual self-expression, self-determination, and democratic participation) of the movements for democratic inclusion (feminism, civil rights, gay/lesbian rights) with new struggles over material needs (for healthcare, for childcare and paid prenatal leave, for living-wage jobs, for a clean environment)" (1993: 157). Crucial to this renewed socialist-feminist agenda is the fostering of "grassroots networks and solidarities" which will be enabling, and which will support a kind of snowball effect whereby those engaged in organized struggle grow and develop as members of more self-determining communities. Political organization, then, is not to be understood instrumentally, but as part of a self-transformative process: "The main point of organizing people around their immediate needs is to develop the capacities of women activists, their critical understanding and confidence in collective action, their commitments to ways of organizing social life that are democratic and participatory" (1993: 149). And among the conditions of a healthy and vibrant democracy are social commitments for shared domestic and childcare responsibilities to enable equalized access to economic and political life for both men and women.

To what degree have these sorts of materialist feminist critiques and positions been reflected in the debates surrounding "globalization"?

Feminist activists challenge neoliberal globalization

Mainstream US women's groups such as NOW—the National Organization for Women—have been slow to engage the public deliberations on issues of globalization, and in particular were conspicuously absent from the NAFTA debates. Marianne Marchand (1996) has argued that this may have been a consequence of the manner in which the NAFTA debates were discursively framed. Marchand argues plausibly that these debates were cast in the peculiar language of economics, econometric models of job losses or gains were accorded a privileged position in the deliberations, and less "scientific" or quantifiable considerations such as gender were effectively marginalized.

However, this marginalization was not uncontested. The gendered effects of North American free trade—and the neoliberal policy regime which it reflected—were analyzed and publicized by smaller activist groups such as the Alternative Women-in-Development (Alt-WID) Working Group, working in cooperation with Mujer-a-Mujer in Mexico and Canada (on which see Gabriel and Macdonald, 1994: 559; Runyan, 1996: 248). Alt-WID argued that exploitation of Mexican women workers (some 60 percent of the extremely low-wage labor force of the "maquiladora" export-oriented industries) was linked to increasing economic vulnerability of women and the feminization of poverty in Canada and the US, and that NAFTA would accelerate and intensify these tendencies. North American women, among the most vulnerable of the continent's workers due to the pervasive effects of gendered divisions of labor, would be set in competition against one another, ultimately lowering the floor under all workers.

> Society's devaluation of women's work in and outside of the home has been a crucial factor at the heart of this trend to lower wages. In all three countries, the pursuit of a low wage strategy is made easier because women's income is seen as secondary. Also, traditional women's jobs are considered "un- or low-skilled," thereby supposedly justifying lower wages. Because of the multiple home, work, and community demands placed on them, women have been less able to organize effectively to protect their rights. . . . Women are forced to juggle household responsibilities with the need to earn an income, so they often seek temporary and part-time work, which companies use as a means to lower their overall wage and benefit costs. . . . For women, part-time, temporary, contract or contingent work means lower wages, no benefits, and little protection.
>
> (Alternative Women-in-Development Working Group, 1993: 3–4)

Further, Alt-WID argued that the free market political agenda underlying NAFTA, and its dynamic of downward harmonization, would result in reduced levels of public services available to poor families and single mothers in all three countries.

> Public provision or subsidy of child care, housing or training all might be contested as barriers to trade for any country which tries to provide a safer and higher standard of living for its people. This particularly hurts women and the children they care for. First, because women (at least in Canada and the United States) tend to be disproportionately poor. Secondly, because publicly provided services often substitute for domestic work and relieve women's burden at home. So, when public services are reduced or eliminated, often women have to compensate in the home and/or as community volunteers...
> (Alternative Women-in-Development Working Group, 1993: 11)

Finally, Alt-WID argued that NAFTA and neoliberalism more generally were potentially disempowering for women, and profoundly anti-democratic in their political implications. "The policies that NAFTA proposes would subordinate democratically developed standards to those created by supranational and democratically unaccountable entities. The 'impact on trade' would be the only yardstick for judging a large body of public laws with those who benefit from free trade as the judges" (1993: 12). Alt-WID called for transnational organizing initiatives to directly address these and related issues, providing practical suggestions for organizing and contacts for networking in all three countries.

In recent years, gendered critiques of neoliberalism have become more common. For example, in 1992 Pamela Sparr—an activist-researcher associated with Alt-WID and the Women's Alternative Economic Network (WAEN)—published (in the pages of *Ms.*) a wide-ranging critique of neoliberalism in which she explicitly linked the gendered effects of Reagan–Bush era policies to ongoing tendencies of worldwide capitalist restructuring and "structural adjustment" in the global South. Sparr argued that neoliberalism in both North and South tended to increase economic and domestic burdens upon women, and most cruelly upon the poorest women. "What US women are now experiencing bears a striking similarity to what women of highly indebted nations in the 'South' have been experiencing for quite some time" (Sparr, 1992: 32).

Similarly, Shea Cunningham and Betsy Reed (of Focus on the Global South, and *Dollars and Sense*, respectively) have argued that a preoccupation with debt reduction, fiscal conservatism, and austerity characterizes the policies of the US government as well as the World Bank and IMF, with especially disastrous consequences for women globally. The Structural Adjustment Programs (SAPs) imposed upon poor countries by the World Bank and IMF generally require cutbacks in government spending, wage containment, deregulation of the economy and privatization of state-owned enterprise, and increased openness to the world economy in order to attract foreign investment and earn export revenues with which to repay debt. "Since the budget slashing, pro-business SAPs hurt the poor, and, according to the 1995 UN Development Report, 70 percent of the world's 1.3 billion people living in poverty are female, women have suffered disproportionately from their [World Bank—IMF] austere measures" (Cunningham and Reed, 1995: 22; see also Vickers, 1993). Under SAPs women are increasingly drawn into the export sector, working for wages much lower than those typically earned by male workers: "As a worldwide average, women are paid nearly 40 percent less than men for the very same work" (Cunningham and Reed, 1995: 24). Further, SAPs typically reduce the level of public services available, increasing the weight of the double burden on women who must then provide more of the "caring" services needed by family members as well as engage in intensified productive activity. And this has implications for the reproduction of gendered divisions of labor and ideologies of domesticity in future generations: "Among children, it is females again who bear a disproportionate share of the burden. As women must extend their work day . . . school attendance among girls in particular tends to drop as mothers depend on their daughters to ease their own time constraints" (Cunningham and Reed, 1995: 24). Cunningham and Reed liken the effects of SAPs to those of the US government's social welfare policies, forcing poor women into the lowest paid strata of the workforce and intensifying the double burden which they must bear.

Along very similar lines, the transnational women's solidarity organization MADRE has associated globalization with "the raw violence of economic exploitation" and suggested that the same neoliberalism which draws women to work in Third World export enclaves also dismantles social welfare systems in the rich countries, driving women into low-wage labor and undermining wage levels more generally. According to MADRE, intensified inequality—both within countries and on a global scale—has been a direct result of this heightened exploitation. MADRE represents globalization as a political challenge which can be met by a broad-based democratizing response: "Multi-national corporations are able to trample the social and economic rights of the world's majority because the global arena lacks any countervailing democratic structures through which to oppose them. In fact, the creation of effective mechanisms to win transparency, accountability and representation for ordinary people in the workings of the global economy is a central challenge of today's progressive movements" (Susskind, 1998: 8).

Mainstream feminist organizations begin to catch on?

Ms. magazine, the first mass circulation feminist periodical in the US, began publication in 1972. "Using the funding and circulation that a mass-media magazine offered, the *Ms.* founders intended to harness capitalism for the feminist movement. The risk, however, was that capitalism—more specifically, advertisers—would harness *Ms.* first" (Farrell, 1995: 54). And, according to Amy Farrell's intensive study of the history and politics of *Ms.*, that is just what happened. For its first 17 years, *Ms.* was torn by its contradictory location, attempting to mediate between a diverse and vibrant women's movement on the one hand and, on the other, advertisers who were primarily interested in representing women to themselves as consumers. In the uneasy symbiosis which emerged, the women's movement was portrayed as struggling for the inclusion of women in the corporate capitalist world of work, and advertisers "drew on some of the most compelling themes evoked by feminism—equality, freedom, personal transformation, and sisterhood—to justify a consumer ethic" (Farrell, 1995: 56). In the representations predominating in *Ms.*, women were liberated to the extent they achieved career goals and were able to purchase commodities which marked them as successful women. In short, *Ms.* had become a cheerleader for the liberal feminism of middle class, predominantly white women, despite its editorial pretensions to include the voices of "all women, everywhere" (quoted in Farrell, 1995: 60). Farrell documents that many *Ms.* readers were painfully aware of the contradictions of "their" magazine, and voiced strong criticisms in letters published in the magazine.

By the late 1980s, the chronic financial difficulties at *Ms.* were becoming an acute crisis, and the magazine was purchased by a mass-media firm which intended to resolve its problems by moving it away from its roots in the feminist movement and making it more attractive to advertisers and to more upscale readers. The strategy failed as advertisers continued to desert the magazine, and the commercial version of *Ms.* folded in 1989. *Ms.* re-emerged, phoenix-like, in 1990, as a non-commercial publication free of advertising.

Since then, the new *Ms.* has published a number of articles which depart from the liberal feminist model of equal opportunity and individual advancement, and present instead a direct critique of interwoven relations of class and gender in the era of capitalist restructuring and neoliberalism. In addition to Pamela Sparr's broad-ranging critique of transnational neoliberalism (1992), *Ms.* published a gendered critique of trade liberalization which pointedly observed that "women—who fill most of the world's low-pay, low-skill jobs—are most often exploited as a result of unchecked global economic integration"; yet, "the National Organization for Women never offered any comment on [1993's] crucial NAFTA vote" (Kadetsky, 1994: 15). Another feature in the new *Ms.* focused upon one of the gendered aspects of post-Fordist restructuring, highlighting the overrepresentation of women among the growing ranks of underpaid, insecure, and vulnerable part-time and contingent workers (Judd and Pope, 1994). The following year, *Ms.* published Cynthia Enloe's devastating critique of Nike and the pervasive exploitation of mostly female workers by the transnational sports shoe industry. Enloe saw such practices as indicative of larger tendencies within globalizing neoliberal capitalism: "Big business will step up efforts to pit working women in industrialized countries against much lower-paid working women in 'developing' countries, perpetuating the misleading notion that they are inevitable rivals in the global job market" (Enloe, 1995: 11–12). In contrast to the neoliberal ideology of relentless competition, Enloe praised the efforts of working women to adopt positions of transnational solidarity and mutual support. Enloe's feature article was accompanied by a shorter attack on GATT authored by Mary McGinn, a radical labor activist associated with the journal *Labor Notes*. "Unfortunately," McGinn argued, "most US women's advocacy groups took no position on GATT [during the 1994 ratification debate]. But clearly, all women have a lot to lose: expanded freedom for multinational corporations jeopardizes social justice everywhere" (McGinn, 1995: 15). Since the articles by Enloe and McGinn, *Ms.* has published at least six articles of varying lengths on the return of "sweatshops" in the neoliberal world economy, and the particular threat this poses to the health and welfare of women workers and their families.

While *Ms.* was becoming more hospitable to critiques of neoliberal globalization, the mainstream feminist organizations appeared largely inert in the major public debates surrounding NAFTA (1993) and GATT (1994). Finally in 1997 Global Exchange[12] succeeded in organizing a coalition of 15 women's organizations including NOW, the *Ms.* Foundation, the Feminist Majority, the Black Women's Agenda, and the Coalition of Labor Union Women, all of whom joined in taking a public stand against sweatshops, directly addressing Phil Knight, CEO of Nike. In a striking gesture of transnational solidarity, they pointed to the stark contradiction between Nike's advertising strategies—which portray Western women as strong, capable, and independent—and its exploitation of a predominantly female labor force in the Asian factories where its shoes are produced. "While the women who wear Nike shoes in the United States are encouraged to perform their best, the Indonesian, Vietnamese and Chinese women making the shoes often suffer from inadequate wages, corporal punishment, forced overtime and/or sexual harassment" (quoted in Greenhouse, 1997c; see also Feminist Majority, 1997). They called upon Nike to accept independent monitors to insure that its subcontractors pay a livable wage and observe basic standards of worker rights and workplace health and safety. The Feminist Majority has continued to encourage transnational solidarity against sweatshops, and maintains a Feminists against Sweatshops web page designed to educate American women on the dangers of global sweatshop labor (www.feminist.org/other/sweatshops.html). While it is not at all clear that mainstream feminist organizations in the US are adopting as a central part of their agenda a radical critique of neoliberal globalization, it is nonetheless difficult to deny that such critiques have found their way into the feminist press and have fostered some very real, if also somewhat limited, gestures of transnational solidarity.

Christina Gabriel and Laura Macdonald argue that women across North America share common aspects of gendered social subordination: "systematic discrimination gives women unequal access to resources; women's participation in economic activities is largely governed by the sexual division of labor within the household; gender underpins definitions of skills; and women's work in reproduction and production is undervalued." These commonalities of gendered oppression might provide the material basis on which to construct relations of solidarity and mutually supporting struggles. However, Gabriel and Macdonald caution that women in North America are differently situated in relation to the international political economy, that "gender, class and race position groups of women differently and mediate the effects of trade liberalization" (Gabriel and Macdonald, 1994: 536).

Viewed in relation to Mexican women, women in Canada and the US have been relatively privileged, benefiting from higher general living standards, more extensive social safety nets (especially in Canada) and more actively mobilized women's movements. As a consequence, many women in northern North America were somewhat less violently affected by global economic crisis and restructuring than most Mexican women have been. Restructuring has exacerbated differences among northern women, as some middle class professional, technical, and managerial women have done well while working class women and women of color have been disproportionately assigned to the ranks of more intensively exploited secondary or contingent workers. Meanwhile in Mexico, it is rural and indigenous women who bear the brunt of liberalization (Gabriel and Macdonald, 1994). As a consequence of such differences, "there can be no axiomatic unity between groups of women" (1994: 539). Rather, political unity becomes the product of ongoing negotiation, a problematic process of recognizing and mediating these differences in order to realize the potential for solidarity.

Although I have written from an analytic perspective informed by my readings of Marx and Gramsci, I do not presume that capitalist globalization will generate a simple and unproblematic class identity such as a "global proletariat." Rather, I would argue that people in different social and historical settings have been incorporated into global capitalism in a variety of ways, articulating their own historical relations and cultures with those of core capitalism. I believe that the various forms of subordination to transnational capital nonetheless entail structural commonalities which create the *possibility* for the negotiation of common political horizons, common interests, and transnational democratizing projects. If they are to be successful, such strategies must encompass not just the workplace, but also "the intersections of public and private spheres, of production and reproduction" linking work, home, and community. In pursuing this kind of transformative project, progressives have much to learn from feminist and women's movements and, in particular, the transnational organizing efforts of the Canadian National Action Committee on the Status of Women, as chronicled by Gabriel and Macdonald (1994).

My contention in this chapter is that a potential convergence of feminist and class-based politics points toward projects of social and economic democratization. For this potential to be realizable in a globalizing capitalism, democratizing visions will need to be de-linked from strains of popular common sense which emphasize American exceptionalism, and which lead toward economic, cultural, and/or racial nationalisms. As we will see in subsequent chapters, ideological struggles currently underway will determine whether it is possible to develop, clarify, and anchor firmly within popular common sense conceptions of politics, democracy, and political agency which transcend visions of politics centered on state or nation.

5 Fear and loathing in the New World Order

I was sitting at my computer one day in the summer of 1995, skimming through the e-mail traffic and looking for items of interest. I came upon a message urging support for the repeal of NAFTA. Since I had been involved in local opposition to NAFTA, and was about to publish an article on the NAFTA debate in the US, this message caught my attention and I took a closer look. It had been cross-posted over several left-progressive lists until it had arrived at one to which I was subscribed. But I was surprised to find that, despite my experience of anti-NAFTA activism and my research in this area, I had never heard of the organization from which this message originated. Who was the Liberty Lobby and why did they oppose NAFTA? And how was it that the Liberty Lobby was originating anti-NAFTA messages which were being actively circulated through various left-progressive communities where the Lobby itself was little known? I had struck the tip of an iceberg, but didn't yet realize what was just beneath the surface.

There are substantial alternative political cultures in the US, challenging liberal narratives of world order, peace, and prosperity. I had participated in one of these when I worked with local unionists, social activists, and environmentalists to try and stop NAFTA. But much to my astonishment, I discovered that we were not the only organized opposition to liberal globalization. There are communities of far-right anti-globalists active throughout the US and, as I soon discovered, the Liberty Lobby is a producer of racial, cultural, and economic nationalist ideology which is central to many of the networks within the far-right "Patriot" movement. In a real sense, then, what follows is a product of my own political education about the contested meanings of globalization in the USA.

I have argued in preceding chapters that the "historic bloc" of social forces and ideologies which formed the core of the US-centered postwar hegemonic world order is being reconstructed. Historical structures which had institutionalized more or less consensual power relations in the nexus between the US and the global political economy now appear less solid and stable, and out of this more visibly fluid environment may emerge new possibilities for re-imagining and reconstructing social relations on a transnational scale.

It is in this context that popular common sense is being more vigorously contested in the US, and these contests have potentially important implications for the relations linking the US with the global political economy. A reconstructed corporate liberalism—emphasizing a global economy in which states and corporate capital make the rules with minimal interference from more democratic institutions—is being challenged on *at least two* fronts. The cosmopolitan democratic response—discussed in Chapter 4—seeks to link communities, unionists, and citizens across national borders, and to use these linkages to impose some measure of social responsibility upon transnational economic actors. This kind of vision has brought together elements of organized labor, the environmental movement, consumer and citizens groups, and steered them toward more active linkages with their counterparts in other countries. But, I want now to emphasize, this is not the only world-view offering itself as an alternative to the dominance of transnational corporate capital. Far-right ideologies of American exceptionalism represent transnational integration as an insidious threat to the special identity of America as a (white, masculine, Christian) nation. In such ways Americanist ideologies authorize resistance to globalization as well as scapegoating and encouraging hostility toward those seen as outside of, different, or dissenting from their visions of national identity.

The various meanings which might attach to globalization in popular common sense carry direct political significance. To the extent that one or another is able to predominate, it will enable different forms of political action in the nexus of relations linking the US to the global economy: In the twenty-first century will these relations be based mainly upon corporate power, upon multi-level linkages between democratic communities constituted at various scales, or upon economic/cultural/racial nationalism? My primary purpose here is to point out that populist-oriented opposition to a corporate-dominated transnational political economy is not the exclusive terrain of progressive or democratizing political forces. A counter-hegemonic project cannot afford to take this for granted, to be insensitive to the differing inflections of common sense which underlie popular opposition to globalization. In a social context which appears increasingly fluid and in which conditions are favorable for reconstructions of popular common sense, it will be important for a progressive political movement to define itself not only in terms of its opposition to the agenda of corporate-dominated globalism, but also clearly and explicitly to articulate this opposition with a transnational democratizing vision.

Defending American exceptionalism: far-right critiques of globalization

In the US, opposition to NAFTA–GATT and the agenda of liberal globalization was hardly univocal. Some dissident voices explicitly reject globalization in favor of nationalism, and interdependence in favor of autonomy. Such groups have often been caricatured in the mainstream media as "paranoids" and "crazies," as if their perspective on politics and globalization might be explained away by some shared psychological problems. On the contrary, I want to suggest that far-right resistance to globalization is understandable as a response to changing socio-economic circumstances, a response which draws upon the cognitive resources available in popular common sense to understand a complex and changing world in a way which maintains a stable identity. Far-right anti-globalists tap the most individualistic strains of American common sense, articulated often, but not always, with religious, masculinist, nativist, and/or racist understandings of "Americanism." This vision has led these self-styled "Patriots" to interpret globalization as an alien tyranny engulfing the US through a nefarious conspiracy that relentlessly erodes American identity, subordinating Americans to a tyrannical "one-world government." On this view, globalization is profoundly threatening and acts of resistance ranging from ideological struggle to mass violence may be justified in these terms. In a context where working people and large segments of what used to be thought of as the "middle class" are experiencing chronic socio-economic degradation unprecedented in postwar experience, and in which formerly hegemonic ideologies may appear increasingly threadbare, reconstructions of popular common sense which seem to explain a reality otherwise seemingly inscrutable, and which point toward urgent political action, potentially pose far more serious socio-political issues than the widespread image of ridiculous dementia suggests.

The conspiratorial world-view: a far-right family resemblance

While it would be misleading to suggest that the far right shares a single ideology or a unified political program, a conspiratorial world-view underlies various far-right narratives of globalization. As Kenneth Stern has suggested, it may be that the more libertarian versions of Patriot ideology act as the wide end of a funnel, using individualist and anti-statist rhetoric —familiar elements in American popular common sense—to attract larger numbers of potential recruits, some of whom—if they continue to move through the organizing "funnel" of the far-right—will then come into more intimate contact with increasingly hardcore and racialized versions of conspiracism in which the scapegoating becomes uglier and more explicit (Stern, 1996: 107). On this view, it would seem appropriate to map this ideological progression, starting from the more libertarian versions of patriot ideology and then proceeding to examine its articulations with more directly racist and anti-Semitic doctrines.

Interpreting social life from within the limits of a rigidly individualistic ontology, the libertarian tendencies of the far right suggest that "there are really only two theories of history. Either things happen by accident, neither planned nor caused by anybody, or they happen because they *are* planned and somebody causes them to happen" (Abraham, 1985: 9). This conspiratorial rhetoric is directly related to the kind of language used by Senator Joseph McCarthy in 1951 to explain perceived setbacks in the seemingly treacherous world of the early Cold War:

> What can be made of this unbroken series of decisions and acts contributing to the strategy of defeat? They cannot be attributed to incompetence. . . . The laws of probability would dictate that part of [the] decisions would serve this country's interest. How can we account for our present situation unless we believe that men high in this government are concerting to deliver us to disaster? This must be a project of a great conspiracy, a conspiracy on a scale so immense as to dwarf any previous such venture in the history of man. A conspiracy of infamy so black that, when it is finally exposed, its principals shall be forever deserving of the maledictions of all honest men.
>
> (McCarthy, quoted in Stern, 1996: 139)

If events had been largely accidental or random, McCarthy suggested, we would expect at least some of them to have favored American interests. On his view, however, world politics had been characterized by an "unbroken series" of setbacks and defeats for the interests of America and the free world. The only reasonable explanation, he asks his listeners to imagine, is that this string of disasters is the deliberate product of a sinister conspiracy which has penetrated American government, sabotaged its policies, and led the US toward a capitulation to internationalist socialism.

This kind of reasoning is reflected in the common sense of grassroots Patriots. One member of an Ohio militia group explained to a *New York Times* reporter that he was increasingly inclined to view the world in terms of the conspiratorial belief system he had encountered:

> Nothing in government occurs by accident. If it occurs, know that it was planned that way. To be planned . . . there must be planners. If you have planners, you must have a conspiracy.
>
> (quoted in Janofsky, 1995)

As a consequence of this agent-centered world-view, Patriots are unable to envision, explain, or critique the interrelated structures and processes which left-progressives see at work in the nexus between the US and the global economy. Conspiratorial authors dismissively equate structural explanations with belief in "mysterious and unexplainable tides of history" (Abraham, 1985: 9). The only apparent alternatives, then, are a view of history as essentially random, accidental, a string of implausible coincidences, or a view which looks for "cause and effect" in terms of the purposeful and morally significant actions of individuals and groups. In this way, conspiracy theory and its manichean construction of the world elevates itself to the status of scientific analysis of cause and effect (Abraham,

1985: 7–16; see also North, 1985: x–xi; Perloff, 1988: 207–8; Robertson, 1991: 8–9).[1]

Libertarian strains of far-right ideology generally take it as axiomatic that the American system of government is properly understood as a *republic* and not as a democracy: the latter is seen as dangerous and even evil insofar as it subjects God-given individual rights and liberties to the will of the community, and hence to potential usurpation. As one subscriber to a Patriot listserv wrote, "Democracy is . . . the foundation of communism" (USA-Forever, 16 June, 1995; see also John Birch Society, 1985; and Welch, 1986). The US founding fathers designed a republican system of government to protect individual rights and economic liberty. The design of strictly limited government and a "free enterprise" economy are understood to be divinely inspired and the best possible social arrangement (Abraham, 1985: 31, 84; North, 1985: x–xi, 246–9; Robertson, 1991: 59, 203–5, 239–47; Jasper, 1992: 101–3, 261–9; McManus, 1995a: 91, 99–100). If something is terribly wrong in America it can't be due to flaws intrinsic to this providential social system; rather, somebody somewhere must be corrupting America's political legacy.[2] John F. McManus, president of the John Birch Society—long the most influential source of conspiracy doctrine on the far-right (see Mintz, 1985: ch. 7; Diamond, 1995: 51–8, 147–52)—points toward "treasonous" and "satanically inspired" forces as the cause of America's ills (McManus, 1995a: 12, 70; see also Perloff, 1988: 220–1; Robertson, 1991: 9; Jasper, 1992: 212–29):

> most Americans know something is eating away at the foundations of this great nation. Unemployment, national and personal indebtedness, economic slowdown, loss of faith, declining national stature, a vaguely defined "new world order," broken families, and much more have stimulated worries from coast to coast . . . Sadly, we witness the presence of powerful forces working to destroy the marvelous foundations given us by farseeing and noble men 200 years ago.
>
> (McManus, 1995a: ix–x)

The basic conspiracy theory which circulates widely on the far right holds that cliques of evil individuals have been scheming to subjugate and exploit the world at least since 1776, when Adam Weisshaupt, a Bavarian scholar, formed a secret society known as the Illuminati.[3] Allegedly plotting to "overthrow . . . civil governments, the church, and private property" (Robertson, 1991: 67) and to supplant these institutions with their own power and control, the Illuminati infiltrated European Freemasonry in order to insinuate themselves into elite networks of social power. This sect of Illuminated Freemasons, including the fabulously wealthy Rothschild family, are said to have been associated with the French Revolution and the Terror. Subsequently, they reputedly provided the model—and the funding—for the Marxist-Bolshevik conspiracy for global domination. "All

Karl Marx really did was to update and codify the very same revolutionary plans and principles set down seventy years earlier by Adam Weisshaupt" (Abraham, 1985: 41; see also Still, 1990: 69–91, 129–38; Kah, 1991: 24–30, 106–19; Robertson, 1991: 67–71, 115, 180–5, 258; Mullins, 1992: 3–4, 282–7; John Birch Society, 1996). Organic intellectuals of the libertarian far right are able to assimilate Marxism into a global elite conspiracy because they do not recognize meaningful distinctions between political ideologies of "left" and "right." Rather, they see the world in terms of a continuum which stretches from complete and anarchic individual liberty on one end to total government domination on the other. The most desirable point on the spectrum is the "Constitutional Republic"—that is, sufficient government to avoid the extremes of anarchy but not enough to destroy individual liberty or to constrain the "free market." Monarchy, socialism, fascism, and elite-dominated and government-supported cartel capitalism are not seen as significantly different, but as forms of the same anti-individualistic monopoly of power (Abraham, 1985: 32; John Birch Society, 1985; Perloff, 1988: 44–6; Still, 1990: 16–20; Robertson, 1991: 71, 183).

So it is not inconsistent for far-right intellectuals to claim that international bankers and the super-rich are also part of the conspiracy to undermine individual liberties and their republican–free-market sanctum. Indeed, the second major tentacle of the conspiracy involves the rise of a clique of international bankers, whose almost unfathomable wealth allows them to grant or deny credit to governments, manipulate economies, extract super-profits, and exercise world-historical power. The Rothschilds, Morgans, Rockefellers, and their agents are said to have advanced the conspiratorial design first laid out by the Illuminati by institutionalizing their financial powers through the creation of a US central bank. Thus they sought to control the money supply, manipulate the macro-economy, and to facilitate the creation of credit-money and the expansion of private and public debt. They were also putatively the driving force behind the establishment of an income tax through which hardworking citizens could be made to pay for public debt and enrich the mega-bankers. Also, Patriots allege that this cabal of the super-wealthy bankrolled the Bolshevik revolution, providing an "enemy" against which the governments of the West had to defend themselves, further deepening public debt, expanding the scope of centralized government activity, and laying the basis for comprehensive social control by the financial elite (Abraham, 1985: 43–87; Perloff, 1988: 19–48; Still, 1990: 139–51; Kah, 1991: 12–22; Robertson, 1991: 61, 65, 71–3, 117–43; Mullins, 1992: 6–9, 64–75, 101–9, 214–15).

The third major tentacle of the conspiracy has involved the fostering of an international "establishment" which would promote a "New World Order," the comprehensive political unification and socialization of the world under the domination of the elite conspirators, "a one-world government that scorns individuality, personality, nationhood, and even private property" (Robertson, 1991: 156). In 1891, the Rothschilds and Cecil Rhodes allegedly established the Round Table—"a semi-secret internationalist group headquartered in London" (Perloff, 1988: 36)—as a vehicle for promoting their global agenda. The Round Table then spawned both the Royal Institute of International Affairs in Britain and the Council on Foreign Relations (CFR) in the US. The CFR was putatively dominated by the American members of the Round Table group and associates of the Rothschilds, such as J. P. Morgan and, later on, the Rockefellers. Members of this international establishment have occupied influential posts in government, business, law, journalism, and academia, and have quietly but profoundly influenced the policies of the world's most powerful states. In the aftermath of World War II, this shadowy elite promoted the United Nations, the Bretton Woods system, the Marshall Plan, NATO, the entire institutional infrastructure of postwar world order. More recently, the CFR has worked in parallel with the Trilateral Commission and the Bilderberg Group towards the globalist agenda (Abraham, 1985: 89–108; Perloff, 1988: 3–38, 71–4, 81–6; Still, 1990: 151–74; Kah, 1991: 30–56; Robertson, 1991: 33–58, 65–7, 95–115; Jasper, 1992: 45–58, 178–81, 241–53; Mullins, 1992: 22–3, 49–53, 163, 192–3, 293; McManus, 1995a: 1–24, 61–3, 81–2; Tucker, 1995; John Birch Society, 1996).

McManus makes it clear how some Americans may perceive that individual liberty requires resistance to this global agenda, and thus how the more libertarian strands of far-right ideology are led to conflate individualism with nationalism:

> The world government sought by the architects of this new world order would mean an end to the nation we inherited, and the destruction of the greatest experiment in human liberty in the history of mankind. World government would also establish socialism in place of the free market system, a certain route to conversion of this nation into another Third World deadend. . . . The stakes are nothing short of a future marked by national independence and personal liberty.
>
> (McManus, 1995a: 70, 103)

Preserving an individualistic, capitalist, Christian USA in the face of an insidious transnational threat is the necessary condition for avoiding the destruction of individual liberty, limited government, free enterprise, and religious freedom and forestalling their replacement by the unlimited power of global monopoly-socialism and its Godless humanism.

This anti-globalist perspective is reproduced in the literature of various grassroots Patriot groups. For example, the Council on Domestic Relations declared that

> most, if not all, of the problems that our country is facing are due to the deliberate migration away from the supreme law of our land—the

Constitution for the United States. . . . the promoters of this migration are the ultra-rich and ultra-powerful international banking and multi-national corporations who seek to increase their power and control by promoting a one-world socialistic government. (Pardon the over-simplification).

(Druck, 1993)

Variants of this basic anti-government, anti-globalist conspiracy narra-tive—more or less explicitly anti-Semitic or racist—circulate within and among the following (partially overlapping) communities:

1   The John Birch Society, which claims 40,000 to 60,000 members and a readership of more than 50,000 for its magazine, *The New Ameri-can*. JBS claims to have sold "over half a million copies" of the *New American* special issue entitled *Conspiracy for Global Control* (John Birch Society, 1996).[4]
2   The Liberty Lobby, which has a membership of approximately 20,000 and claims a circulation of 120,000 for its tabloid, *The Spotlight*.[5]
3   The Patriot/Militia/Gun-Rights/anti-Tax movements: The Militia Task Force of the Southern Poverty Law Center identified 858 Patriot groups active nationwide in their peak year of 1996, declining to 523 in 1997 and 435 in 1998.[6]
4   Neo-nazi and affiliated white supremacy groups (e.g., Aryan Nations, National Alliance, White Aryan Resistance), with around 10,000 to 20,000 hard-core members and perhaps ten times as many sym-pathizers.[7]
5   Pat Robertson's Christian Coalition, which claims over two million active members and supporters (a figure which is now widely believed to have been substantially inflated); the Coalition claimed to have distributed some 40 million voter guides in 1998; and Robertson's publisher claims over half a million copies of his conspiracy text, *New World Order*, are in print.[8]
6   The populist Presidential campaigns and proselytizing punditry of Pat Buchanan.[9]

Chip Berlet provides a useful overview of the Patriot movement. According to Berlet, the armed militias which received so much media attention in the wake of the 1995 Oklahoma City bombing are an

offshoot of the larger and more diffuse Patriot movement [which] is bracketed on the moderate side by the John Birch Society and the conspiratorial segment of Pat Robertson's audience, and on the more militant side by the Liberty Lobby and groups promoting themes histori-cally associated with white supremacy and anti-Jewish bigotry.

(Berlet, 1995: 2–3)

Estimates of the total number of persons in the US who are influenced by far-right movements and their conspiratorial anti-government and anti-globalist ideology vary from a few hundred thousand to several million.[10] Whatever the actual number, it is clear that in the mid-1990s the world view of right-wing populism made inroads into mainstream politics through the influence within the Republican Party of Pat Robertson's Christian Coalition (Lind, 1995a; Boston, 1996; Wilcox, 1996), members of the 1994 Republican Congressional majority who were sympathetic to far-right ideology (Egan, 1995; Stern, 1996: 128, 212–14), and Pat Buchanan's right-populist Presidential campaigns (J. Bennett, 1995).

Americanism in peril: NAFTA, GATT, and the New World Order

Viewed from the anti-globalist perspective of the far right, the significance of trade agreements such as NAFTA and GATT far exceed their economic costs or benefits, as Dan Druck of the Council on Domestic Relations explained to fellow Patriots in 1993:

> The passage of NAFTA would be a giant step toward a one world socialistic government. With the jelling of the European Economic Community . . . in Europe, NAFTA and GATT in the Americas [sic] and the formation of an Asian economic consortium, the three legs of the Tri-Lateralist plan for global unification of commercial and banking interests are rapidly coming to fruition. It is also an overall giant leap toward the New World Order's one world government. NAFTA impacts far more than our jobs and our economy.
>
> (Druck, 1993)

Similar interpretations are relatively easy to find on the internet. According to the Militia Task Force of the Southern Poverty Law Center (1999), hundreds of computer bulletin boards and news groups, and almost 250 World Wide Web pages propagate the world views of various far-right sects from anti-government Patriots and militias to white supremacists and neo-nazis. More or less articulate, the authors of Patriot documents on the internet express common fears that their rights and liberties are under assault by a federal government which is out of control and/or that their standard of living and identity as Americans are being corroded by processes of global economic and cultural integration driven by the secretive machinations of transnational elites.

Such interpretations echo the ideological leaders of the far right, such as the John Birch Society and its journal, *The New American*. One JBS writer claims that:

> the whole NAFTA–APEC–GATT trade waltz has been expertly choreographed by the same globalist Insiders of the Council on Foreign

Relations (CFR) and Trilateral Commission (TC) who are also using concerns over supposed "crises" involving the environment, security, population, poverty, refugees, debt, and nuclear proliferation to empower the United Nations.

(Jasper, 1993: 19)

Another *New American* writer argues that both NAFTA and GATT "call for bigger and more costly government, greater intrusions into the daily affairs of the American people, and a substantial transfer of US sovereignty to a host of new international governmental institutions" (Eddlem, 1994: 23). These agreements shift the weight of taxation even further away from tariffs, allegedly favored by the Founders, and toward more intrusive and freedom-destroying income taxes. Still more grave, NAFTA and GATT mire the US in "an artificial state of economic dependency" which, like quicksand, inexorably draws the US economy and political system into a global order dominated by the Insiders. "The underlying strategy employed by the CFR–Trilateral alliance is that economic power leads to political control, and economic union is a necessary step toward political union" (Eddlem, 1994: 27; see also 1992). John McManus, president of the JBS, assesses economic globalization in stark terms: "The goal is the breakdown of national sovereignty via economics. In the end, unless all of this is stopped, the 'new world order' will emerge and freedom will be a mere memory" (McManus, 1995b: 19).

The JBS and the Liberty Lobby are the most important "Americanist" organizations promoting conspiratorial world-views, but there are significant differences between them. JBS membership tends to be disproportionately well-educated, relatively affluent, and professional.[11] The Birch Society eschews explicit racism or anti-Semitism in its well-produced materials. However, the Liberty Lobby and its founder, Willis Carto, are longstanding participants in pseudo-populist politics promoting (more or less thinly veiled) anti-Semitism, Holocaust revisionism, and racialized views of history (Carto, 1982; see also Mintz, 1985; Campbell, 1992; McLemee, 1994; and Diamond, 1995: 140–60, 261–5). For the JBS, nationalism is a means to protect fundamental values of individualism: the meaning of American exceptionalism involves traditions of strictly limited republican government and free market, entrepreneurial capitalism. For the Liberty Lobby, however, nationalism becomes intrinsically significant insofar as its vision of Americanism constitutes an ethnic or racial identity, threatened by "alien forces promoting culture distortion" (Carto, 1982: ix). Through its lurid tabloid *The Spotlight*, Liberty Lobby represents itself as defending a "populist and nationalist agenda" which expresses "the point of view of the unorganized exploited middle class—the 'producers'." These hardworking American taxpayers are doubly exploited by two classes of (essentially alien) social parasites: the wealthy elite of stateless international bankers (read: Jews) who profit from interest payments on national and personal debt, and welfare recipients (read: Blacks and Hispanics) who live off the public dole.[12] Carto defines his populism as "Government by the producers and taxpayers of society, not by the super-rich, tax-free exploiters or the tax-eating, indolent parasites or powerful organized minorities" (1982: 204). Carto's populism "holds free enterprise to be a sacred property right" (1982: 193), but identifies free enterprise with the American middle class whose interests are unalterably opposed by "stateless, predatory" super-capitalists who "see nations as mere objects for plunder" (1982: 189–90).

Writers associated with the Liberty Lobby stressed the loss of American sovereignty in their interpretations of NAFTA and GATT, as did the Birch publications; but the Lobby's populist pitch more directly addressed the fears of America's working "middle class" in this period of de-industrialization and internationalized production.

> There used to be an unwritten social contract between the middle class and the Establishment that went like this: America's capitalist economy would provide jobs—good paying jobs in a factory or office—that enabled an American worker to support his family on one income. . . . In return, the middle class worked hard, paid taxes and raised the next generation to follow in their footsteps. . . . But sadly, so much has changed.
>
> (Hudson, 1993: 16)

In the context of a vision of history where nothing happens unless some agent causes it to happen, *Spotlight* readers are led to ask: who killed the American Dream? In a signed article featured in the special NAFTA issue of *Spotlight*, Liberty Lobby founder Willis Carto explained:

> An extremely powerful political lobby has developed among the community of international traders. Their loyalty is only to their money, wherever it may be and derived from whatever source. These capitalists are the greatest advocates of free trade and are implacable enemies of national sovereignty. They are far more dangerous to the nation than communists ever were.
>
> (Carto, 1993: 4)

Suggesting that the political debate over NAFTA was being orchestrated as part of a globalist conspiracy, *Spotlight* claimed that the corporate moguls behind powerful and well-funded lobbies such as USA*NAFTA "are internationalists who also have membership in the Council on Foreign Relations, the Trilateral Commission and the Bilderberg Group" (Arnold, 1993: 12).

> Together, the Trilateralists and the Bilderbergers constitute a shadow world government, meeting secretly and in concert each spring. David

Rockefeller dominates the Trilateralists; he shares power with the Rothschilds of Europe in the older Bilderberger group. . . . The Bilderbergers
ordered the secret collection of international financiers, political leaders,
media personalities, and business leaders to establish an "American
Union," modeled after the [EC].

(Tucker, 1993: 1)

Spotlight has published the commentaries of Eustace Mullins, a notorious
anti-Semitic writer,[13] who asserts that the real powers pressing for globalization are stateless financiers whose only loyalty is to money (again, readers
are invited to fill in the blank).

Behind these groups are . . . the super rich. They are internationalists
and have no loyalty to any country. . . . They see governments come
and go, but they protect their interests. They are essentially monopolists.

(Mullins, 1993: B-14)

For *Spotlight* readers who may not have been taking notes, Carto spelled it
out in comic book terms:

Today, it is obvious that NAFTA is part of the overall plan for the
"New World Order . . .". Today, the operating plan is a step-by-step
progression to the final goal of ownership and control of all natural
resources and every square inch of land and everything on it by a
consortium of international supercapitalists: a gigantic holding company, a super-Bilderberg Society of mega-plutocrats.

(Carto, 1993: 22)

If NAFTA was a step toward the dreaded one-world government, then
GATT was a giant leap into "the global plantation," in which "the non-
productive global overseers will be siphoning the resources, financial and
otherwise, of the world's producers" (Katson, 1994: 16). Trisha Katson,
Liberty Lobby's point person on GATT, described it as "a world economic
government" unencumbered by the Constitutional limitations from which
the American republic drew its governmental legitimacy. Thus, rather than
being the institutional infrastructure of a globalizing capitalism, GATT
was seen as "the very fulfillment of international socialism, the nationless
world envisioned by Karl Marx" (Katson, 1994: 6, 8; see also Tucker,
1994).

In sum, Liberty Lobby and the Birch Society emphasize economic policies to support "free enterprise" and a strong "middle class." Both interpret NAFTA–GATT as part of a conspiratorial subversion of American
sovereignty by forces dedicated to economic and political globalism. Yet
the pseudo-populism of Liberty Lobby has a stronger nativist-racist colora-
tion than Birch Society ideology.

The most disturbing narratives of globalization, however, are those explicitly constructed in terms of a white supremacist political project. In
these ideologies, the far-right articulation of individualism and nationalism
is explicitly incorporated into a view of the world in which environmental
differences have—through evolutionary processes—produced biologically
unequal races. As Jessie Daniels makes clear in her study of white
supremacist publications, a primary goal of these narratives is the construction of "whiteness" as a privileged—if also endangered—social identity by juxtaposition with groups who are ascribed with essential and
invariant characteristics in order to define them as other than "white." The
resulting racialized vision of Darwinian biological competition has significant implications for the politics of gender and sexuality, for its vision of
white men as agents of a racialized bio-politics implies their power and
control over the sexual and reproductive capacities of white women. Along
with racial supremacy, then, this vision presumes a rigidly patriarchal
family structure and compulsory heterosexuality. "The highest duty of a
white man, according to white supremacist discourse, is to preserve the
white family and with it a hierarchy of race, gender and sexuality" (Daniels,
1997: 39). Such racialized and gendered world-views—seeking to stabilize
and control gender relations and women's bodies as an integral part of the
project of constructing a racially hierarchic world—resonate strongly with
the cultural supports of colonialism and Western imperial domination of
the modern era. As Jan Jindy Pettman explains, "White women's bodies
were subjected territory in colonized and racialized societies where
dominant-group men strove to guarantee the reproduction, physically and
socially, of the boundaries of colonial race power" (Pettman, 1996: ch. 2).
This has enabled dominant white men to construe non-white men as a
threat, generating an obsessive fear of the "rape" of white women and of
their own emasculation, and rationalizing in these terms the most brutal
acts of violence.[14]

In contemporary white supremacist discourse, white men are identified
as the victims of racialized others—primarily African-Americans and Jews—
and as the privileged warriors who are anointed to defend their race and
its cultural and biological survival against the threats allegedly posed by
these others. It is this construction of threat which enables white supremacist
men to assume the dual identity of warrior-victim. With great vulgarity,
white supremacist literature represents African-American men as primitive
and sexually voracious, a danger against which white men must protect
"their" women. But, Daniels explains, in white supremacist ideology it is
the presumed "Jewish conspiracy" which controls finance, government, and
the media, and poses the gravest threat to white Americans' way of life:

> Even as viciously as African-Americans are portrayed in white supre-
> macist discourse, it is widely agreed that they are *not* the "real enemy"
> of the white race . . . [Rather, on this view] Jews populate or control

the United States government [often referred to as ZOG, or Zionist Occupation Government—MR], "international banking and finance," and most industry. This power enables them to wield enormous influence over the course of world events. In white supremacist accounts, Jews were responsible for both the Lincoln and Kennedy assassinations, for the Vietnam as well as Persian Gulf wars, as well as for the moral decay of American society at the end of the twentieth century.

(Daniels, 1997: 108)

Further, there is a class-based dimension to this understanding of "whiteness": White American men are understood to be the productive workers who "built this nation," and whose labors are undermined by parasitic, unproductive, and culturally degenerate races, and their institutionalized oppression of white male workers. "What emerges in the discourse is a melding of working- and middle-class concerns forged in opposition to an elite class, associated with corporations and the government, and in opposition to racialized others who may also be members of the working-middle classes" (Daniels, 1997: 43).

These kinds of world-views and self-understandings are evident in the narratives of Americanism and globalization which circulate within the more explicitly racist segments of the far right. In its programmatic statement of goals and principles, the neo-nazi National Alliance (n.d.) declares that "we [white Americans] have an obligation to our race as a collective agent of progress." On this view, then, "we need an economic system which, in contrast to Marxism, allows individuals to succeed in proportion to their capability and energy, but which, in contrast to capitalism, does not allow them to engage in socially or racially harmful activity, such as stifling competition or importing non white labor." Individual enterprise and initiative are to be encouraged, so long as this occurs within a context of racial awareness and responsibility to the racial community. To the extent that they are seen to conflict, then, possibilities for individual gain through free trade may be overridden by racial responsibility.

I encountered these currents of racist anti-globalism when, at an anti-NAFTA rally primarily organized by and for Syracuse-area unionists, local neo-nazis circulated through the crowd distributing audio cassettes. I was handed a recording of the radio program *American Dissident Voices*, produced by the National Alliance and featuring its now infamous leader, William Pierce.[15] On the program, Pierce (1992) speaks of long-term decline of the US economy which he represents as the result of basic forces "which any high school drop-out can understand"—the impenetrable mumbo-jumbo of academic economists notwithstanding. According to Pierce, internationalization of production and de-industrialization of the US are two sides of the same coin and have for the last 45 years been the deliberate policy of a "power elite." He describes this elite as "New World Order schemers" seeking to "permanently fasten their grip on the power and wealth of the world." There are, he tells listeners, "men in Washington and New York and London and Tel Aviv who are behind the policies which are exporting American jobs to Mexico and Hong Kong because they want to create a one-world economy in which Mexicans and Chinese and white Americans will have the same living standard." None too cryptically, Pierce describes members of this hidden elite as "the eternal outsiders, the eternal parasites whose strength always has been in their ability to manipulate and deceive rather than in their ability to build things." Stealthily, they control the media, public opinion, and the agendas of both major political parties in the US. They support free trade agreements like NAFTA because they are "hell-bent" on creating "a world without national boundaries or even national distinctions, a world in which every national economy has been submerged in a global economy, a world with a single homogenized labor force and a uniform standard of living." The inevitable result of global economic integration, Pierce tells his listeners, is racial integration and leveling, the mongrelization of the US workforce and a corresponding loss of racial-national identity among US workers, declining harmony and vigor in the workplace, lowered productivity, and growing social costs for the support of "non-productive" elements in society. In tones of shock and alarm, his radio co-host characterizes this as "a long-term economic disaster for white American workers." Pierce suggests that the American people blunder into this ultimately self-defeating policy of free trade because "they like being able to buy consumer goods at low prices." These short-term benefits for individual consumers mask the long-term consequences for white American workers, whose standard of living is suppressed to Third World levels and whose national independence and capacity for racial agency is undermined.

To stop their impoverishment and subordination into an interdependent and mongrelized New World Order, Pierce (1992) urges white Americans to educate themselves about their racial identity and interests and to organize accordingly, whereupon, he chillingly suggests, "you can be sure that we'll have a national cleaning day." What he has in mind here may resemble an episode described in Pierce's now infamous novel, *The Turner Diaries*. After insurgent "Aryan" forces secure politico-military control of southern California, they immediately drive non-whites into the desert and annihilate those whose racial identity appears ambiguous. Then, during what Pierce calls "the day of the rope," tens of thousands of white "race traitors" who may have supported a political agenda of social equality or been involved in trans-racial relationships are hanged from lamp posts, trees, and traffic lights all over the Los Angeles area and left to dangle as object lessons in the importance of racial consciousness and fidelity (Pierce, 1980: 153–6, 160–9). Thus the construction of "White Americans" as political agents entails the systematic use of violence against "non-Whites" as well as potential "Aryans" whose practices seem to defy the perceived imperatives of their presumptive biological identity.

Once white Americans regain awareness of and control over their racial destiny, Pierce envisions an economic policy of higher tariffs to protect white American jobs from non-white countries with lower standards of living and thus to end insidious de-industrialization. "We might even justify the elimination of trade barriers between a racially cleansed United States and a selected group of other White countries" provided that these racially similar nations were united under a single political authority which Pierce calls "the Aryan World Order" (Pierce, n.d.). And what of the rest of the world? To prevent Third World overpopulation from endangering the global ecosystem and thus the racial living spaces of white nations, Pierce explicitly advocates genocide on a global scale. Without equivocation he calls for "the radical depopulation of the non-White world" using "modern chemical and biological means" (Pierce, n.d.).[16]

This horrifying vision of a white supremacist response to globalization—a final solution in the US, to be followed by global genocide and an "Aryan World Order"—illustrates the extremes to which the scapegoating tendencies implicit in conspiratorial narratives so readily lend themselves. Clearly, Pierce and his neo-fascist ilk have left behind the libertarian impulses which animate much of the Patriot movement. Pierce is little concerned with individual rights and liberties, and heaps scorn upon "responsible conservatives" whose distrust of the state is motivated primarily by free-market ideology and/or crass self-interest (Pierce, 1980: 52, 64, 103, 173–4). For Pierce, state power as such is not the enemy, nor are individual rights and liberties the fundamental values to be protected. Rather, Pierce's enemy is a state which he views as being under the control of essentially "alien" forces who are systematically attacking the racial interests of "White Americans." As Pierce's description of the "Day of the Rope" makes clear, when individual rights and liberties come into conflict with perceived imperatives of racial destiny, he has no compunctions about the most brutal and direct exercise of state power. "Our struggle is to secure the future of our race, and . . . the issue of individual freedom is subordinate to that one, overwhelming purpose" (1980: 52).[17] For Pierce and other white supremacists on the far right, coercive violence plays a central role in the construction of an "Aryan" political movement and the realization of its political project. Whereas the libertarian wing of the conspiratorial far right may envision itself in a cultural battle with the forces of leftist Godless humanism—the John Birch Society, for instance, explicitly invokes Gramsci in its conceptualization of this kind of ideological struggle over "the very core of our civilization" (McManus, 1994: 44)—it is clear that the white supremacist project places greater emphasis on coercion relative to consent and is, in Gramscian terms, a movement aimed more at domination than ideological hegemony.

Some versions of Christian Patriot ideology are grounded in an obscure racialized theology known as Christian Identity. Identity doctrine teaches that white Anglo-Saxons are the true chosen people of God and the descendants of the lost tribes of Israel. Jews are understood to be the direct biological descendants of Satan, fraudulently presenting themselves as the chosen people but actually offspring of Cain, spawned in the liaison between Eve and the Satanic serpent, the product of original sin. Jews are seen as the primary agents of an ancient Satanic conspiracy to destroy the chosen people and frustrate God's design. Pawns in this conspiracy are "pre-Adamic" peoples, "non-whites" who are said to have been created prior to Adam and who are understood to be not fully human. In this racialized view of Genesis, "race mixing" between "Adamic" peoples—whites—and others is seen as profoundly evil insofar as it undermines the identity of God's chosen people and corrupts their bloodlines with those of inferior and evil races allied with Satan (see Barkun, 1994; Ridgeway, 1995). Among the most prominent evangelists of Identity doctrine is Richard Butler of Aryan Nations, but Christian Identity has a much broader influence within the Patriot movement and in citizens' militias, and some see this influence becoming stronger (Southern Poverty Law Center, 1999).

Less explicitly racist or anti-Semitic Patriots may wish to distance themselves from the bile-churning politics of a William Pierce, or a racialized theology such as Christian Identity, but the identification of scapegoats is implied in the very structure of a conspiratorial narrative and its central questions: Who is to blame for our problems? How can "they" be stopped? One caller to a Patriot-oriented radio talk show had apparently grasped this logic at its root: "The problem we have right now is who do we shoot . . ." (quoted in Stern, 1996: 223). The libertarian vision which serves as the starting point for much Patriot ideology may not be able to contain the violently anti-liberal implications of its conspiratorial narrative.

Mainstreaming far-right ideology?

Conspiratorial ideologies of globalization are hardly the exclusive province of tiny sects of paranoid mountain men or platoons of weekend warriors, as sound-bite stereotypes might suggest. One of the most important conduits channeling far-right conspiratorial ideology toward a more mainstream mass audience has been evangelist Pat Robertson, founder of the Christian Broadcasting Network and the politically powerful Christian Coalition (see Diamond, 1995: 228–56, 289–306, 310–12; Lind, 1995a; Boston, 1996; Wilcox, 1996). In his best-selling book, *The New World Order*, Robertson echoes Birch Society rhetoric, claiming that political events "are not the accidents and coincidences we are generally led to believe." Tendencies toward globalization "spring, instead, from the depth of something that is evil" (Robertson 1991: 9):

> the common strain that permeates much of the thinking about a new world order involves four basic premises: (1) the elimination of private property, (2) the elimination of national governments and national

sovereignty, (3) the elimination of traditional Judeo-Christian theism, and (4) a world government controlled by an elite group made up of those who are considered to be superior, or in the occultic sense, "adepts" or "illuminated."

(Robertson, 1991: 71)

The Establishment (especially the Council on Foreign Relations (CFR)) seeks "to form a world system in which enlightened [i.e., Illuminated— MR] monopolistic capitalism can bring all the diverse currencies, banking systems, credit, manufacturing, and raw materials into one government-supervised whole, policed of course by their own world army" (1991: 97). This is deeply troubling to Robertson because the Constitutional order which protects the God-given rights of individual Americans rests in turn upon the foundation of US sovereignty (1991: 203–5, 239–47). To undermine that foundation is to imperil God's order. Yet this appears to be precisely the project of the Establishment with its cosmopolitan and Godless humanism (1991: 95–115, 167–85). Robertson concludes: "The stream of world order flowing from the Illuminati [through the Establishment] is clearly occult and satanic" (1991: 115). Globalization is part and parcel of a diabolical plan to create "a new order for the human race under the domination of Lucifer and his followers" (1991: 37).

While readers impressed with Robertson's conjuring of demons might infer that he would take a dim view of global economic integration, he has expressed instead a quite conventional liberal commitment to the principle of free trade as a way to increase the total global product (1991: 267; *700 Club*: 10 November, 1993; 28 November, 1994; 29 November, 1994). His positions on specific trade agreements were ambivalent, however. In the case of NAFTA Robertson reaffirmed his general support for free trade and endorsed the agreement on his television talk show (*700 Club*: 10 November, 1993). But he later described the Uruguay Round of GATT as "flawed" insofar as the WTO could effectively undermine US sovereignty. He lamented that US trade negotiators and Fast Track legislation had put Americans in a take-it-or-leave-it position where rejecting this problematic agreement would "blow up world trade." Pondering how we got into this mess, Robertson explained that "there are a group of people in America that just cannot stand American sovereignty. They just have to have a world government that somehow dominates America" (*700 Club*: 28 November, 1994).[18] Clearly, then, Robertson represented GATT as a step toward the New World Order, a step away from God's design as manifested in the US Constitution, and, in that sense, a victory for the forces of evil.

Another important vehicle for the injection of New World Order ideology into the political mainstream has been the right-populist punditry and Presidential campaigns of Patrick Buchanan (J. Bennett, 1995, 1996; Sanger, 1995; Frantz and Janofsky, 1996; Gladwell, 1996). With generous financial support from ultra-conservative textile magnate Roger Milliken,[19] Buchanan has focused attention on the plight of American working people and described NAFTA, GATT, and globalization in terms of a narrative of elite perfidy, the destruction of national identity and individual liberty, and the creation of a tyrannical New World Order.

While he made much of the impoverishment of American workers by globalizing corporations, for Buchanan—as for the conspiratorial far right —the primary significance of NAFTA was that it brought with it "the virus of globalism" (Buchanan, 1993b). "Though advertised as 'free trade,' [NAFTA] is anti-freedom, 1,200 pages of rules, regulations, laws, fines, commissions...setting up no fewer than 49 new bureaucracies...it is part of a skeletal structure for world government" (Buchanan, 1993a).

> NAFTA is about America's sovereignty, liberty and destiny. It is about whether we hand down to the next generation the same free and independent country handed down to us; or whether 21st Century America becomes but a subsidiary of the New International Economic Order.
>
> (Buchanan, 1993b)

In his 1996 Presidential campaign, Buchanan vigorously denounced globalization and declared: "When I raise my hand to take the oath of office, this whole new world order is coming crashing down" (quoted in Sanger, 1995). Describing what he meant by "new world order," Buchanan explained:

> The UN is its political arm. The so-called International Monetary Fund is going to be the Federal Reserve of the world. The World Bank will provide the income transfers from the United States all over the world...The World Court will prosecute and convict people and their countries, take their citizens and try them in international tribunals. The World Trade Organization...will eventually get...more and more control of world trade, until one day we wake up like Gulliver, find ourselves tied down...with tiny silk strands that by the thousands have been done up during the night, with the strongest nation on earth suddenly immobile.
>
> (Buchanan, 1996)

If elected, Buchanan vowed he would restrict foreign aid, curtail US participation in multilateral institutions and UN peacekeeping missions, withdraw the US from NAFTA and GATT, and constrict the flow of immigrants into the US which, he claims, suppresses the wages of US workers (Buchanan, 1995c). He promised to levy selective tariffs upon specific competitor nations who enjoy a trade surplus with the US, especially Japan and China. Like some progressives, he also suggested "a social tariff on Third World manufactured goods" to protect US workers from downward pressure on wage, health and safety, and environmental standards (Buchanan, 1995b; Gladwell, 1996). Buchanan called on Americans to ride to the sound of the guns in his "second war of American independence, to recapture US sovereignty from faceless global bureaucrats who view our country as but a vast, rich province to be plundered and looted on behalf of their New World Order" (Buchanan, 1994).

How is it that the US, with its extraordinary Constitutional system and its exceptional power, has "handed off its sovereignty" to global institutions? Who "is pulling the strings?" Buchanan points the finger at "the multinational corporations and the Wall Street financial elite."

> Real power in America belongs to the Manhattan Money Power, the one power to which neither party is any longer able to say "No!" [Former Treasury Secretary Robert] Rubin said, "There must be a broad understanding that we really and truly are in a new world where we are dependent on other nations in ways that we never were before." That is the authentic voice of Goldman Sachs, and regrettably, of our own Republican elites. They are saying, all of them, that America's sovereignty, independence and liberty are things of the past. . . . We must all accept our dependency on the New World Order. . . . But we never voted our sovereignty away. If it is gone, they sold us out; they traded it away, without our permission.
>
> (Buchanan, 1995a)

Asked by interviewers if his rhetoric included far-right "code words," Buchanan responded directly: "There is nothing code-word about it, I don't need to speak in code . . . there are embryonic institutions of world government being formed even as we speak" (quoted in Bennett, 1996). Buchanan denies anti-Semitism or links to far-right or white supremacist groups, but his campaign was plagued by a series of revelations about unseemly statements and unsavory connections among his staff (Buchanan for President, 1996; Frantz and Janofsky, 1996; Zeskind, 1996). Whether or not Buchanan actually subscribes to the conspiratorial vision of the far right, he clearly speaks in terms which lend themselves to a conspiratorial interpretation. In his language, far-right anti-globalists can readily situate themselves and find reflections of their xenophobic ideology. Thus his 1996 candidacy drew the endorsement of the Liberty Lobby's *Spotlight* and was supported by members of the JBS, various self-described Patriots, and some white supremacists.[20] Buchanan was far and away the most popular Presidential candidate among readers of the far-right magazine *Media Bypass* who responded to a 1995 survey. Among respondents to the magazine's reader survey, 99 percent supported citizen militias while fewer than 1 percent favored the United Nations (Pitcavage, 1996): this suggests Buchanan's appeal to those under the influence of New World Order ideology.

Buchanan stunned the Republican Party in 1996 with his wins in Louisiana and New Hampshire, and his strong second-place showings in the rust belt states of Michigan and Wisconsin, but the significance of his Presidential campaigns cannot be summarized in terms of vote counts. At a time when the historical structures underlying postwar prosperity are visibly degenerating and ideologies of liberal internationalism appear increasingly dubious to average Americans, Buchanan continues to deliver the Americanist ideology of right-populism to their doorstep along with their morning paper.

In a recent book about globalization and the US entitled *The Great Betrayal*, the master polemicist Buchanan adopts a tone at times almost scholarly, and the conspiracist overtones so evident in his earlier commentaries recede into the background. In a passage which would not seem out of place in many mainstream "realist" international relations texts, Buchanan explains that a world of nations is fundamentally a competitive and dangerous place in which policies of economic nationalism have been legitimate and successful instruments of state power: "Nations are rivals, antagonists, and adversaries, in endless struggle through time to enhance relative power and position. So it has been; so it shall ever be" (Buchanan, 1998: 66, also 48, 83). Failure to recognize this timeless reality is leading America toward disaster. "By accession to NAFTA, GATT, the UN, the WTO, the World Bank, the IMF, America has ensnared itself in a web that restricts its freedom of action, diminishes its liberty, and siphons off its wealth" (1998: 107). Liberal globalization has resulted in de-industrialization, job loss and falling wages, working moms and the weakening of the traditional family, destruction of the American Dream, and enfeeblement of American national power and sovereign independence. On these grounds, Buchanan asserts, "free trade is truly a betrayal of Middle America and treason to the vision of the Founding Fathers" (1998: 45). Unsparing in his criticism of the internationalist elites who dominate both major political parties, Buchanan is at pains to shield corporate America from the fire and brimstone he unleashes. "Many of our greatest corporations were driven out of America, whipped into exile by government policies that mandated ever higher costs of production here and by trade policies which told US executives that they could avoid such costs if they moved overseas. For forty years the US government has been stacking the deck against industries that wanted to stay home and hire Americans, and it bears the primary responsibility for the de-industrialization of this country" (1998: 86).

Despite occasional (and in the American political context, quite refreshing) references to class struggle, Buchanan abjures a systematic critique of transnational corporate power and its roots in the structures of capitalism and instead opens the door to the subplot of *The Great Betrayal*. The agents of globalization he identifies would be readily recognizable to anyone remotely familiar with Patriot ideology: a "rootless transnational elite" organizing its political influence through the Council on Foreign Relations, the Bilderberg Group, and the Trilateral Commission, "one-worlders" committed to a "deeply un-American" agenda of "free trade, military disarmament and world government" (Buchanan, 1998: 32, 97, 105, 191, 192). Under their domination since the 1930s, the US government has abandoned the economic nationalism responsible for making this country a great power and an exemplar of liberty and prosperity, and has pursued a globalist agenda destructive to the economic, political, and cultural foundations of American exceptionalism. The end result of these policies will be a "new world order," the "death of the nation state," and the rise of world government, "global-socialist centers for the redistribution of American wealth" administered by "faceless foreign bureaucrats of the WTO or the UN" (1998: 17, 72, 108, 113, 174, 260, 264, 266, 313, 315). True to his roots in the messianic traditions of American exceptionalism, Buchanan holds out hope that America may yet hold the key to universal salvation: "If this greatest of nations is ensnared in the Global Economy, and unable to break free, no nation will ever escape. But if America can restore her national sovereignty and independence, nations all over the world will one day be able to do so. Truly, we are deciding not for ourselves alone but for all mankind" (1998: 301).

With the apparent resurgence of more widespread economic prosperity at the peak of the long business cycle expansion of the late 1990s, and with the memories of Ruby Ridge and Waco fading into the historical distance,[21] the avatars of Patriot ideology are struggling to maintain a place in popular consciousness. The Christian Coalition is reeling from multimillion dollar debt, leadership problems, and legal challenges to its tax-exempt status which have prompted major organizational restructuring (Berke, 1999; Goodstein, 1999; Rosenbaum, 1999). While Pat Buchanan's 2000 Presidential campaign ran into a roadblock within the Republican Party mainstream, his political influence is hardly exhausted. He bolted the Republicans and declared his intention to continue—through the vehicle of Ross Perot's neo-populist Reform Party—the struggle against the subsumption of the American constitutional republic into a "new world order" (Buchanan, 1999). According to the Southern Poverty Law Center, the number of Patriot and militia groups in the US appears to have declined sharply in 1997–8; but the influence of racist doctrines such as Christian Identity may be much stronger among the remaining hard-core memberships. Further, the number of Patriot publications is holding steady and the number of internet sites devoted to Patriot ideology has increased substantially (Southern Poverty Law Center, 1999). Federal law-enforcement officials are not ready to presume that threats to public safety emanating from the more hard-core elements of the far right have expired. The FBI warned police chiefs around the country that the turn of the century may bring with it renewed dangers from the most hard-core elements of the far right: "The volatile mix of apocalyptic religious and [New World Order] conspiracy theories may produce violent acts aimed at precipitating the end of the world as prophesied in the Bible" (FBI report quoted in Vise and Adams, 1999). We need not presume that the end of the world is at hand to acknowledge the continuing political significance of these resilient nodes of far-right anti-globalism.

Indeed, it is important to recognize that the power of far-right ideology in America has wellsprings much deeper than the political imaginaries of particular contemporary spokesmen (or gunmen). Political scientist Rogers Smith has argued that the core political traditions in America include not just the rights-based discourse of liberal individualism on the one hand, and the participatory democratic vision of civic republicanism on the other, but also a deeply rooted strain of racialized and gendered "Americanism," privileging white male Americans above all other social identities.

> The liberal tradition involves limited government, the rule of law protecting individual rights, and a market economy, all officially open to all minimally rational adults. The republican tradition is grounded on popular sovereignty exercised via institutions of mass self-governance. It includes an ethos of civic virtue and economic regulation for the public good. Adherents of . . . ascriptive Americanist traditions believe true Americans are in some way "chosen" by God, history or nature to possess superior moral and intellectual traits, often associated with race and gender. Hence many Americans believe that nonwhites and women should be governed as subjects or second-class citizens, denied full market rights, and sometimes excluded from the nation altogether.
> (Smith, 1993: 563, n. 4)

Smith argues that "an evolving mix of these traditions is visible in America's political culture, institutions, and the outlooks of Americans of all backgrounds." Far from being essentially aberrant or marginal, the "Americanist" preoccupations of the far right have longstanding residence at the very core of political culture in the US, and speak in a voice already familiar to most Americans.

Further, as historian Dana Frank has documented, Americanist doctrines have been successfully articulated with economic nationalism at crucial historical conjunctures going back to the revolutionary period. In Frank's analysis, such Americanist articulations have always been contested by more solidaristic visions of politico-economic community, but have nonetheless effected a powerful recurrent influence in American political culture. Their effect has been to suggest to American working people that the sources of their economic problems were "alien" workers both at home and abroad, and that the appropriate response was to join with their employers under the guise of protecting the privileges of "American working men" from the threat of alien competition. This strategy of exclusion has been aimed especially but not exclusively at African-Americans and Asians, but has had important gendered dimensions as well, all with devastating effect on possibilities for a politics of solidarity (D. Frank, 1999). We cannot afford to assume that only the most ignorant or delusional would see the world in this way, that the broad American public is somehow inoculated against far-right ideologies by virtue of the pervasive influence of liberal democracy (which is itself, after all, profoundly contradictory), or that these kinds of doctrines will disappear with the fading visibility of particular individuals or groups, for ideologies of "Americanism" are deeply rooted in popular common sense and continue to provide a reservoir of resources for the articulation of nationalist, racist, and masculinist political projects.

Tensions and possibilities of post-Fordist common sense

We are witnessing the long and painful demise of the Fordist socio-political regime through which American industrial workers were incorporated into the hegemonic bloc which constructed the postwar global order (Rupert, 1995). The social conditions of life for average Americans are shifting in ways almost unthinkable only a generation ago. Finding their economic security and their political identity increasingly problematic, the easy certainties of the Cold War no longer providing fixed ideological reference points, American working people are trying to make sense of a rapidly changing world. It is in this context that alternative narratives of globalization increasingly challenge the blandishments of liberal internationalists. Some of these interpretations emphasize the anti-democratic character of transnational capitalism and the need to construct popular-democratic institutions within the world economy. Others view globalization as a process infused with evil intent, the product of alien treacheries designed to undermine the special character of the American republic, its culture, or its "true" (white, male, Christian) citizenry. My claim is that these alternative visions of globalization are circulating within and among various segments of the US population, seeking to articulate themselves within popular common sense and thus to define the horizons of political action—and that current socio-political conditions create a much more favorable environment to such counter-hegemonic ideologies.

The world-view of neoliberal internationalism—in which states and corporations create the rules for global economic integration—is facing challenges which emphasize different aspects of popular common sense in order to envision alternative possible worlds. Drawing on the democratic strains of popular common sense, what I have called the left-progressive position would construct a world in which the global economy is explicitly politicized, corporate power is confronted by transnational coalitions of popular forces, and a framework of democratically developed standards provides social accountability for global economic actors. The anti-globalist position of the far right, on the other hand, envisions a world in which Americans are uniquely privileged, inheritors of a divinely inspired socio-political order, an Anglo-Saxon culture or gene pool, which must at all costs be defended against external intrusions and internal subversion. This latter vision also entails a challenge to corporate power, but it implicitly constructs this challenge from within the bounds of capitalism's structural separation of politics and economics. Unable to understand capitalism in terms of historical structures and the progressive possibilities they may entail, the far right offers instead a reactionary vision which implies a reversal of processes of capital concentration and the transnational socialization of production which have been central to the historical development of capitalism. Insofar as it seeks to preserve capitalism while reversing its central processes, we might anticipate the ongoing frustration of the reactionary vision, and an attendant intensification of scapegoating and hostility toward those seen as outside of, different or dissenting from its vision of national identity. If I am correct in my belief that the restructuring of the postwar order is creating conditions which are increasingly favorable for reconstructions of popular common sense, then it will be important for a progressive political movement to define itself not only in terms of its opposition to corporate power and neoliberal internationalism—which are themes readily co-opted into the radical right world-view—but also clearly and explicitly to distinguish its democratizing vision from the reactionary nationalism of the populist right.

In these ideological contests, the future shape of transnational political order may be at stake. The real danger of the far right, as I see it, is not so much that they will succeed in constructing a thousand-year *Reich* in America or an "Aryan World Order." Rather, they threaten to submerge the democratic aspects of popular common sense beneath longstanding currents of cultural, racial, or economic nationalism. To the extent that they succeed in doing so, the potential for democratizing transnational political projects will be blocked. American workers will look upon other segments of the global labor pool and will see competitors, rivals, or enemies rather than potential partners in the construction of a new world. They will see themselves and their jobs more closely identified with their employer (and, of course, its profits) than with "foreign" workers, whose alleged willingness to work harder for less will be blamed for the misfortunes of God's chosen people—the "productive" American "middle class." Despite its anti-corporate banners, far-right ideology not only fails to challenge the power of global capital effectively, but actually augments it. Any movement which means to contest that power must then also challenge the ideological claims of the nationalist right.

6   Competition or solidarity?

The new populism and the
ambiguities of common sense

The ambiguities of populism cum conspiracism

The story of Chuck Harder and the United Broadcasting Network illu-
minates the central ambiguities of populism and its articulation with
conspiracism.[1] Before I tell that story, however, it would be helpful for me
to set the stage with a brief conceptual discussion, drawing on the insight-
ful cultural analysis of Mark Fenster. Fenster has argued that it is a mistake—both analytical and political—to trivialize conspiracist thinking by
framing it in terms of metaphors of pathology, especially paranoia; for
framing it in this way draws attention away from the real social circumstances to which conspiracism might otherwise be seen to respond. Patho-
logizing conspiracism not only produces inadequate explanations of it but
is also politically self-limiting, for the appropriate response to pathology
is treatment of the individual(s) suffering symptoms. Rather than being
symptomatic of pathology, Fenster argues that contemporary conspiracism
articulates, in distorted and self-limiting ways, a populist critique of contemporary social conditions and a desire for a meaningful political space
which can be inhabited by ordinary "citizens." Fenster writes: "just because overarching conspiracy theories are wrong does not mean that they
are not on to something".

> Although conspiracy as a totalizing, instrumental entity might not
> exist, . . . relatively secretive, and at times quite open, concentrations
> of power, built through economic and social connections among elite
> groups, do. Conspiracy theory is thus ideological in that it substitutes
> the populist discourse of an antagonism between the people and pow-
> erful elites for the analysis of specific structures of power and the
> processes of struggle, particularly, though not exclusively, concerning
> class. . . . Conspiracy theory as a theory of power, then, is an ideologi-
> cal misrecognition of power relations, articulated to but neither defin-
> ing nor defined by populism, interpellating believers as "the people"
> opposed to a relatively secret, elite "power bloc." Specifically, [con-
> spiracy theories] ideologically address real structural inequities, and

constitute a response to a withering civil society and the concentration
of the ownership of the means of production, which together leave the
political subject without the ability to be recognized or to signify in
the public realm . . .

(Fenster, 1999: 63, 67)

On this view, conspiracy theory ought not to be pathologized and treated;
it should, rather, be understood as a distorted populism, framed in response to real social conditions but contradictory and deeply ambiguous in
its political implications. "Articulating a necessary distance between 'the
people' and 'power,' conspiracy theory draws on the most simplistic, disabling, and dangerous interpretations of political order, including fascism,
totalitarianism, racism, and anti-Semitism—yet it also represents a populist
possibility, a resistance to power that implicitly imagines a better, collective future" (Fenster, 1999: xiii). Fenster's analysis points toward ways in
which this populist impulse might be de-articulated from conspiratorial
reasoning and re-articulated to visions of more progressive, socially enabling possible futures.

Populist Inc.

The unfolding struggle over the meaning of globalization in popular common sense, with all its tensions and possibilities, is represented in micro-
cosm in the story of Chuck Harder and the United Broadcasting Network
(UBN), referred to by the *Wall Street Journal* as "Populist Inc." According
to UBN promotional bulletins, Harder has been a professional broadcaster
since the 1960s. As a consumer affairs reporter, he is said to have become
disillusioned with "the 'velvet hammer' of corporate media," which dampens
anti-corporate messages to avoid offending advertisers. Harder left his
mainstream media job in 1987, and invested his life savings to start a radio
program for "the little guys who had no voice" (Davis, 1996a; UBN online
promotional bulletin: ww2.audionet.com/pub/ubn/harder.htm).

Controversially, in 1989 Harder sold a majority stake in his first ven-
ture, the Sun Radio Network, to another network controlled by the Liberty Lobby—a group which calls itself "populist" but pushes an anti-Semitic
agenda of Holocaust denial and tales of global conspiracies by stateless
"international bankers" (Harder, 1994; Cooper, 1995b; Davis, 1996a).
After a brief partnership, Harder broke with Liberty Lobby and left Sun to
start the People's Radio Network (PRN). Founded in 1991 with 72 stations, PRN grew to around 300 radio stations in all 50 states, as well as 77
TV stations. Writing in April, 1995, journalist Marc Cooper reported:

> More than 40,000 listeners pay a minimum of $15 a year to belong to
> [Harder's] *For the People* organization. For an extra $19 a year an-
> other 30,000 followers subscribe to the biweekly, full color, thirty-

two-page *News Reporter* ... From merchandise sales and memberships, People's Radio Network grossed more than $4 million in 1994.
(Cooper, 1995a: 488)

Broadcast industry surveys showed Harder outperforming such high-
profile personalities as Michael Reagan and Oliver North, some ranking
him among America's top ten radio talk-show hosts (DeRosa, 1995; Davis,
1996a).

Harder's radio show represented itself in the following terms: "*For the
People* seeks to provide a forum for the average citizen to learn about
consumer information and the workings of our government. Because the
program is financially supported by listeners rather than advertisers, Harder
speaks without fear of corporate censorship or reprisals" (Harder, quoted in
UBN online promotional bulletin ww2.audionet.com/pub/ubn/harder.htm).
Harder said: "Our goal is to save the middle class, save the little guy"
(quoted in Cooper, 1995a: 488). Harder and his guests—including such
heavy hitters as Ralph Nader and Pat Buchanan—routinely excoriated
corporate power and a government which they represented as unresponsive to popular needs and concerns. He and his guests have, on a variety of
grounds, been sharply critical of recent trade agreements such as the General Agreement on Tariffs and Trade (GATT) and the North American
Free Trade Agreement (NAFTA). During the NAFTA debate, Harder ex-
cited the interest of his listeners to such a degree that 7,000 of them
bought copies of the full 2,000 page text of the NAFTA agreement which
Harder made available at low cost (Davis, 1996a).

In May 1996, Harder's network was purchased by a consortium of
investors including the United Automobile Workers (UAW). One of the
most historically progressive of American industrial unions, the UAW
invested "several million" dollars for a share of about 10 percent in the re-
named United Broadcasting Network which, according to the *Wall Street
Journal*, was "designed to bring Mr. Harder to a wider audience by up-
grading technology and buying stations in major markets" (Davis, 1996a).
As UAW public relations chief Frank Joyce explained to me (24 May,
1996), the union viewed UBN as a broad-based effort to present diverse
perspectives on themes important to American working people, especially
preserving American jobs. The new network's chairman was economic
nationalist Pat Choate, who left UBN temporarily to run for Vice-Presi-
dent in 1996 on Ross Perot's Reform Party ticket. The original team of
commentators for UBN included highly visible opponents of transnational
corporate power: Choate himself; Bay Buchanan, sister and political advi-
sor of Pat Buchanan; left-populist Jim Hightower; and, of course, Chuck
Harder (Baker, 1996; Gladstone, 1996; Rosier, 1996).

This story was intriguing to me because Harder has been characterized
as a promoter of far-right conspiratorial ideologies of globalization. Re-
visiting Harder's brief association with the Liberty Lobby, critics suggested

that this might be interpreted as part of a pattern in Harder's activities. They pointed out (correctly) that Harder's radio show *For the People* offered a receptive atmosphere for far-right organizers and militia activists such as John Trochmann, Linda Thompson, Ken Adams, and Larry Pratt, and even provided a forum for the noxious anti-Semitic conspiracist, Eustace Mullins. Further, Harder has marketed an array of far-right conspiratorial literature to his listeners (including for a time several of Mullins' books). Critics allege that Harder has told his listeners that the Council on Foreign Relations "controls the world" and that he routinely promotes the view that America is being led toward incorporation into the New World Order by "New York power brokers," "New York bankers," "the global elite," suggesting that Harder speaks to his audience in the lexicon of far-right conspiracists (Cooper, 1995a, 1995b; Davis, 1996a).[2]

Harder has maintained that he does not promote conspiracy theories or anti-Semitism, and he is supported in this by Arthur Teitelbaum, of the Miami office of the Anti-Defamation League, who told the *Wall Street Journal* that his office had not "seen anything that would cause us to label Chuck Harder as an anti-Semite" (quoted in Davis, 1996a). Moreover, Harder has disavowed any association with far-right armed militias: "I have never been to a militia meeting. I have no idea who they are. I have no idea what they do" (quoted in Davey, 1996). He claimed that his radio network presented a forum for a variety of populist voices which "promote American core values, morality and economic nationalism"—including, for example, *both* Pat Buchanan and Ralph Nader (Harder, 1995). Critical of politicians from both major parties whom he characterized as "puppets of the multinational corporations that have brought this country to its knees in the name of profits and globaloney" (in Cooper, 1995a: 488), Harder described himself as "non-partisan," "politically neutral." "I'm on no side. They all despise me. The left-wingers hate me. The right-wingers hate me . . . It's very simple. I'm for what's right for the American people" (in Davey, 1996). Harder and his network, it seems to me, represented the tensions and ambiguities of the new populism, a confluence of such currents as the far-right conspiratorial ideologies of the "Patriot" movement, the economic nationalism associated with Buchanan and Perot, as well as the potentially more progressive and cosmopolitan world-views of Naderites and unionists. It is precisely this sense that the ambiguities and tensions of popular common sense are being played out in the productions of Harder's network that led me to a closer reading of some of those materials.

Reading the new populism: The News Reporter

Chuck Harder and Richard Osborn[3] of *For the People* made available to me the complete print run of the program's biweekly tabloid, *The News Reporter*, which was first published in August, 1992. Most of the paper consisted of articles and commentary reprinted from Knight–Ridder and other news services, but each edition also contained commentary by Harder, Osborn, and/or others associated with *For the People*. My interpretations here are based primarily upon a perusal of articles authored by Harder between August, 1992 and November, 1995. I read this material as an embodiment of the tensions and possibilities which have historically resided in the American populist tradition.

According to historian Michael Kazin, the primary characteristic of populist discourse in the American political tradition is its claim to speak for "the people"—represented as citizen-producers, the social foundation of the American republic—against arrogant and malevolent elites. On this view, populism is "a language whose speakers conceive of ordinary people as a noble assemblage not bounded narrowly by class, view their elite opponents as self-serving and undemocratic, and seek to mobilize the former against the latter" (Kazin, 1995: 1). Kazin describes successive instantiations of populist language in American political history, speaking on behalf of (often white, male) farmers, craftsmen, and small businessmen whose arduous labors are seen to create the material wealth of the republic. The great "other" of these populist narratives is an aristocratic (and hence implicitly "un-American") elite, producing nothing and living off the sweat of the average man even as they mocked his manners and mores.

American populist movements have been "rooted in contradiction," Kazin suggests: "they championed 'individual enterprise' or equal opportunity in the marketplace but decried the division between haves and have-nots as a perversion of democratic spirit" (Kazin, 1995: 17). Thus they have on the one hand envisioned a small town main street version of capitalism as their social ideal, while, on the other, they have railed against the undemocratic social power implicit in capitalism's core structure.[4] The former position seems less likely than the latter to serve as a vehicle for the construction of a broad-based social movement encompassing the poor as well as the "working middle class" and which might aim at the democratization of economic relations. The construction of such a movement, and of cross-border alliances with other people's movements for economic democracy, seems to me a prerequisite for effectively challenging the power of transnational corporate capital. To the extent, then, that the new populism can be reconstructed in such a way that it contributes to this agenda, I would assess its impact as potentially progressive. If, on the other hand, it scapegoats the poor as parasites on the middle class, and takes refuge in an economic nationalism which represents underpaid and under-protected workers in other countries as somehow to blame for deteriorating conditions in America, then the new populism is serving to divide rather than unite the dispossessed and its effect is to enhance still further the power of transnational capital.

In attempting to sort out the various currents of neo-populist ideology running through *For the People*, it seems to me important to ask questions such as the following. Who are "the people" in whose name claims of injustice are being made, and who are represented as the people's oppressors? Are "the people" understood in the fashion of a narrowly ethnocentric "Americanism"—as, for example, the white "middle class" burdened not only by the exploitation of super-rich bankers but also by an unproductive underclass? Or are "the people" broadly construed as those whose life chances are constrained by pervasive social inequalities, within the US and transnationally? Is that oppression represented as being rooted in a particular socio-political order, or is it attributed to the intrinsic characteristics of malevolent individuals or groups? What kinds of political strategies seem to flow from these analyses; what kinds of possible worlds do they point toward?

Who are "the people" addressed by Harder and *For the People*? In a statement of "editorial and broadcast philosophy," *The News Reporter* put it like this: "It is our simple belief that all Americans of all colors and creeds must work together to face the problems and rebuild our country and regain our previous standard of living" (5 October, 1992). In another context, Harder wrote "Our broadcasts are for the sake of advancing the welfare of the American people and their standard of living. We take the logical position that no matter if you are white, black, brown, or any color in-between, and no matter if you go to church, temple, synagogue or mosque, or don't go at all, we're still all American people.... Hatred has no place in our organization" (quoted in Hilliard and Keith, 1999: 212). Thus, unlike racist elements of the Patriot movement who (more or less explicitly) address "white Americans," Harder's brand of populist Americanism appears more inclusive. For example, rather than drawing on the familiar racist trope which associates crime and violence with non-whites, Harder suggests a more sociological perspective in which crime is linked with poverty and desperation. Constructing prison cells for non-white citizens thus seems less important than rebuilding the productive base which supports all working Americans. This approach is also reflected in Harder's comments on the roots of the Los Angeles riots: "Unless all people in the USA have a fair and equal chance at the American Dream, there is no way to avoid more riots of the kind that swept through Los Angeles" (*The News Reporter*, 19 October, 1992). Such language contrasts markedly with Pat Buchanan's view of the social unrest in Los Angeles: at the 1992 Republican national convention, Buchanan glorified military force used to suppress those he characterized as a lawless "mob" (Buchanan, 1992). Harder's representation suggests instead that issues of social justice uniting middle class and poor Americans of all races are more fundamental than their differences, thus keeping open the possibility of cross-race solidarity.

Harder's version of "the people," however, does not seem to be a concept sufficiently elastic to encompass workers in the Third World, who were frequently characterized in *The News Reporter* as "coolies" and "peasants," language suggesting that the labors of such unsophisticated peoples could not be worth more than some bare minimum (sub-American) wage. To the extent that American workers are brought into competition with "coolies" and "peasants," this seems to imply, the American standard of living will inevitably suffer. Accordingly, Harder consistently advocates a more militant economic nationalism, urging his audience to "fix America first" and to "buy American."

> Right now we're losing tool and die makers, industrial engineers, draftsmen, and all other support staff that industry requires. Instead we only need people to put stuff on the shelf at Wal-Mart. Well sir, those jobs would still be there if the product was made in the USA instead of China. Countries like ours that sell raw materials abroad and then import finished goods are known as "colonies." The fix is easy. Put a tariff on all incoming goods that protects USA citizens. Have it so that NO COMPETITOR can move offshore and cut the throat of a US-based factory-produced item.
>
> (Harder in Hilliard and Keith, 1999: 216)

At a minimum, this kind of nationalism reinforces feelings of American exceptionalism and does little to encourage cross-border solidarity amongst those dominated by the growing power of multinational corporate capital. In the worst case, it could be interpreted by the racist right as validation of their view of white Americans and Europeans as genetically superior and thus entitled to a higher standard of living than the rest of the world.

Similarly ambiguous are Harder's representations of the causes of popular oppression. While occasionally disavowing conspiracism, Harder consistently uses language which lends itself quite readily to interpretations grounded in far-right conspiracist ideology. "The people" were seen as being oppressed by an elite whose disproportionate power is based in finance, and whose interests diverge from those of "middle class" Americans. In a sociological sense, of course, this is hardly an outlandish or even implausible claim. Indeed, responding to published critiques which associated him with far-right conspiracism, Harder's language took on an analytical tone: "Wall Street has come to dominate national policy-making in Washington, both through the way we finance our elections and the force of money in the economy. The decision-making, moreover, is highly concentrated. It is not a conspiracy theory . . . but a well-documented reality" (Harder in *The News Reporter*, 8 May, 1995). Yet, at the same time, Harder repeatedly told of an anti-democratic "shadow government" in which "David Rockefeller and his power group" stealthily influence government policy through such organizations as the Trilateral Commission and the Council on Foreign Relations. "These groups serve as a 'Chamber of Commerce' for the ultra-rich industrialists and the world's elite," wrote Harder. "Our concern is that the everyday citizen has no voice, input, or real opportunity to balance their doctrines and goals that, historically, become law and official US policy" (Harder in *The News Reporter*, 11 July, 1994). According to Harder, American electoral democracy is hollow insofar as "both parties are controlled and owned by the David Rockefeller crowd—the global greedsters and world industrial overlords who love slave labor and big profits" (31 July, 1995). Under their influence, "The USA is turning into a 'Third World Banana Republic'" (14 August, 1995). Echoing the conspiracists' dichotomy of either coincidence or conspiracy, Harder asserts: "Current USA policy—to export jobs and benefit only the ruling class—didn't happen by accident. It was all planned!" (25 January, 1993).

Rhetoric of this latter sort moves away from a more sociological perspective focusing on structured imbalances of social power and moves back toward the scapegoating of nefarious individuals or groups who are held to be ultimately responsible for the deteriorating circumstances faced by ordinary Americans. Thus in another discussion of globalization and de-industrialization, Harder asked: "Who's doing this? The answer is the global bankers and influence peddlers" (19 October, 1992). Globalization, and the concomitant de-industrialization of America, was seen as the financial elite's deliberate policy of self-enrichment at the expense of American working people—"the disposable victims of global corporations chasing larger profits and lower labor costs" by moving factories abroad to take advantage of "desperate people" in impoverished countries (19 June, 1995). Free trade agreements (NAFTA and GATT) were depicted as instruments of this elite strategy: "It's obvious to us that the bankers, who control our USA public policy via their front organizations, have implemented deals like NAFTA" (13 December, 1993). "Good jobs in the US are exported to sweatshops where frightened, docile, unarmed peasants do exactly as they are told. This slave-labor force ... establishes the *base line* for the economic yardstick called 'global competitiveness.' It is where the US is headed" (20 September, 1993). Global competitiveness may then be used by corporate employers to batter down the middle class aspirations of American working people: "War was silently declared on the 'American Dream,' as the wealth and lifestyle of the middle-class was drained and turned into profit for a select financial global elite in New York and Tokyo" (19 June, 1995). In "corporate America's New World (fascist) Order," Harder warned his readers in language which resonates even more strongly with far-right visions of imminent enslavement, "People in America could literally be forced to live in poverty at gunpoint in a federal police-state" (8 May, 1995). Harder cautioned, "Don't call it a conspiracy because it was just consensus by the elite to do good business" (19 June, 1995). Yet, there was little analysis of the social conditions under which such practices could be seen as "good business," or of social transformations which might redefine the conditions of "good business." Instead, echoing *The Spotlight*—the hard-core conspiracist tabloid of the anti-Semitic Liberty Lobby—Harder referred to this New World Order as the elite's "global plantation dream" (19 June, 1995). In language which would warm the blood of any far-right "Patriot" or armed militiaman, he condemned globalization boldly and simply as "TREASON" (2 November, 1992).[5]

When it was announced in 1996 that German air force pilots would be stationed at Holloman Air Force Base in New Mexico for training, Harder suggested to his radio audience that this could be understood in terms of the New World Order narrative in which the United Nations subsumes US sovereignty as part of the establishment of an elite-dominated one-world government: Harder described the basing of foreign forces on US soil as a watershed event, a cession of US sovereign territory, "the first part of a global plan by the United Nations nitwits to control the world" (Harder quoted in Mintz, 1996). Harder's tabloid *The News Reporter* devoted a great deal of attention to issues preoccupying the radical right, such as the FBI killings at Ruby Ridge, Idaho and the disastrous siege of the Branch Davidian compound outside Waco, Texas. It reprinted articles from the organ of the conspiracist John Birch Society claiming that the federal government was constructing a "police state" as part of a "march toward global tyranny," and lent its credibility to the suggestion, commonplace in far-right circles, that the Oklahoma City bombing might have been perpetrated or instigated by forces within the federal government, an American version of Hitler's Reichstag fire (24 January, 7 February, 1994; 19 June, 17 July, 1995).

Further, although Harder's organization appears to have stopped selling the most bilious of the conspiracy literature it had once advertised, he continues to market texts which promote an explicitly conspiratorial vision of globalization. In August, 1996, I contacted the *For the People* bookstore and was told that Eustace Mullins' books were no longer available for purchase, nor were several other hard-core conspiracy titles previously advertised through the *News Reporter*. They were, however, selling what might be considered softer conspiracy texts such as *The Shadows of Power: The Council on Foreign Relations and the American Decline*, produced by the publishing house of the John Birch Society (Perloff, 1988). Visiting the online book catalogue at Harder's *For the People* web site in June 1999, I found conspiracist tracts such as Gary Kah's *En Route to Global Occupation* and *Demonic Roots of Globalism*, along with Jim Keith, *Black Helicopters over America*. Further, the online *For the People* program schedule indicated that these and other conspiracist and millenialist authors had enjoyed Harder's on-air hospitality between September 1997 and April 1999 (www.forthepeople.org).

From conspiracist representations like these Harder's audience might readily infer that the solution to America's problem is to neutralize the perpetrators who are usurping governmental power in order to subject "the people" to an exploitative global government. Resistance to such treason and tyranny may require an armed and militant citizenry as the final defense of freedom, as Harder's friendly reception of militia-related guests seemed to imply.[6] On this view, constructing broad-based social movements could appear less relevant than building heavily armed bastions from which to strike against the forces of globalization and tyranny. Despite Harder's disavowal of violence and calls for peaceful political resolution of America's problems, there is evidence which suggests that *For the People* contributed to the environment in which far-right ideology has incubated (Freivogel, 1995; Goodman, 1995). For example, an officer of the Michigan Militia told the *St. Louis Post-Dispatch* that Harder's show

> gives people like me . . . a chance to call in and talk about . . . the fear they have of their government . . . They are trying to destroy this country . . . some of the people who are in power . . . some of the world bankers . . . If they break my constitutional . . . rights to come into my house, to take my weapons, yes, I feel like I have the right to resist.
>
> (quoted in Freivogel, 1995)

It appears that Harder, his radio network, and his marketing of conspiracy texts have helped to establish among far-flung Patriots a sense of simultaneity, of sharing a common historical situation with distant, unmet fellows. Borrowing from Benedict Anderson (1991), then, we might say that Harder has contributed to the formation of an "imagined community" of Patriots on the far-right wing of American populism. Harder's stature within the conspiracist discourse community is widely acknowledged. He appears to enjoy a measure of respect from more hard-line conspiracist radio figures such as the Liberty Lobby's Tom Valentine and neo-fascist William Pierce (author of the notorious *Turner Diaries*), the latter perhaps intending to pay Harder a compliment by situating him in a historical "movement to free America from international domination" which traces its roots back to Henry Ford's populist anti-Semitism (quoted in Hilliard and Keith, 1999: 175, also 226). Harder is cited as an authoritative source of New World Order information on the internet bulletin boards of the far right, and I found numerous conspiracy-oriented world wide web sites which recommended *For the People* or provided links to the show's home page. A survey done by the far-right, pro-militia magazine *Media Bypass* in November, 1995 revealed that Chuck Harder was the most popular radio talk show host among its readers, almost all of whom also expressed strong sympathy for citizen militias and disapproved of the United Nations (Pitcavage, 1996).

I offer the following anecdote as further evidence suggestive of the disposition of at least some segments of Harder's audience. On 15 May, 1997, I was contacted by the legal defense team for Timothy McVeigh, then being tried for the bombing of the Federal Building in Oklahoma City. The attorney I spoke to told me they were considering whether to call Chuck Harder as a witness and were interested in my research into

Harder and UBN. Near the end of the conversation, I asked the attorney whether McVeigh had been a frequent listener of Harder's program. The lawyer would not confirm this explicitly, but responded positively when I asked him whether this would be a reasonable inference for me to make on the basis of his entire line of questioning. That someone as radically far right as Tim McVeigh—someone who considered himself to be at war with the US government and the New World Order—might find political sustenance in Chuck Harder's radio program suggests to me that Harder's populism, ambiguous as it is, finds some resonance with the most danger-ous tendencies of the far right.

The decline and rise of Chuck Harder and the new populism

Whether or not Mr. Harder actively sympathizes with the far right, what is important to me is the fact that his talk-radio networks have served as a vehicle for the contending counter-ideologies of globalization. In this populist stew, the Americanist anti-globalisms of Pat Buchanan, the Patriot-militia movement, and Eustace Mullins were juxtaposed with the potentially cosmopolitan democratic ideologies represented by Ralph Nader, Jim Hightower, and others. The tensions within this populist melange could not be contained at UBN, as Harder almost immediately came into conflict with Choate and the network's new management. Choate's UAW-backed team quickly took editorial control of *The News Reporter* from Harder's staff and purged it of its conspiratorial themes while retaining its populist tone and economic nationalist orientation. On the air, they began to under-cut some of Harder's message, and encountered dissonance from the more conspiratorially-minded segments of Harder's audience. According to the *Wall Street Journal*, Choate "spent much of his time on-air dispel-ling conspiracy theories involving Whitewater, trade officials and Hillary Rodham Clinton that were put forward by the network's callers" (Davis, 1996b). With tensions also building over managerial and money matters, Harder reportedly broke with the Choate team after they "reprimanded" him for his vociferous anti-Clinton rhetoric. In September, 1996, Harder was taken off the air by UBN and sent on "extended vacation." He has since begun broadcasting his populist message on a new network of over one hundred stations and hopes to rebuild his audience independent of Choate and UBN (Davis, 1996b; DeGeorge, 1996).[7] Harder's departure has not resolved the tensions within the neo-populist movement addressed by UBN, however. The network began advertising the talk show of left-populist commentator Jim Hightower in the March 1997 issue of *Solidar-ity*, the magazine of the UAW. In that issue, one could find both UBN's "Buy American" brand of economic nationalism (p. 15) and William Grieder's call for "an aggressive campaign to win labor rights for the impoverished new industrial workers in developing countries" (p. 24). The tensions and possibilities of populism remain evident in Harder's new network as well. In addition to conspiracist and millenialist authors who would be familiar to an audience of Christian Patriots, Harder's 1999 book catalog and program list also included progressive critics of capitalist and corporate power such as Holly Sklar, Tom Ferguson, Alexander Cockburn, and Charles Derber (www.forthepeople.org).

In my view, UBN failed because it was premised on an untenable pluralist approach to a profoundly conflicted populist politics. When confronted with these tensions in the form of Harder's on-air persona, UBN tried to de-link populism from conspiracism (by muzzling Harder) without systematically re-articulating the populist impulse with a critique of the historical structures of globalizing capitalism. Instead of helping its audience to reframe their populist commitments in terms of a more systematic and transformative critique—a critique which might have led beyond the contradictory concatenation of nationalism and conspiracism with populism's democratizing impulse—the UAW's allegiance to the Democratic Party and Choate's alliance with Perot's reform party meant that the new management at UBN tried to remain within the bounds of the respectable, conventional politics of liberal capitalism, even as it offered up a menu of populisms some of which pointed toward more radical, and divergent, forms of politics. When Harder refused to be thus contained, the populist network broke apart.

In venues such as this, the world-view of neoliberal internationalism—in which states and corporations create the rules for global economic integration—is facing challenges which emphasize different aspects of popular common sense in order to envision alternative possible worlds. Drawing on the democratic strains of popular common sense, what I have called the left-progressive position would construct a world in which the global economy is explicitly politicized, corporate power is confronted by transnational coalitions of popular forces, a framework of democratically developed standards provides social accountability for global economic actors, and, perhaps most importantly, working people (both waged and unwaged) come to understand themselves as politically engaged and potentially self-governing even in their "economic" relations. The anti-globalist position of the far right, on the other hand, envisions a world in which Americans are uniquely privileged inheritors of a divinely inspired sociopolitical order which must at all costs be defended against external intrusions and internal subversion.

In such ideological contests, the future shape of transnational political order may be at stake. The emerging historical structure of transnational capitalism may generate the potential for the construction of political identities and projects which transcend state-centric understandings of politics and facilitate transnational movements to contest the global dominance of capital. To the extent that the ambiguities of the new populism are resolved in ways which reconstruct political identities on the basis of economic, cultural, or racial/ethnic nationalism, this potential will be undercut. If, on the other hand, this ambiguous populism can be reconstructed in ways which broaden its core understandings of "the people" and affirm core values of popular self-determination, it could provide a necessary (but not sufficient) condition for the emergence of transnational social movements oriented toward the democratization of the world economy.

7 The New World Order

Passive revolution or transformative process?

Fear and loathing in reverse: the global power bloc and the new populism

By 1996 there were clear signs that the world's most powerful social forces were getting worried. Why? Their agenda of global economic openness and integration via the free flow of trade and investment has been progressively realized over half a century. Over the postwar period world trade has grown more rapidly than output, and foreign investment has in recent decades expanded still more dramatically. In the early decades of this emerging global order, its architects could justify their project in terms of the manichean categories of Cold War ideology as well as the stories of generalized peace and prosperity associated with the classical liberal tradition. And indeed, American working people (or, at least, a substantial proportion of them) were integrated into a hegemonic global order through access to postwar prosperity and through the stark representations of Cold War politics (Rupert, 1995).

But the Cold War is over and its unambiguous political narrative no longer seems to make sense of the world in ways which are adequate to the realities of life faced by many people in the US and elsewhere. Among those realities has been a major shift in socio-political power at various scales from the local to the global. The "historic bloc" of social forces and ideologies which formed the core of the US-centered hegemonic world order is being reconstructed. American industrial labor is no longer secure in its position as a relatively privileged junior partner in this global power bloc, as prevailing interpretations of liberal ideology have shifted away from a version which had endorsed more activist and growth-oriented state policies and which legitimized collective bargaining by mass industrial unions. In place of the kinder, gentler liberalism which was hegemonic during the postwar decades we now find instead a hard-edged liberalism which strives to focus the violence of market forces directly upon working people through policies which emphasize public fiscal retrenchment, containment of inflation, and "flexible labor markets" in a context of rigorous global competition.

It is in this context that a new populism is emerging to challenge the formerly hegemonic narratives of liberal peace and prosperity. The new populism, stoked in the US by Pat Buchanan and company, is not going unnoticed by the constellation of capitalists, state managers and intellectuals who have fostered economic globalization as part of a transnational hegemonic project. Even as Buchanan made himself a symbol of popular discontent a steady stream of critical commentaries appeared in the mainstream press bashing his policy proposals as atavistic, crude, isolationist, protectionist, and dangerous. Among these was a warning from James Bacchus, American member of the World Trade Organization appeals panel, who characterized Buchananism as a threat to the system of global liberalization painstakingly constructed through postwar decades: "It would be economic suicide to throw it all away now" (quoted in Nordheimer, 1996; see also Friedman, 1996; Hormats, 1996). Evidently, Buchanan's populist nationalism provoked real anxiety among the global power bloc.

Ethan Kapstein, then Director of Studies for the Council on Foreign Relations, has suggested that the new populism increasingly evident across the OECD countries represents a backlash against the combination of intensified global competitive pressures and a political climate dominated by the interests of investors. The growth-oriented "embedded liberalism" compromise has been abandoned in favor of anti-inflationary policies which effectively suppresses the real standard of living of working people while maintaining the long-term profitability of investments. Kapstein warned readers of *Foreign Affairs*: "if the post-World War II social contract with workers—of full employment and comprehensive social welfare—is to be broken, political support for the burgeoning global economy could easily collapse." In the absence of growth-oriented and internationally coordinated measures to ease the plight of those hardest hit by the new global competition—primarily less skilled workers and middle managers—politics in the industrial countries could well take an ugly turn. "Populists and demagogues of various stripes will find 'solutions' to contemporary economic problems in protectionism and xenophobia" (Kapstein, 1996: 16–17). Were that to occur, he suggested, the result would be a loss of the potential aggregate income made available by an extended Smithian division of labor, and the emergence of a zero-sum world in which both peace and prosperity would become more difficult to realize.

And Kapstein was not the only representative of the global power bloc expressing such fears. The World Economic Forum (WEF) has become increasingly preoccupied with the politics of globalization. Evolving out of the European Management Forum which Swiss business professor Klaus Schwab founded in 1971, the WEF has become a membership organization for over one thousand major international firms, each of which pays substantial annual fees to the Forum.[1] The Forum explains in its promotional literature why such shrewd business people see this as money well spent: "As a member of the World Economic Forum, you are part of a real

Club, and the foremost business and public-interest network in the world" (World Economic Forum, 1997a: 10). In keeping with its program of promoting "entrepreneurship in the public interest," the WEF brings its members together at the annual Davos extravaganza, which Thomas Freidman calls "the ultimate capitalist convention" (Friedman, 1999a: 268). The Davos meetings offer WEF members "intensive networking in a privileged context allowing for the identification of new business opportunities and new business trends." At Davos, WEF members hobnob with their fellow global capitalists, but also with leaders from political and civil society to whom the Forum refers as "constituents" (to distinguish them from WEF "members"): while corporate "members" are entitled to attend WEF events, heads of state and government ministers, academics and policy experts, media figures, and cultural leaders from around the world may attend by invitation only. Thus the WEF offers its members privileged access to "high-level interaction between political leaders and business leaders on the key issues affecting economic development" on regional and global scales (World Economic Forum, 1997a: 10).

> The key to Forum activities is direct access to strategic decision-makers, in a framework designed to encourage economic development via private sector involvement. This direct interaction between public and private sector and experts leads to the creation of a partnership committed to improving the state of the world.
>
> (World Economic Forum, 1997b)

Representing itself as being at once a private club and a kind of global public sphere, the Forum is an organization in which the various segments of the global power bloc can come together to construct a unifying political vision, and present to the rest of the world the interests of global capital in the guise of a universal vision—"entrepreneurship in the public interest." In short, it attempts to organize the hegemony of a global ruling class, as Kees van der Pijl has argued (van der Pijl, 1998: 132–5).

At the 1996 Davos conclave, the central theme was "sustaining globalization." As the meetings opened, Forum organizers Klaus Schwab and Claude Smadja published an essay in the *International Herald Tribune* suggesting that the process of economic globalization "has entered a critical phase" in which economic and political relationships, both globally and within countries, are being painfully restructured. Schwab and Smadja acknowledge that these changes are having a devastating impact on large numbers of working people in "the industrial democracies," with heightened mass insecurity resulting in "the rise of a new brand of populist politicians." They fear that in the absence of effective measures to address the social circumstances of working people and the weakened ideological legitimacy of global capitalism, the new populism may continue to gain strength, threaten further progress toward the agenda of globalization, and "test the social fabric of the democracies in an unprecedented way." The social forces leading globalization, then, face "the challenge of demonstrating how the new global capitalism can function to the benefit of the majority and not only for corporate managers and investors" (Schwab and Smadja, 1996). In the spirit of this analysis, Schwab addressed the opening session of the 1996 forum: "Business has become a major stakeholder of globalization and has a direct responsibility to contribute to the stability of our global system" (World Economic Forum, 1996; see also Economist, 1996).

As early as 1995, the World Bank's *World Development Report* had focused its attention on "Workers in an Integrating World." While maintaining its basic commitment to "market-friendly" policies and international openness, and representing such policies in familiar liberal terms as generally beneficial, the Bank conceded that "within the industrial countries there is a small but vocal minority who fear that they will lose from the introduction of new technologies, the growth of international trade, and movements of capital and people across national boundaries" (World Bank, 1995: 4–5, 56). This "vocal minority" the Bank viewed as posing a potential political threat to international openness and the prevalence of "sound" economic policies. "Ensuring that a commitment to open trade remains politically acceptable sometimes requires policy measures to ease the plight of the minority that loses out." The Bank warned that such policies should not foster welfare dependence, but should "encourage workers to upgrade their skills, educate their children, and support the mobility of workers into new jobs," thus making themselves more useful and attractive to transnational capital (1995: 60). Further, to insure that the gains from liberal globalization were seen to spread as widely as possible, governments were warranted to deal with inequality, especially that linked to discrimination based on ethnicity or gender. Betraying the fundamental liberal fear of "special interests," the Bank explicitly declined to link trade and international labor standards (1995: 6, 79), but called upon governments to protect (if not necessarily to encourage) basic worker rights such as the right to form unions for purposes of (enterprise-level) collective bargaining (1995: 71, 79–86).

In these remarkable statements—by representatives of the constellation of social forces whose hegemony acted as midwife to long-term processes of capitalist globalization—the importance of ideological struggle and the potential threat of populism and nationalism to a sustained liberal hegemony are frankly acknowledged. Even before the 1997–8 financial crises which rocked Asia and the world, and the two-time defeat (in 1997 and then again in 1998) of Presidential Fast Track authority in the US, expressions of popular disaffection had awakened some among the dominant bloc to the fragility of neoliberal globalization and of their continued global social power.

The Asian crisis

Through 1997–8, a series of financial panics swept through several newly industrializing countries (NICs) and, as the confidence of the investor class was shaken, reverberations from the crisis were visible in industrializing economies and major financial markets around the world. Among the countries most seriously affected were Thailand, Indonesia, Malaysia, the Philippines, and South Korea—countries which only a short time before had seemed to be rising stars of the new international division of labor. Massive inflows of foreign investment have fueled rapid growth in these economies, including growth in manufacturing for export but also including a great deal of more speculative and unproductive investment, especially after 1985 when Japanese foreign direct investment was increasingly displaced by international portfolio investment and bank capital. As part of their strategy to attract international capital, several Asian NICs had linked the values of local currencies to the US dollar, but when the dollar appreciated this arrangement put pressure on the trade balances of Asian NICs (whose exports became more expensive as a result). As trade balances deteriorated, business confidence became further clouded by the relative magnitude of unproductive investment (especially speculation in real estate) and fears of a bursting bubble began to spread. Investors increasingly fled these economies, dumping local currencies and assets denominated in those currencies.

Smelling blood in the foreign exchange markets, packs of predatory speculators attacked the Thai baht, Malaysian ringgit, Indonesian ruppiah, and the Philippine peso by "selling short." That is, speculators contracted to deliver at future dates currencies which they did not actually hold at the time, betting that by the contractually specified delivery date the market value of the currency would have deteriorated to such a degree that it could be bought more cheaply than the price specified in their contracts to deliver. Near the delivery date, the speculators would buy the promised quantities of currency and deliver them at the previously contracted price which, if they bet successfully, would be higher than the heavily devalued market price which the speculators actually pay for the currency prior to delivery. With increasing volumes of their currencies being dumped onto foreign exchange markets by fleeing investors and speculators selling short, defense of the dollar-linked currency values became untenable, and governments with depleted foreign exchange reserves were compelled to turn to the International Monetary Fund for help in addressing their balance of payments crises. The price of such help was submission to the IMF's standard policy template, a draconian program of austerity designed to reduce inflation and imports, attract foreign capital and expand exports by raising interest rates, slashing public spending, and suppressing wages and consumption (Bello, 1998; Henwood, 1998a, 1998b; on selling short, see Soros, 1998: 136–7).[2]

As the ramifications of the financial crisis spread around the world, George Soros wrote a series of articles and a book in which he made the remarkable claim that financial markets are inherently unstable, and that free market capitalism constitutes a threat to liberal, pluralist values. Soros attacked the atomistic assumptions upon which economic theory is based, arguing that markets, and especially financial markets, operate not on the basis of pre-given individual preferences but rather "reflexively." By this he meant that the preferences of market actors are shaped by the very markets in which they participate, creating the possibility of self-reinforcing cycles of boom and bust. Soros denounced what he calls "the capitalist threat" which results from conjoint influence of the instability of global markets, the erosion of civic values and resistance to regulation in the public interest which arise from the ideology of "market fundamentalism," and the likelihood of political backlash among those in the "periphery" most dependent upon, and vulnerable to, international capital.

> I can already discern the makings of the final crisis. It will be political in character. Indigenous political movements are likely to arise that will seek to expropriate the multinational corporations and recapture "national" wealth. Some of them may succeed in the manner of the Boxer Rebellion or the Zapatista Revolution. Their success may then shake the confidence of financial markets, engendering a self-reinforcing process on the downside. Whether it will happen on this occasion or the next one is an open question.
>
> (Soros, 1998: 134)

Much like the apostasy of John Gray—the former Thatcherite political philosopher who penned a bitterly critical attack on neoliberal globalization and its corrosive effects upon deeper social bonds and traditional institutions (Gray, 1998)—Soros' critique is remarkable not so much for its originality, but rather for its source. Soros—billionaire, financier, philanthropist, and amateur philosopher—has been a major player in the new world of global finance and was deeply implicated in the currency speculation which contributed to the Asian crisis.

The crisis not only unleashed fears about the instability of globalizing markets, it also called into question the institutional infrastructure of neoliberalism. In particular, a storm of controversy raged around the International Monetary Fund (IMF) and its invariant prescriptions of austerity in the face of crisis (Kristof, 1998; Miller, 1998; Sanger, 1998). The Fund's deflationary measures were originally designed for countries with large public deficits and high inflation, neither of which were characteristic of the Asian NICs. As a result of rigid IMF policies, critics claimed, the Asian NICs were subjected to recessions more severe than they might otherwise have had to endure, deepening economic pessimism and generating worldwide ripple effects. Prominent among these critics were officials of the

World Bank, especially its chief economist Joseph Stiglitz and its president James Wolfensohn. The latter went so far as to advocate a Comprehensive Development Framework which would link financial bailouts with integrated programs to maintain employment and facilitate access to healthcare and education. "If we do not have greater equity and social justice," Wolfensohn said, "there will be no political stability, and without political stability no amount of money put together in financial packages will give us financial stability" (quoted in Friedman, 1998).

In the US, both conservatives and progressives attacked the IMF when the issue of further US funding arose in Congress, illustrating once again the ambiguities of populist politics. Conservatives such as Senator Lauch Faircloth (Republican, North Carolina), representative Les Paul (Republican, Texas), and the Heritage Foundation (a prominent right-wing think tank), claimed that IMF bailouts amounted to welfare for Wall Street and distorted the operation of a free market (presumably based on individual responsibility for one's economic endeavors). Progressives, on the other hand, criticized IMF programs as not going far enough. Representative David Bonior (Democrat, Michigan) declared: "The American people are going to be very skeptical of any plan to bail out international speculators and repressive regimes that simply encourages them to repeat the same pattern of abuse and excess all over again. We cannot support a bailout that imposes an economic stranglehold on working people, tramples democratic rights, ignores the underlying causes of instability and then asks the American taxpayer to foot the bill" (quoted in Sanger, 1998). Some progressives called for replacement of the IMF by a new institution which would be funded by a modest tax on all international capital flows, which would dampen short-term speculative flows and make financial aid to investors and governments conditional upon their commitment to encourage long-term productive investment, pay living wages, and respect international labor standards. Others suggested a global equivalent of the Federal Deposit Insurance Corporation, funded by levies upon international banks and investment firms (Borosage, 1998; Miller, 1998).

While the IMF was subjected to extraordinary critical scrutiny, and there was for a time much talk of a "new architecture" for the global financial system, the storm seems largely to have blown over without effecting major change (Sanger, 1988). The administration and its major allies, such as the Business Roundtable, lobbied strenuously for immediate US support for the IMF. In return for IMF promises of greater disclosure of the terms of its bailout loans, and stiffer terms to act as a disincentive for borrowers, Congress agreed to continue funding with billions of dollars (Blustein, 1998).

Fast Track and stalemate in the US

The Clinton administration envisioned extending the North American Free Trade Area to encompass the whole of the hemisphere, and of entering into a new Asia–Pacific free trade area. For serious negotiations to proceed, however, the administration believed that it needed "Fast Track" authority from Congress: with the granting of such authority the President could proceed to negotiate trade agreements with other countries which Congress could subsequently accept or reject without amendment. The point of this procedural provision is to reassure potential bargaining partners that agreements reached with the US executive branch will not be picked apart in Congress. Every US President since 1974 had enjoyed repeated Congressional grants of this authority, but Clinton had allowed Fast Track authority to lapse without renewal in 1994. He had found himself trapped between progressive members of his own party, who insisted on making further liberalization contingent upon strong provisions protecting workers' rights and environmental standards, and intransigent Republicans and business interests dead set against any such provisions. In combination with its strong commitment to continued liberalization, the administration's lukewarm stance toward such protections did little to reassure progressive forces but was sufficient to alienate pro-business conservatives (Dunne, 1994). Between the proverbial rock and hard place, Clinton postponed confronting this divisive issue until after the 1996 Presidential election. Then, in the fall of 1997, he sought renewal of Fast Track authority in order to continue the agenda of neoliberal globalization.

The President had powerful backers. The business community was strongly united behind the neoliberal agenda in general and Fast Track in particular. Soon after the President announced his intention to seek Fast Track renewal in 1997, the Business Roundtable—which had played leading roles in USA*NAFTA and the Alliance for GATT Now—announced its plans for a three-pronged campaign of direct lobbying in Washington, grassroots mobilizations in every state, and media blitzes in specially targeted Congressional districts. In a letter to fellow Roundtable members, the CEOs of Caterpillar, Boeing, Proctor and Gamble, TRW, Chrysler, and General Motors estimated that such a campaign might cost as much as $3 million, pledged $100,000 each toward the efforts, and asked their fellows to consider similar contributions.[3] Later in the year, as the fight over Fast Track heated up in the House of Representatives, the Roundtable sent a letter to President Clinton, Speaker Gingrich, and the majority and minority leaders of the House urging passage of Fast Track authorization. For the 45 major corporate CEOs who signed this letter, at stake was whether "the United States will continue to maintain its global economic leadership": "If the United States is forced to the sidelines in future international trade negotiations because we do not have Fast Track, there will undoubtedly be negative economic consequences across the country. We risk being left behind as our trading partners and competitors open up trade and investment for their workers, companies, and farmers while maintaining their barriers against US exports."[4] As it had in the campaigns for NAFTA and GATT, the business community created a specialized umbrella organization to coordinate their efforts in support of Fast Track.

In a press release announcing its foundation in September, 1997, America Leads on Trade (with the apt acronym ALOT) described itself as "a coalition of more than 500 companies, associations, small and medium-sized businesses, organizations and individuals dedicated to securing America's leadership role in the international marketplace through the destruction of trade barriers and the creation of better and more highly-skilled US jobs" (America Leads on Trade, 1997; see also Neal, 1997).

The broad populist front which first emerged in the battle against NAFTA coalesced again in 1997 to fight against Fast Track. On the right-wing of this front, Pat Buchanan denounced Fast Track as part of a long-term program for "the steady transfer of wealth from industrial America and its workers to a new financial elite." Buchanan cast the Mexican Peso crisis of 1995 as paradigmatic of the new regime of global finance:

> Capital once invested in US industry is now poured into "hot" Third World economies. When those regimes, like Mexico, squander the money and need a bailout to pay off their wealthy Yankee investors, Washington lends the bankrupt regime the money, puts US taxpayers on the hook and makes the investors whole. To keep up interest payments, the bankrupt regime then devalues its currency to cut its prices, exports more to the United States and runs a trade surplus. Thus, America's industrial base and the best jobs of our manufacturing workers are sacrificed on the altar of finance.
>
> (Buchanan, 1997)

Translating this kind of right-populist pitch into its own peculiar code (see Chapter 5 above), the Liberty Lobby's *Spotlight* cast Fast Track as part of the plan by global "plutocrats" to "help multinational corporations further the exploitation of the world's masses" (Temple, 1997). Both Buchanan and the Liberty Lobby implied that the appropriate response to neoliberalism was a reassertion of American exceptionalism and protection of the special qualities of the working middle class.

As Robert Borosage pointed out, however, among the leading critics of Fast Track were Jesse Jackson, Paul Wellstone, and Richard Gephardt— "progressives, not protectionists . . . supported by the labor movement, environmental groups and consumer and human rights activists" (Borosage, 1997: 20). For this wing of the opposition, the issue was not so much *whether* the US should participate in globalization, but *how*. In particular, progressive forces objected to the double standards codified within trade regimes whereby property rights received explicit and enforceable protections, but labor and environmental standards received little more than lip service (Blustein, 1997). The newly reinvigorated AFL–CIO tackled the issue head-on. Federation president John Sweeney—elected in 1995 on a more activist, progressive platform—rallied the troops at the 1997 AFL–CIO convention: "The battle over 'fast track' is important to every union in this room . . . because trade agreements without worker rights and human rights and environmental standards undermine the wages and jobs of us all just as they damage the communities where we live and work." The unions vowed to oppose Presidential Fast Track authority unless it included explicit commitments to link labor and environmental standards directly to trade, and to enforce them with trade sanctions. In this critical stance, the federation was joined by House minority leader Gephardt (Democrat, Missouri), who declared: "If intellectual property and capital deserve protections in core free-trade treaties, with trade sanctions to enforce it, so do labor laws and environmental laws, on an equal basis" (Sweeney and Gephardt quoted in Greenhouse, 1997b). The AFL–CIO mounted a million-dollar media campaign attacking the administration's Fast Track proposal, and mobilized local union activists nationwide to put pressure on Congressional representatives.

As the debate heated up, former Secretary of Commerce and US Trade Representative Mickey Kantor weighed in on the pages of the *Washington Post*, claiming that the "reality" of "an interdependent, globalized world" is "routinely ignored by those who would have us cower behind walls of fear." Kantor summarized for the *Post*'s readers his vision of this reality, stressing that previous trade agreements had expanded US exports significantly. Over twelve million Americans owed their jobs to US exports, he claimed, noting that export sector jobs tend to pay higher wages. Americans also benefit from imports insofar as consumers face lower prices and US firms are encouraged to innovate and enhance their competitiveness. Kantor claimed that failure to renew Fast Track authority would not halt the progress of globalization, but would simply mean that the US would be left behind as other countries proceeded to liberalize on their own, "at the expense of US market share and jobs." In closing, Kantor explicitly appealed to the historic project of the neoliberal bloc and its ideology of prosperity and peace: "If Congress acts quickly to grant Fast Track negotiating authority, our generation can set the capstone on 50 years of concerted, bipartisan effort to promote open markets and open government. It will enrich our people, and it will promote our security" (Kantor, 1997).

And, as in previous debates on trade and globalization, academic economists lent their intellectual and political support to the cause of liberalization. During the Fast Track controversy, Michael Eisner—past president of the American Economic Association and professor emeritus at Northwestern University—published "A Free Trade Primer" in the *Wall Street Journal*. Eisner sought to debunk what he depicted as prevailing myths about trade deficits, low-wage competition, labor rights, and environmental standards. His arguments were based on "Ricardo's wisdom," the notion that even if a country (like the US) is relatively more productive across a range of activities, it will still benefit from increased openness, specialization according to comparative advantage, and trade. Although acknowledging that some workers will suffer—especially those in low-skill, low-wage occupations which do not constitute US comparative advantage—Eisner maintained that freer trade would "increase the proportion of high-wage jobs in our economy." On this reasoning, then, it is perverse to insist upon "stronger unions and better wages and working conditions in foreign countries" since this would have the effect of keeping US workers in the low-wage jobs they currently occupy. On these grounds, Eisner suggested, critics of Fast Track were misguided and Congress was warranted in granting the authority sought by the President (Eisner, 1997). The following year, a quartet of prominent economists published a book-length attack on the "globaphobia" afflicting much of the US population and threatening progress on the agenda of liberalization. In accessible prose clearly directed at a popular audience, they advanced the standard liberal arguments in favor of greater openness, and argued that although the US faced some serious economic problems (stagnant wages, inequality, insecurity), these were not the result of freer trade and would not be remedied by protectionism. Instead, they advanced "a strategy for making the domestic political environment more amenable to trade liberalization"—through an enhanced social safety net including temporary insurance against lost or reduced wages resulting from greater openness to imports. Lamenting that Fast Track authority had yet to be renewed, these economists reasserted the bottom line that "The United States . . . has much to gain from further reductions of barriers to trade and investment" (Burtless et al., 1998: 32).

As in the debates over NAFTA and GATT, the mainstream media took their cues from academic economists, government officials, and other "credible sources," while generally denying such legitimacy to critics of liberalization. As noted by the media watchdog group Fairness and Accuracy in Reporting (FAIR), "In editorial after heated editorial, virtually every major paper in the country denounced such critics and their concerns as 'protectionist' (*New York Times*, 9/8/97), an 'obstruction' (*Baltimore Sun*, 2/3/97), 'silly' (*Atlanta Journal and Constitution*, 3/4/97) and 'hypocritical' (*Minneapolis Star Tribune* 9/13/97)" (Jackson, 1997). FAIR noted that editorialists tended to lecture their readers on the basic arguments in favor of freer trade, while taking a dismissive tone toward the arguments of critics, who were almost by definition placed outside the bounds of reasoned economic discourse. Thus, when explaining the actions of critics, the newspapers tended to emphasize not their reasoning but rather ulterior motives such as the influence of labor union lobbying and campaign spending within the Democratic Party. There was little suggestion that the enormous power of corporate capital, organized through the Business Roundtable and ALOT, might underwrite arguments in favor of Fast Track and further liberalization; rather, these were represented as the products of scientific reasoning and enlightened public policy (Jackson, 1997). ALOT found such enlightened reasoning quite congenial and reproduced on its web site pro-Fast Track editorials from numerous papers around the country, including the *New York Times, Washington Post, Boston Herald, Chicago*

Tribune, St. Louis Post-Dispatch, Dallas Morning News, Seattle Times, and others (www.fasttrack.org/resources/opinion_editorial).

Despite energetic lobbying and Presidential promise-making, as the scheduled date neared it became apparent that the President's proposal could not muster the votes needed to pass in the House of Representatives. Clinton withdrew the Fast Track bill in November, 1997, to await more propitious circumstances. When he reintroduced it the following year, Fast Track was soundly defeated in the House (Schmitt, 1998). The defeat of Fast Track marked a major political setback for the social forces behind the neoliberal agenda. In combination with the transnational opposition to the proposed Multilateral Agreement on Investment, the defeat of Fast Track has focused their attention on formulating a vision of globalization which would defuse opposition and overcome the populist backlash. Fred Bergsten, director of the Institute for International Economics, explained: "Most trade types thought the merits of free trade were so obvious, the benefits were so clear, that you didn't have to worry about adjustments— you could just let the free market take care of it. The sheer political gains of the anti-globalization side [sic] in the last few years have made the free trade side realize that they have to do something to deal with the losers from free trade and the dislocations generated by globalization" (Bergsten, quoted in Dionne, 1999).

Responses to the new populism: "globalization with a human face"

It is not clear to me that the global ruling class is prepared to abandon its hegemonic doctrine of low inflation and fiscal retrenchment, "flexible labor markets," and free flows of goods and capital, all policies which promote the interests of investors and magnify the impact of market forces on working people. Yet it seems safe to say that its confidence has been shaken and that the ideological grip of neoliberalism is weakening, even among those whose political project it has been. It is in this context that some in the global power bloc are beginning to engage critics of neoliberal globalization on the terrain of ideological struggle.

Addressing the World Trade Organization in May, 1998, President Clinton reassured the WTO membership that despite the ongoing battles over Fast Track, the US was not turning away from the project of global liberalization: "we must pursue an ever-more-open global trading system" which, he said, will bring in train increasing economic opportunity, prosperity, freedom, and democracy. But Clinton was clearly impressed by the resistance to liberal globalization, and sought to co-opt some of their central arguments:

> We must do more to make sure that this new economy lifts living standards around the world and that spirited economic competition

among nations never becomes a race to the bottom in environmental protections, consumer protections and labor standards. We should level up, not level down. Without such a strategy, we cannot build the necessary public support for the global economy. Working people will only assume the risks of a free international market if they have the confidence that this system will work for them.

(Clinton, 1998)

Clinton called on the WTO to create a forum in which the voices of labor, consumer, and environmental groups might be heard, along with that of business, and he urged the organization to make its deliberations more open and public. In his 1999 State of the Union address, Clinton returned to this theme of legitimating the global economic order. He bemoaned the divisiveness of the trade issue and called for the construction of a new consensus: "Somehow we have to find a common ground. . . . We have got to put a human face on the global economy" (Clinton, quoted in Dionne, 1999).

The first US President to address the International Labor Organization (ILO) in Geneva, in the summer of 1999 Clinton reiterated his "firm belief that open trade is not contrary to the interest of working people" insofar as it brings with it efficiency gains, faster growth, better jobs, and higher incomes. "Unfortunately, working people the world over do not believe this," he lamented, reiterating his call to "put a human face on the global economy." Clinton proposed a three-pronged program. First, he advocated closer cooperation between the ILO and the other major institutions of the global economy, especially the IMF and the WTO, in order to promote more widespread respect for "core labor standards." He called for generalized adoption of the ILO's new *Declaration on Fundamental Principles and Rights at Work*—which he described as "a charter for a truly modern economy"—and for abolition of "the worst forms of child labor." And to assist the world's poorest countries, Clinton prescribed some measure of debt relief (Clinton, 1999).

While some observers saw in these declarations evidence that fundamental changes were afoot in US policy toward the world economy (Dionne, 1998, 1999), others have greeted Clinton's declarations with a healthy measure of skepticism, for Clinton's new global charter is weak beer indeed. In the anticlimactic debate over GATT–WTO in the US, the Clinton administration had purchased the quiescence of Lane Kirkland's AFL–CIO by promising to introduce the issue of labor standards into the deliberations of the WTO. And so they did: in the 1996 Singapore Ministerial Declaration, marking the first ministerial-level conference of WTO members, the ministers rhetorically renewed their commitment to internationally recognized labor standards, but made it absolutely clear that any such commitment would in no way be allowed to impede the agenda of liberalization. The WTO deferred to the ILO any active role in institutionalizing such standards, and flatly declared, "There is currently no work on the subject in the WTO" (World Trade Organization, 1998: 51). No direct connections would be forged between labor rights and access to the global trading system.

The ILO's attempts to implement the conventions defining fundamental labor rights have depended upon the willingness of member states to ratify the conventions and bring national labor laws into conformity with them. And this has been uneven at best. Of the seven "fundamental" ILO conventions, ratification rates range from 44 percent of member states up to 86 percent. The Convention on Freedom of Association and Protection of the Right to Organize (which one might imagine to be the *sine qua non* of membership in such an organization) has been ratified by only 71 percent of ILO members. The United States, ostensibly an advocate of international labor standards, has ratified only one of the seven fundamental conventions—Convention 105 proscribing forced labor.[5]

The approach to international labor standards which Clinton has been pushing, then, does not necessarily build into the global trading order mechanisms for enforcement of the standards, nor does it require adoption of ILO conventions and their inscription into national labor laws. Rather, the President has endorsed the ILO's non-binding *Declaration on Fundamental Principles and Rights at Work*, which makes it possible rhetorically to embrace the seven core labor standards without endowing them with the force of law or backing them with the possibility of trade sanctions. International trade union activists have attacked the new Declaration as "a toothless voluntary accord" made up of "hollow principles and rights at work detached from concrete implementation in national labor legislation" (Open World Conference of Workers, 1999). On these and other issues, progressive critic Robert Borosage sees a larger strategy at work in the performative contradictions of the President: "the gulf between word and deed . . . is essential to the administration's struggle to contain the growing revolt against corporate-defined globalization at home and abroad" (Borosage, 1999).

In calling for a version of "globalization with a human face," the President is not alone among card-carrying members of the neoliberal bloc. This trope was explicitly invoked as a central theme of the 1999 World Economic Forum. In their annual contribution to the opinion page of the *International Herald Tribune*, highlighting the theme of each year's Davos conclave, Forum president Klaus Schwab and managing director Claude Smadja struck a note of urgency:

We are confronted with what is becoming an explosive contradiction. At a time when the emphasis is on empowering people, on democracy moving ahead all over the world, on people asserting control over their own lives, globalization has established the supremacy of the market in an unprecedented way. . . . We must demonstrate that globalization is not just a code word for an exclusive focus on share-holder value at the expense of any other consideration; that the free flow of goods and capital does not develop to the detriment of the most vulnerable segments of the population and of some accepted social and human standards. . . . If we do not invent ways to make globalization more inclusive, we have to face the prospect of a resurgence of the acute social confrontations of the past, magnified at the international level.

(Schwab and Smadja, 1999)

As interesting as the acuity of the WEF's diagnosis, however, was the banal infirmity of its prescribed treatment. In his opening address, Schwab exhorted members of the global power bloc to "try to define a responsible globality" based on an ethic of "caring for the neighbors in our global village" (Schwab, 1999). In the absence of global standards enforceable through international economic institutions or ILO Conventions inscribed into national laws, it seems that we are reduced to pleading for niceness from the world's largest and most powerful enterprises and their allies. And indeed, Schwab's call for new corporate values was echoed in UN Secretary-General Kofi Annan's plea to the businessmen and women gathered in Davos: "I call on you—individually through your firms, and collectively through your business associations—to embrace, support and enact a set of core values in the areas of human rights, labor standards, and environmental practices" (Annan, 1999).

The United Nations Development Program has become another major global institution to embrace the metaphor of "globalization with a human face." In the 1999 edition of its annual *Human Development Report*, UNDP notes the dramatic worsening of global inequalities which have been attendant upon neoliberal globalization. By the late 1990s, the fifth of the world's population living in the highest-income countries had 86 percent of world GDP, 82 percent of world market exports, 68 percent of foreign direct investment, and 74 percent of the world's telephone lines; while the poorest fifth had only about 1 percent of each of these (United Nations Development Program, 1999: 3). According to UNDP, these inequalities have been deepening as the neoliberal project has unfolded: the wealthiest 20 percent of the world's people received 74 times as much income as the poorest 20 percent in 1997; up from a ratio of 60 to 1 in 1990, and 30 to 1 in 1960. It is frequently claimed that the current period of economic internationalization is not so different from that around the turn of the last century, but UNDP claims that the income gap in 1870 was 7 to 1, and 11 to 1 in 1913. If these figures are even remotely indicative, it would seem that the inequalities fostered by the current processes of globalization are manifoldly more intense than anything witnessed during its nearest historical analog.[6]

According to UNDP, "poverty is everywhere," with more than one-quarter of the population of developing countries facing conditions of dire poverty, and one-eighth of the people of the richest countries confronting significant effects of poverty. Further, UNDP notes that these inequalities have gendered dimensions. As market-led development increasingly integrates producers into the formal labor market, women are more subject to the double burden of paid work outside the home in addition to unpaid work of caregiving and domestic production within the household. At the same time, fiscal pressures associated with the neoliberal global order result in widespread cutbacks in publicly-provided care services, further aggravating the gendered inequalities of neoliberal globalization. Women are more likely than men to be poor, undereducated or illiterate, and politically underrepresented (United Nations Development Program, 1999: 7, 28, 77–83).

But UNDP is not attacking globalization, which it represents as a process pregnant with opportunities for human progress, producing unprecedented levels of wealth and technology, improving health and education, exposing people everywhere to a rich variety of cultural practices, expanding the scope of individual choice, and offering "enormous potential to eradicate poverty in the 21st century." For this potential to be most fully realized UNDP argues that the current, imbalanced form of globalization must be supplanted by one in which the development of competitive markets is matched by the fostering of communal values and construction of institutions of governance. "When the market goes too far in dominating social and political outcomes, the opportunities and rewards of globalization spread unequally and inequitably—concentrating power and wealth in a select group of people, nations and corporations, marginalizing the others" (United Nations Development Program, 1999: 1, 2). In the dramatically imbalanced globalization of recent decades UNDP explicitly implicates "a global ideological shift" toward liberalization and market-driven development, embodied in the norms and practices of the governing institutions of the global economy. It notes the apparent double standard within global regimes by which state governments are bound to respect the rights of firms, but firms are bound by no norm of social responsibility and public accountability (1999: 29, 34–5).

UNDP prescribes better governance at all levels, emphasizing the values of "human development." National governments should complement market-friendly policies with programs which improve productivity, enhance equity, and shelter the vulnerable. For example, by investing in the education of a broad spectrum of their populations, developing countries will attract more long-term investment from transnational capital, enhance the productivity of their labor force, and thus make it possible to raise wage levels and labor standards without putting upward pressure on unit labor costs or undercutting the competitiveness of exports. Further, processes of

governance should be extended and made more inclusive, fostering participation by non-governmental organizations (NGOs), allied with local and
national governments and entering into negotiations with multinational
firms and foreign investors. These negotiations might take place in the
context of regionally established frameworks setting out basic labor and
environmental standards. Firms and investors ought also to be subject to a
global code of conduct, monitored through a global forum in which NGOs
and other actors in civil society (for example, labor unions) would be
empowered to participate. And governance of international institutions
should be reformed so that voting rights correspond more closely to population than wealth, providing poorer countries with a stronger voice. Finally, UNDP called for major institutional innovations at the global level,
including the creation of a global central bank to regulate financial flows
and act as lender of last resort during liquidity crises, a global investment
trust to insure more equitable long-term capital flows to developing countries, a world environment agency to promote sustainable development,
and an expansion of the WTO's mandate to enable closer regulation of the
operations of multinational firms (United Nations Development Program,
1999: 97–114).

The trope of "globalization with a human face" is then invoked in a
variety of contexts, and is associated with various meanings. For the World
Economic Forum, it appears to represent a public relations strategy aimed
at making the global dominance of corporate capital more palatable; for
the President of the United States, it is a public relations strategy wedded
to some very modest institutional reforms; and for the United Nations
Development Program, it is associated with a somewhat more ambitious
set of proposed reforms aimed at making market-based globalization more
socially responsible and equitable. It is in the latter view of globalization
that the "human face" most prominently features the public visage of the
participatory citizen, the NGO activist, the labor unionist. This signifies to
me that global institutions are themselves terrains of ideological struggle in
which alternative meanings may be associated with globalization and its
"human face."

To the extent that "globalization with a human face" can pre-empt
grassroots mobilizations and transnational coalitions aimed at the explicit
politicization of the world economy and the democratization of its governance, it will have effected what Antonio Gramsci referred to as a "passive
revolution"—social reform initiated from above for the purpose of forestalling popular political mobilization and thereby disabling a potentially
transformative, self-empowering social movement. On the other hand, as
we have seen, not all versions of this trope are equally anti-democratic. In
particular, the vision represented by the UNDP appears to offer some
scope for politicizing and democratizing the global economy. Such visions
are not in themselves progressive; but they represent openings for progressive global politics. Their progressive potential can be realized by articulation

with vigorous and active transnational grassroots movements—embracing NGOs, labor unions, women's groups, and various other populist initiatives enacting a critique of the anti-democratic character of transnational capitalist power. It is these latter, and their ideologies of globalization as an open-ended project of democratization, which represent the potential for a post-liberal, and conceivably post-capitalist, New World Order.

Seattle and beyond

During 1999, there was much talk of a "Millennium Round" of negotiations which might emerge from the WTO ministerial-level conference in Seattle and define the horizons for renewed efforts toward global economic liberalization. Instead, what emerged in Seattle was diplomatic deadlock within the conference, and a high water mark of mass organized resistance without.

Prior to the Seattle events, a "Statement from Members of International Civil Society" had circulated via the internet, collecting (as of 27 November, 1999) 1,400 endorsements from non-governmental organizations located in at least 89 countries, all of whom found common ground in a critique of the undemocratic character of the WTO and the inequalities it promotes:

> In the past five years the WTO has contributed to the concentration of wealth in the hands of the rich few; increasing poverty for the majority of the world's population; and unsustainable patterns of production and consumption. The Uruguay Round Agreements have functioned principally to prise open markets for the benefit of transnational corporations at the expense of national economies; workers, farmers, and other people; and the environment. In addition, the WTO system, rules and procedures are undemocratic, untransparent and non-accountable and have operated to marginalize the majority of the world's people.
>
> (Members of International Civil Society, 1999)

Together, these NGOs called for a moratorium on negotiations for further liberalization until a comprehensive review of the WTO and its effects could be concluded—a review which, they insisted, should be "conducted with civil society's full participation."

As trade ministers and their delegations arrived in Seattle from 135 member states, they were met by crowds of demonstrators at least forty-thousand strong, many engaging in what the *Washington Post* called "one of the largest acts of mass civil disobedience in recent US history" (Burgess and Pearlstein, 1999). Among the demonstrators were environmentalists, labor unionists, advocates of Third World debt relief, consumer activists, indigenous peoples' groups, farmers, Lesbian Avengers, religious groups, student anti-sweatshop activists, animal rights defenders—a rich stew representing, by some estimates, over 700 various grassroots organizations from many countries (Economist, 1999; Henwood, 1999; Longworth, 1999; Moberg, 1999). Simultaneous protests against the WTO occurred in London and numerous other places around the world.

In Seattle, while some staged marches and rallies, organized groups of protesters successfully interrupted traffic in the city center and for a time precluded access to the convention center. The protests discomfited delegates and forced the cancellation of the conference's opening ceremonies. In response to this loss of control over city streets, and to some relatively isolated acts of violence against property, the city's mayor declared a state of emergency, put downtown under a curfew, and called in state police and National Guard troops. Meanwhile Seattle police unleashed clouds of tear gas, pepper spray, and rubber bullets—along with the more traditional boots and batons—at demonstrators and bystanders. Although protests continued on subsequent days, mass arrests by riot police in gas masks and body armor enabled the delegates to go about their business.

The official business soon bogged down, however, as the US clashed with Europe and Japan over agricultural protection and anti-dumping measures, and developing countries expressed frustration with the heavy-handed domination of the WTO and its agenda by the US and the developed countries (Henwood, 1999; Khor, 1999; Pearlstein, 1999b; Sanger, 1999). Most controversial, however, was the Clinton administration's attempt to place core labor standards on the WTO agenda by proposing a working group to study the relationship between trade and labor, a move which would call into question the "Singapore consensus" that labor issues are outside the ambit of the WTO. While the International Confederation of Free Trade Unions and over 100 labor unions from around the world supported it (Cook, 1999), diplomats from developing countries vociferously opposed any such proposal, seeing it as a cover for protectionism designed to discriminate against their products and maintain the privileges of workers in the US.[7] With evident suspicion the Egyptian trade minister asked "Why all of a sudden, when third world labor has proved to be competitive, why do industrial countries start feeling concerned about our workers?" (quoted in Greenhouse and Kahn, 1999). Business interests breathed a sigh of relief as a Presidential remark envisioning the eventual use of trade sanctions to enforce labor rights was greeted with hostility from developing country governments, and representatives of the European Union made it clear they would not support labor-related sanctions. Deadlocked and beleaguered, the ministerial meetings adjourned with little progress toward an agenda for a new round of liberalization.

As in the debates over NAFTA, GATT, and Fast Track, some commentators aligned themselves closely with neoliberal ideology and adopted a posture of near-papal infallibility, refusing to grant the critics' perspective even a measure of legitimacy. With the epic self-certainty characteristic of his profession, Robert Litan, economist of the Brookings Institution, proclaimed: "However well-intentioned many of the protestors might be, they are on the wrong side of the facts and of world history" (Litan, 1999).[8] Litan feared that the protests might be harbingers of "backsliding toward protectionism." Celebrity economist Paul Krugman ridiculed the WTO's critics by likening them to simple-minded conspiracists: "The WTO has become to leftist mythology what the United Nations is to the militia movement: the center of a global conspiracy against all that is good and decent" (Krugman, 1999). Thomas Friedman—foreign affairs columnist for the *New York Times* and captain of the neoliberal globalization cheerleading squad—could not contain his contempt for the protesters and heaped calumny upon them, calling them "ridiculous," "crazy," "a Noah's ark of flat-earth advocates, protectionist trade unions and yuppies looking for their 1960s fix" who, if they only "stopped yapping" long enough to think, "would realize that they have been duped by knaves like Pat Buchanan" (Friedman, 1999b).[9]

While neoliberal positions such as these clearly dominated the preceding instances of public debate over globalization, in the discussions surrounding the events in Seattle some in the mainstream media seemed to glimpse that what is at issue is precisely the *political* limits imposed by the neoliberal ideology exemplified above. Writing in the *Los Angeles Times* and the *International Herald Tribune*, William Pfaff hit the nail on the head: "The prevailing assumption . . . has been that trade issues should be dealt with in isolation from social and political context and consequences. This idea has been dealt a blow from which it will not recover" (Pfaff, 1999). This revelation has potentially radical implications: if trade relations are intrinsically political, then they are properly issues of public concern and need not be governed by criteria of private profit or "efficiency." Moreover, the Seattle protests may at last have revealed as a hoary canard the formerly widespread presumption which equated opposition to neoliberal globalization with atavistic tribalism and xenophobia. Thomas Friedman notwithstanding, Pat Buchanan's appearance in Seattle was barely noticed, as the unprecedented coalition of left-progressive forces dominated the agenda of protest (Economist, 1999; Henwood, 1999; Longworth, 1999; Moberg, 1999). After witnessing the transnational coalition of groups protesting the WTO, and their agendas of global scope, a *Newsweek* reporter reflected: "Hitherto, it's been easy to insist that anyone opposed to 'trade' was by definition a protectionist, happy to hide behind the walls of the nation-state. That simple equation no longer holds good; one of the most important lessons of Seattle is that there are now two visions of globalization on offer, one led by commerce, one by social activism" (Elliott, 1999). At stake in these debates, a *Washington Post* correspondent recognized, might be things much more fundamental than trade: "People are now openly discussing how the world's political architecture—up to now built around the sovereignty of the nation-state—may have to be reworked to provide for a more global economic governance system that is open and democratic enough to gain legitimacy in the eyes of voters around the world" (Pearlstein, 1999a). Writing for the *Boston Globe*, Ellen Goodman framed succinctly the central question raised in Seattle: "Whose world is it, anyway?" (Goodman, 1999). Since before NAFTA, progressive activists have struggled to suggest that neoliberal globalization had profound implications for the future of democratic self-government on every scale from the local to the global; the Seattle protests seem finally to have placed this issue on the agenda of public debate.

In a stunning editorial statement, the *Seattle Post-Intelligencer* first apologized to the WTO delegates for the "unfriendly" reception they received, and then proceeded to endorse the major demands of the protesters: institutionalized and effective labor and environmental protections, along with openness and inclusion in the negotiation of trade policies and the settlement of disputes (Editorial Board, 1999). The editors of the nation's two leading papers were less inclined to adopt the agenda of the demonstrators, but acknowledged that the WTO had serious problems of "legitimacy." In order to sustain what the *New York Times* (6 December, 1999) called "the main vehicle of international economic progress," both the *Times* and the *Washington Post* prescribed limited reforms and greater institutional openness at the WTO. But, the *Post* cautioned, "The WTO should not seek to buy legitimacy by taking all criticisms to heart. If it took on as much of the role of protecting labor standards and the environment as its critics want, it would quickly lose focus" (1 December, 1999). For the *Post*, it seems, "loss of focus" is too high a price to pay for democratization, so the WTO should enact strictly limited reforms in order to resolve its legitimacy crisis and move on with the fundamental agenda of global liberalization.

If the more optimistic among the progressives are correct, a passive revolution such as the tepid reform agenda envisioned by the *Times* and the *Post* may not suffice. In the wake of Seattle it may be difficult to sustain a depoliticized global economy. Scholar and labor activist Elaine Bernard argues that the rise of "international advocacy networks" so clearly evident in protests against the WTO are of enormous long-term significance, for they represent "a forum for debating, negotiating and deliberating global solidarity. They are the beginnings of an emerging international civil society" which "provides space for the development of public values, and is the process by which a public self, or citizenry, is created" (Bernard, 1999). The process by which such transnational social spaces are constructed, and the negotiation of explicitly political identities and projects within those sites, is a necessary (if not sufficient) condition of global democratization.

A New World Order: (r)evolutionary change?

As it is conventionally posed, the distinction between "evolution" and "revolution" represents, I think, something of a false dichotomy. As Paul Thomas has pointed out, in its Leninist form this dichotomy is rooted in a fetishized understanding of politics and the state, one which accepts as the grounds of its own political practice the reified forms of capitalist social life. On this view, the state appears as "an object, an instrument, a 'finished thing' that is capable of being 'seized' and turned to good account once it is seized by the right hands" (Thomas 1994: ix). Lost from view in this understanding of "revolution" is the sense in which the modern political state has been embedded in state–society relations and cannot be transformed apart from a transformation of its relational context through the concomitant politicization and democratization of civil society and the economy. Only in this way can capitalism's structured separation of politics and economics be overcome. It is misguided, then, to identify transformative social change with a discrete event focused upon possession of state power (*a fortiori* possession of that power by a self-declared vanguard); rather, if it is to emerge at all, such transformation will emerge from processes which enable explicit social self-determination in spheres of life where it is currently precluded by the structures of capitalism and their articulations with relations of racial or gender dominance.

Potentially transformative, then, are those forms of social change which entail the political self-empowerment of dominated groups and their allies and, by reforming social identities and self-understandings, which open up new possibilities for political practice and make possible new forms of political and social organization. To the extent that such possibilities are realized through concrete political practices—and this will be the crux of political struggles—both agents and structures may be transformed, bringing into view new horizons of political action which may lead to still further transformation. Understood as progressive (although not necessarily singular, linear, or monotonic) processes of social self-determination, (r)evolutionary change needs to be distinguished from reforms which may result in significant redistribution of resources, but which have the political effect of demobilizing grassroots movements, pre-empting transformative processes of struggle and collective self-empowerment, and contracting the horizons of political possibility. And here, it seems to me, we arrive at the crux of the contemporary political conjuncture.

Resistance to globalizing capitalism has opened up possibilities for new forms of political practice which are not circumscribed by the territorial state or by the conventional separation of politics from the economy. A system premised on endless accumulation for its own sake, capitalism has never been easily contained within conventionally recognized geographic boundaries. Yet, its expansionist tendencies do not operate in the abstract or automatically. Capitalism has political conditions which must be secured if it is to reproduce itself and expand. Among these are the institutionalized protections of private property and the attendant social powers of employers and investors. These institutionalized conditions, enabling accumulation, are enacted by historically situated social agents, whose political projects and representations are subject to the resistance and re-articulation of others.

In the second half of the twentieth century, a transnational historic bloc of internationally-oriented capitalists, liberal statesmen, and their allies began to construct the institutional framework of a globalizing capitalism. Despite bouts of resistance, their project has succeeded spectacularly. Trade and investment, cultural products and practices, and relations of social power now span the globe, unevenly and imperfectly to be sure, but nonetheless in ways historically unprecedented (Held et al., 1999). Yet, this project now faces forces of resistance and alternative world-views which appear to pose an increasing threat to the realization of the global liberal vision.

In the United States—the country which has been arguably most closely associated with this project—the social power and hegemonic vision of the liberal internationalist bloc was secured through a complex historical process in which two factors were especially crucial. First, Cold War liberalism fostered the identification of US national interests with the peace and prosperity of the "Free World," presented liberal capitalism as the social system best able to resist the totalitarian threat of Soviet communism, and de-legitimized left-progressive alternatives as un-American, subversive, and treacherous. Second, a broad swath of American industrial labor was subordinated within the historic bloc through the politics of prosperity and the mobilization of "free trade unions" in Cold War struggles to defend liberal capitalism.

As the Cold War and its manichean world-view fade into historical memory, and the neoliberal turn toward market fundamentalism undermines the politics of prosperity which once helped to secure the social hegemony of the liberal capitalist bloc, counter-ideologies circulate through popular discourse, challenging the basic premises and the political implications of transnational liberalism. One family of such ideologies emphasizes American exceptionalism, understands globalization as a mortal threat to this special identity and its attendant privileges, and prescribes a circling of the wagons through economic, cultural, and racial/ethnic nationalisms. Conspiracist narratives of the New World Order generally share this genealogy. Another family of counter-ideologies understands globalization as both an opportunity and a danger. It is seen as dangerous insofar as it extends, deepens, and strengthens the anti-democratic structures of capitalism. But this is not seen to be ineluctable, a done deal. Rather, it is seen as being contingent on the outcomes of social struggles in which those similarly subordinated and exploited under capitalist systems of production and exchange might conceivably find common ground, build relationships

of solidarity and mutual support across manifold socially significant differences, and create new social movements and institutions through which to
negotiate a common future. The potential convergence evident in Seattle
has brightened these hopes.

Each of these political visions is active in the nexus between the US
and the global political economy, drawing on the resources of popular
common sense in order to address and mobilize political subjects. These
contests over the meaning and future of globalization—and other similar
struggles in other sites—have been recognized by the global power bloc as
potentially significant threats, especially in the wake of the Seattle WTO
debacle. As a consequence, elements within that bloc have begun attempting to formulate a vision of globalization which might counteract these
ideological challenges, and re-incorporate potentially rebellious subjects
within the global liberal vision. These new ideologies of "globalization
with a human face" are not seamless or univocal, however. Fraught with
contradiction, they may themselves become terrains of struggle on which
more enabling, participatory, and democratic visions may be articulated
and fought for. To the extent that progressive social forces are able to
stress the contradiction between capitalism and democratic self-determination, and to apply ongoing pressure through their social movements for
realization of the latter within the very social relations which globalizing
capitalism has brought into being, they will have begun a process of self-
empowerment and social transformation which has no necessary end.

Notes

1 Introduction

1 Note, however, that the actual production and reproduction of such ideological effects is problematic, contestable.

2 We should pause here to note the implicit masculinism of this formulation, which neglects relations of gender and unwaged labor in the domestic sphere. I am grateful to an anonymous reviewer for calling this to my attention.

3 Useful discussions of the concept of ideology, and especially Gramsci's articulation of it within the historical materialist tradition, include: Larrain, 1979, 1983, 1996; Hall, 1988a, 1996a; Eagleton, 1991; McNally, 1995.

4 For a helpful overview of the British cultural studies movement with which Hall's work is associated, see Turner, 1996. My claim that Hall's version of historical materialism is viable and helpful does not mean that it is uncontested: for critiques of Hall's work and tendencies toward "ideologism" to which his approach may lend itself, see Jessop et al., 1984; and Smith, 1997: 152–7. I gratefully acknowledge the collegial support of Shampa Biswas and Mark Laffey, both of whom steered me in the direction of Hall's work at a time when I was becoming open to it. Particularly noteworthy is Laffey, 1991—the first attempt, to my knowledge, to use Hall's work as a vehicle for critically rethinking Gramscian international studies.

5 On possible articulations of a regressive populist political agenda in the US, see Chapters 5 and 6 below.

6 It is important to emphasize here that the thesis of "no necessary correspondence" is not the same as claiming a necessary non-correspondence.

7 In the public discourses of "globalization," there are in fact more than two positions. Among those which I will not deal with at any length are pseudo-progressive positions which tend to dichotomize global and local, and to fetishize the local as against the global, romantically associating small-scale capitalism with ecological sustainability and stronger bonds of community. In particular, I have in mind here Korten, 1996. Doug Henwood has provided a scathing critique of Korten and company—to whom Henwood refers as "greenish postmoderns"—and their seemingly willful blindness to the systemic dynamics of capitalism, and the deeply entrenched relations of power which underlie them (Henwood, 1996).

8 Here, and throughout this text, I rely on "critical realist" philosophy to enable me to sketch a materialist dialectic of real, effective social structures and active, interpretive social agents. For more on this philosophy and methodology of social inquiry see: Isaac, 1987; D. Sayer, 1987; A. Sayer, 1992; and Collier, 1994.

2 Americanism, Fordism, and hegemony

1 The irony in this is monumental. Only the year before *Why We Fight* was released, workers at Ford Motor Company had overturned Ford's brutally coercive factory regime by successfully organizing a recognition strike which shut down the giant River Rouge plant and compelled the bitterly anti-union firm to negotiate (see Rupert, 1995: chs 6–7). Labor rights in America were won through long and difficult struggles in the face of intense and often violent opposition; they were in no sense attributable to the innate justice or demo-cratic essence of the American way, as *Why We Fight* disingenuously suggests.

2 As feminist theory would suggest, it is almost exclusively male children who are depicted engaging in martial ritual and simulated combat, being socially consti-tuted thereby as gendered subjects of violence, distancing themselves from pu-tatively feminine characteristics of passivity and submissiveness, and embodying a state premised upon militarized masculinity (Pettman, 1996: ch. 5).

3 In Capra's world of light, women's bodies may not be directly subject to claims of the state, but this hardly amounts to gender emancipation. Some of the most memorable images of American women in the film represent them as avatars of domestic ignorance and parochiality, the embodiments of misguided isolation-ism. In a series of newsreel "man on the street" [sic] interviews, one woman is shown sitting in a lawn chair with a baby on her knee, and confesses to the newsreel camera, "I haven't the slightest idea of European affairs," while another responds to the reporter's questions about potential involvement in impending war by shouting "No!" and slamming closed her window sash, re-enclosing herself in the domestic sphere. Capra seems less to be challenging the domestication of women than telling his audience that to embrace isolationism is to be like a housewife. These representations call upon meanings associated with the masculinization of politics and the state, the feminization of child care and the home, and the social valorization of the former to the detriment of the latter (Pettman, 1996: ch. 1).

4 Note the implicit gendering of Capra's great American "we," whose liberties, families, and lives were seen to be imperiled: it is the public liberties and private privileges of American *men* which are primarily at stake in these representations.

5 In the lexicon of Marxian value theory, productivity gains in the consump-tion goods sector have the effect of cheapening labor-power by decreasing the labor-time socially necessary to produce the workers' means of subsistence. As a result, the unpaid proportion of the working day—the value of which accrues to the capitalist as "surplus value"—is expanded. This is known as "relative surplus value" and contrasts with the relatively straightforward method of increasing "absolute surplus value" by driving workers to ever longer working days without transforming the process of production itself. By increasing the rate of exploitation along with productivity, the production of relative surplus value may to some degree counteract the notorious tendency for the rate of profit to decline. On relative surplus value, see Marx, 1977a, parts four and five. For more accessible introductory treatments, see: Wolff and Resnick, 1987: ch. 3; Fine, 1989; and Sayer, 1991: ch. 1.

6 The AFL–CIO is the largest labor federation in the US, formed by the 1955 merger of the American Federation of Labor—representing predominantly craft-based unions—and the industrial union-based Congress of Industrial Organiza-tions. Currently the AFL–CIO consists of 68 unions and represents over 13 million members. See the AFL–CIO web site: www.aflcio.org/about.htm

7 For various plausible accounts of the demise of Fordism, see: M. Davis, 1986; Harrison and Bluestone, 1988; Harvey, 1989; Bowles *et al.*, 1990; Gordon, 1996; but compare Brenner, 1998. While not denying the potential significance

of a variety of factors, my own interpretation emphasizes the importance of relative surplus value to the profitability of Fordist capitalism, and hence its need to maintain rapid productivity growth through effective combinations of coercion and consent in the workplace. I wish to call attention to the political roots of profitability, and the ways in which class struggles may be mediated by historical structures such as the socio-political institutions of Fordism.

8 In the late 1990s, the real wages of working people once again began (modestly) to grow. I will explain near the conclusion of this chapter why the significance of these gains should not be exaggerated.

8 Harvard political economist Dani Rodrik has translated this argument into the language of mainstream economists, explaining that globalization "results in an inward shift in the demand curve for low-skilled labor in the advanced countries" as comparative advantage in more skilled occupations takes effect. Perhaps more importantly, however, it also makes unskilled workers more substitutable, increasing the "elasticity of demand" for their labor—i.e., making the demand for that kind of labor more price-sensitive and thereby weakening the bargaining position of unskilled workers (Rodrik, 1997: 11–27).

3 The hegemonic project of liberal globalization

1 This analysis is premised upon a "critical realist" reading of Marxism and its theory of social powers grounded in real material relations or structures. On this view, these structures are neither static nor self-reproducing. As Jeffrey Isaac explains, the reproduction of social power relations "is *always* problematic" and depends in part upon struggles surrounding the social meanings which are attached to them (Isaac, 1987: 93, 101).

2 I am grateful to Scott Solomon for helping to clarify my thinking on this issue. See Solomon and Rupert, 1999.

3 On the profoundly conflicted relationship between liberal capitalism and democracy, see Rupert, 1998.

4 On the role of orthodox economic analysis, and its claim of authoritative scientificity, in the selling of NAFTA, see Cypher, 1993.

5 For a very similar formulation by another leading international economist, see Krugman, 1993a: 16–17.

6 Letter to President Clinton signed by 283 economists, dated 1 September, 1993, obtained from USA*NAFTA as part of its standard packet of lobbying materials. See also the various works of Hufbauer and Schott, Krugman, and Dornbusch, cited earlier.

7 The intellectual influence of orthodox economics is transmitted through both governmental and private channels. According to Cypher (1993), economic modeling studies suggesting generalized gains from NAFTA were selectively promoted as authoritative by such US government agencies as the International Trade Commission and the Trade Representative, as well as the departments of Commerce and the Treasury; by private think tanks (Brookings, Heritage Foundation, Institute for International Economics); and by the lobbying organizations of big business (Business Roundtable, USA*NAFTA, Coordinating Council for Mexican Foreign Trade Associations).

8 In a full-page advertisement advocating NAFTA, Citibank claimed that 136 newspaper editors had endorsed the agreement: *New York Times* (24 October, 1993). A Lexis/Nexis search of major newspapers during mid-November, 1993 turned up the following editorial endorsements: *Boston Globe* (14 November); *Atlanta Constitution* (16 November); *Chicago Tribune* (11 November); *Chicago Sun-Times* (11 November); *St. Louis Post-Dispatch* (16 November); *Houston Chronicle* (16 November); and *San Francisco Chronicle* (11 November); in

addition to the *New York Times* (14 November) and *Washington Post* (16 November).

9 Materials from USA*NAFTA lobbying packet: quotations are from 1993a, 1993b. See also Lewis and Ebrahim, 1993; and Weisskopf, 1993.

10 For explicit references to Smoot–Hawley, see Hufbauer and Schott, 1993a: 110; also Kantor, 1993, obtained as part of the USA*NAFTA lobbying packet. During their televised "debate," Vice President Gore presented Ross Perot with a framed photo of Senators Smoot and Hawley.

11 The Oliphant cartoon was published along with Rowen, 1993b. Conjuring stereotyped images of labor corruption and violence, Oliphant's trademark gnome says to the unionists: "Say Hi to Mr. Hoffa."

4 From liberal globalization to global democratization

1 I make no pretense here of scholarly disinterest, much less the mythical "objectivity" of the empiricists. I was active as a partisan in these debates, contributing to the anti-NAFTA efforts of the Fair Trade Coalition of Central New York, and such perspectives are reflected in my writing.

2 On Fordism and the ideology of "Americanism," see Rupert, 1995: chs 5–7. For discussions by labor activists of the degeneration of this hegemonic identity, see Cantor and Schor, 1987: ch. 4; Moody, 1988: 294–5; and Sims, 1992: 91–2.

3 The ambiguity of US organized labor's stance on NAFTA is suggested by a statement of the AFL–CIO Executive Council which, on the one hand, includes the relatively cosmopolitan declaration that a continental trade agreement should include enforceable transnational standards for labor rights, as well as consumer and environmental protection; and, on the other hand, asserts that federal, state, and local "Buy American" laws and regulations should be preserved (AFL–CIO, 1993). I experienced these tendencies first hand during my work with the Fair Trade Coalition in 1993: unionists distributed "Buy American" materials at Coalition meetings; imported cars were barred from the parking lot of the union hall where Coalition meetings were held; vehicles parked in the lot bore nationalistic bumper stickers including one equating Japanese auto makers with "the people who brought you Pearl Harbor"; and sombreros were worn by unionists during anti-NAFTA demonstrations. In such ways as these, foreign workers were represented as a threat to American jobs and living standards. Such "Buy American" movements—effectively submerging a politics of solidarity beneath presumptive privileges of nationality, race, and gender—draw upon tendencies longstanding in US political history (D. Frank, 1999).

4 Economist Gary Burtless and his co-authors (1998) argue that fears of a global "race to the bottom" are overstated, partaking of "Globaphobia." In their view regulation need not undermine competitiveness nor provoke capital flight so long as the benefits provided "are valued by firms and people that are mobile or are paid for by those that are not" (Burtless et al., 1998: 117). In other words, you can have any regulations you want so long as: (a) it isn't vetoed by multinational capital or (b) working people are willing to accept lower real incomes. Of course, it is the power relations underlying this conditionality to which the critics are calling attention.

5 Full-page advertisement entitled "8 Fatal Flaws of NAFTA," *New York Times* (15 November, 1993), emphasis in original. For some background on this Group of 25 and their opposition to NAFTA, see Wallach, 1993: 41–50.

6 In addition to the umbrella groups responsible for producing the Initiative—Alliance for Responsible Trade, Citizens Trade Campaign, and The Mexican Action Network on Free Trade—the statement was endorsed by the Action

Canada Network, Border Ecology Project, Development GAP, Greenpeace (US), Institute for Policy Studies, Instituto Latinoamericano de Servicios Legales Alternativos (Colombia), Inter-Hemispheric Resource Center (Albuquerque), International Labor Rights Fund, National Consumers League, Resource Center of the Americas (Minneapolis), United Electrical Workers (UE), United Methodist Church, and others. In addition, the drafters of the Initiative acknowledged significant input from the Canadian Center for Policy Alternatives, the Center of Concern, the Alternative Women-in-Development working group (Alt-WID), the Economic Policy Institute, and a variety of other groups and institutions which may not have been directly represented at the July 1992 meeting in Mexico City where the document was promulgated.

7 Examples from the *New York Times* include Bowles and Larudee, 1993; Cavanagh and Anderson, 1993; and Schlefer, 1993; as well as regular columns by Bob Herbert; in the *Washington Post*, see especially Nader, 1993a.

8 Under the rubric "left press," I mean to include such US-based journals as *The Nation*, *In These Times*, *Z Magazine*, *Against the Current*, *Dollars and Sense*, *Multinational Monitor*, and *Left Business Observer*.

9 These publications circulated among participants in the fair trade movement: for example, I learned of the Nader book from a unionist attending an anti-NAFTA rally in Utica, New York.

10 The Inter-Hemispheric Resource Center now has its directories of transnational solidarity groups online at www.irc-online.org/cbl/index.html

11 I am troubled by Greider's apparent alternation between a democratizing vision which points toward an open-ended process of social reconstruction, and one which focuses more narrowly upon underconsumptionist tendencies in the global economy and points toward a macroeconomic regime of global Keynesianism which might stabilize global capitalism.

12 Global Exchange maintains an extensive web site at www.globalexchange.org. An activist group promoting fair trade and human rights on a transnational scale, Global Exchange was founded in San Francisco in 1988 and became active in the campaign against Nike's sweatshop labor practices (which they saw as an avatar of neoliberal globalization) in 1996. Since then, Global Exchange has been a leader in an extensive grassroots campaign which has brought together Asian-American, students', women's, and religious groups. Together, they relentlessly challenged Nike's public self-representations as an exemplar of "progressive" capitalism, damaged the firm's carefully constructed public image, and pressured it into a series of modest, if also non-trivial, labor reforms. On the Nike campaign and the role of Global Exchange, see Shaw, 1999: 13–96. On transnational anti-sweatshop campaigns more generally, see Ross, 1997. For an overview of the issue from a gendered perspective, and a comprehensive set of links to No Sweat web pages, see the Feminist Majority Foundation's *Feminists Against Sweatshops* page: www.feminist.org/other/sweatshops.html

5 Fear and loathing in the New World Order

1 It is important to distinguish conspiracism from analysis of power bloc formation rooted in the method of historical structures. For example, Kees van der Pijl (1997, 1998) has argued for the political significance of elite conclaves such as the Rhodes–Milner Roundtable group, the Bilderberg group, the Trilateral Commission, and the Council on Foreign Relations, while Stephen Gill (1990) has been particularly attentive to the Trilateralists. In contrast to the conspiracists' presupposition that such activities are to be understood in terms of the malevolent acts and sinister underlying characteristics of particular individuals or "alien" groups, van der Pijl and Gill discuss elite fora in the context of pains-

taking and theoretically-grounded analyses of the formation of a transnational ruling class: "transnational planning groups prove to be not a conspiratorial world government, but class organizations constantly adjusting to the real balance of forces confronting them" (van der Pijl, 1998: 134). They are crucial in forging a unity of purpose—a potentially hegemonic world-view centering on a "comprehensive concept of control"—among differently situated class fractions and their allies in the state, in international organizations, in the media, academia, civil society more generally. It is not conspiracism to suggest that structured relations of inequality permeate our social world, and that those who are privileged by such relations may organize to frame common interests, construct political projects, and coordinate their activities. Most importantly, however, historical-structural analyses differ from conspiracism in the political projects which they enable: whereas conspiracism typically leads toward nationalism (and, in its extreme form, racial nationalism) as a defense against a conspiracy of "others," historical-structural analyses prescribe the construction of solidarities across exploited groups such that, together, they might transform the structures of their oppression.

2 While some variants of this conspiracy narrative are explicitly racist or anti-Semitic, others have attempted to distance themselves from overt anti-Semitism (e.g., Larry Abraham, Pat Robertson, John Birch Society). On Robertson's attempt, see Lind, 1995a, and the ensuing controversy: Lind, 1995b; Heilbrunn, 1995, and the *New York Times*: 2, 4, 5, 9, 20 March, and 6, 18, 27 April, 1995. On anti-Semitism in the Patriot-militia movement more generally, see Stern, 1996: 224–7.

3 The Illuminati, it seems, actually existed in Germany between 1776 and 1785. According to the *New Columbia Encyclopedia* (Harris and Levey, 1975: 1315), it was a briefly popular "rationalistic society" with "affinities" toward freemasonry. Tales of the "Illuminism conspiracy" have been a part of American nativism since the late eighteenth century (D. Bennett, 1995: 22–6).

4 Conversation with John Birch Society officials (13 October, 1995); phone query to *New American* (20 May, 1996); and JBS summer 1997 publications flyer. On JBS more generally, see Mintz, 1985: 141–62; D. Bennett, 1995: 315–23, 430–31; and Diamond, 1995: 51–8, 147–51. The JBS officials with whom I spoke in 1995 claimed that membership had been growing at an increasing rate, which they attribute to a general sense among US citizens that the federal government is out of control (13 October). Chip Berlet told me that his estimate of JBS membership was in the range of 40,000 to 50,000, up from a low of about 20,000 in the 1980s (10 June, 1995).

5 Telephone query to *Spotlight* circulation department (31 October, 1995). On the Liberty Lobby, see Mintz, 1985; Campbell, 1992; Center for Democratic Renewal, 1994; D. Bennett, 1995: 356–7, 430; Diamond, 1995: 85, 140–60, 261–5, 295. Material from *Spotlight* is accessible at a number of Patriot movement web sites, although the Liberty Lobby is controversial among Patriots, some of whom explicitly denounce its anti-Semitic tendencies.

6 Southern Poverty Law Center, 1999; on the militia-Patriot movement, see also Berlet, 1995; Berlet and Lyons, 1995; D. Bennett, 1995: 446–75; Wills, 1995; Dees, 1996; Stern, 1996.

7 Based on 1989 estimates compiled by Elinor Langer and reported in Diamond, 1995: 257; see also D. Bennett, 1995: 431–45.

8 On Christian Coalition membership, see their web site at www.cc.org/about.html; but compare Boston, 1996: 87, and Goodstein, 1999. *New World Order* copies in print from phone interview with Thomas Nelson Publishers (23 July, 1995). On the rise of the Christian right more generally, see Diamond, 1995: 228–56; Boston, 1996; Wilcox, 1996.

9 During Buchanan's 1996 Presidential campaign, a large cache of useful documents was available at the official Buchanan for President Campaign web site: www.buchanan.org/; and some more controversial items appeared at the unofficial Buchanan site: www.iac.net:80/~davcam/pat.html. In recent years, Buchanan has maintained an extensive web site for his tax-exempt organization called *The American Cause*: www.theamericancause.org/index.html. Buchanan's web page for his 2000 presidential bid is at: www.gopatgo2000.org

10 My colleague Michael Barkun is one of the leading students of Christian Identity theology and the racist right (see Barkun, 1994), and believes that the conspiratorial far-right comprises no more than two hundred thousand persons. Chip Berlet of Political Research Associates estimates that the so-called Patriot movement—broadly understood as persons or groups under the influence of conspiratorial ideologies—may embrace as many as five million persons (Berlet, 1995).

11 Conversation with John Birch Society officials (13 October, 1995), who described JBS members as drawn from the ranks of businessmen, doctors, dentists, police officers. This is generally corroborated by the findings in Kraft, 1992, a study based on the 1987 membership mailing list of the JBS obtained by Political Research Associates, and using zip codes as surrogates for socioeconomic status.

12 The wording I quoted is from two pamphlets: "Liberty Lobby ... Looking Forward"; and "Why Subscribe to *The Spotlight*?." On producers vs. parasites, see Campbell, 1992; Berlet, 1995. On the Lobby's "populism" more generally, see Diamond, 1995: 140–52, 261–2.

13 On Mullins' role in the propagation of anti-Semitic conspiracy theories, see Mintz, 1985: 100; Heilbrunn, 1995. It is hard to imagine that anyone even dimly aware of the long history of Western anti-Semitism could read Mullins' venomous characterization of cosmopolitan conspirators biologically predisposed toward parasitism without inferring that he was talking about Jews and suggesting a final solution (Mullins, 1992: 286–97).

14 White American men have perpetrated acts of racial violence ranging from lynchings to virtual pogroms on the basis of this morbid fear of the rape of white women. It has recently been (re)discovered, for example, that rumors of such a "rape" were the pretext for a massive episode of what contemporary discourse might describe as "ethnic cleansing" directed at African-American residents of Tulsa, Oklahoma in 1921. As many as three hundred blacks were killed and an entire section of the city was razed by an army of rampaging white citizens numbering in the thousands (Staples, 1999). I mention this case not to suggest that gender and race-based violence is a thing of the past, but rather that its historic presence in America has been even more virulent than is commonly imagined (among whites, at any rate).

15 Pierce has gained a measure of national notoriety as the pseudonymous author of *The Turner Diaries*, a fictionalized account of white supremacist guerrilla war against the federal government, which includes a vivid account of the fertilizer bombing of a federal office building (Pierce, 1980). Pierce's book, along with *The Spotlight*, were widely reported to be Timothy McVeigh's favorite reading material. On Pierce's career and influence, see Mintz, 1985: 129; D. Bennett, 1995: 348–9, 437–8; Dees, 1996: 135–70, 176–8, 202–3; Stern, 1996: 53–5, 192.

16 That chemical and biological warfare on a scale sufficient to annihilate the great bulk of the earth's population might entail negative consequences for the global ecosystem and thus defeat its putative purpose seems not to have occurred to Pierce; or perhaps the ecological rationale is simply a pretext covering genocide for its own sake.

17 I am grateful to Mark Pitcavage for reinforcing this important distinction between the libertarian and neo-fascist wings of the Patriot movement.

18 I am grateful to Mr. Gene Kapp of the Christian Broadcasting Network for making available to me relevant excerpts of *700 Club* transcripts.

19 Billionaire Roger Milliken is patriarch of the family textile firm, Milliken and Company, and is an archetype of the nationally-oriented capitalist engaged in intra-class struggle against transnational factions of capital, and representing his politics in terms of the defense of the American worker (his rabidly anti-union track record somehow notwithstanding). A founder of the "Crafted with Pride in USA" labeling campaign during the 1980s, in the 1990s Milliken contributed substantial sums to Pat Buchanan's Presidential campaigns and even more to his tax-exempt organization, *The American Cause*. He has also backed the nationalist populism of Ross Perot and Pat Choate, and is perhaps the most reliable corporate supporter of the Birch Society's *New American* magazine, regularly buying full-page advertisements. Milliken is, then, a long-time supporter of economic nationalism and of tendencies within the far-right which might be capable of mainstreaming that agenda (D. Frank, 1999: 192–7; Paulsen, 1999: 15).

20 For favorable coverage of Buchanan's candidacy in far-right media, see Piper, 1995; McManus, 1996; and Black, n.d. *The Spotlight* web site featured the Buchanan for President campaign logo: nethomes.com/Miracle/Spotlight/tws.html. In discussions with officials of the John Birch Society (13 October, 1995) I was told that they viewed Buchanan as being as close as they could probably get to a viable candidate who reflected their perspective. For several months during 1995, I subscribed to a Patriot listserv called USA-Forever: many subscribers expressed their support for Buchanan, although several hard-core Patriots refused to endorse a candidate unless he/she promised to attack the citadel of financial power by abolishing the Federal Reserve, and others were suspicious of Buchanan's Catholicism—one denouncing him for allegedly swearing an (presumably un-American) oath of allegiance to the Knights of Malta.

21 Recent disclosures that, despite years of explicit denials, federal agents did in fact use incendiary tear gas shells during the Waco siege promise to give new life to conspiratorial accounts of what happened there (Boyer, 1999).

6 Competition or solidarity? The new populism and the ambiguities of common sense

1 In the conceptual context of critical cultural studies, and especially those currents strongly influenced by Stuart Hall, the concept of "articulation" carries special significance inasmuch as it defines a crucial terrain of ideological struggle. It is used to signify non-necessary, historically contingent connections forged between ideological elements brought together into a more-or-less coherent discourse (for example, populism and conspiracism), and also the anchoring of this discourse in the popular common sense of particular social groups, enabling them to understand themselves and their place in the world in terms which may predispose them toward some kinds of political projects and away from others. As Stuart Hall puts it, the theory of articulation "enables us to think how an ideology empowers people, enabling them to begin to make some sense or intelligibility of their historical situation, without reducing those forms of intelligibility to their socio-economic or class location or social position" (Hall, 1996b: 141–2); on Hall's influence within contemporary cultural studies, see Turner, 1996.

2 Recall that the phrase "New World Order" carries special significance in far-right ideologies, "both dreaded and fetishized by conspiracy theorists" (Fenster,

1999: 166). It is understood to imply a "one-world government" dominated by super-rich "international bankers" and their creatures (e.g., the Council on Foreign Relations, Trilateral Commission, United Nations, etc.) who will use their secretive transnational power to escape the political limits of a constitutional republic and to exploit the resources and peoples of the world. In this emerging "global plantation," the rights and liberties of average Americans, their standard of living, and their national identity will all be lost irrevocably. In one of the most directly anti-Semitic versions of this conspiratorial world-view, Eustace Mullins calls for the elimination of those he characterizes as cosmopolitan conspirators biologically predisposed toward social parasitism (Mullins, 1992: 286–97).

3 Osborn is a political commentator and associate of Harder's who appeared frequently on *For the People* and edited and wrote for *The News Reporter*. I would like to acknowledge his willingness to speak to me repeatedly and at length about his world-view and the role of the network, and his assistance in acquiring relevant materials.

4 On capitalism's anti-democratic separation of politics from economics, see Thomas, 1994; and Wood, 1995.

5 On the Liberty Lobby's dystopian vision of a "global plantation," see McLemee, 1994; and *The Spotlight, Special NAFTA Issue: The Global Plantation* (17 May, 1993).

6 In fairness, however, I must note that when I raised this issue with a representative of *For the People*, Harder responded by directly and explicitly disavowing violence by armed militias while on the air (*For the People* program tape in my possession).

7 As of July 1999, Harder's program was being carried on a network of over 130 radio stations across the US (www.forthepeople.org/stations.htm).

7 The New World Order: passive revolution or transformative process?

1 Business is booming for the brokers of the global "public sphere": According to a *Washington Post* report (Swardson, 2000), each of the one thousand WEF members pay a basic membership subscription fee of $12,500 and an additional $6,250 for the privilege of sending their executives to the Davos meeting. At least 27 major firms pay an additional quarter million dollars each for the privilege of being designated as "knowledge partners" or "institutional partners." Two dozen others pay $78,000 to become "annual meeting partners." Partners enjoy a leading role in planning the Davos extravaganza and, not surprisingly, are highly visible participants: "They buy sessions," one former WEF staffer told the *Post*. All this generated $32 million in revenue for the WEF in 1999—a 57 percent increase over 1995.

2 When thinking about the international financial crises of 1997–8, it is important to keep in mind that a crucial condition of possibility for such financial follies was the enormous expansion over recent decades of liquid capital sloshing about in the world economy (see Chapter 3), and the cash surpluses piling up in the hands of corporations and investors as a result of neoliberal political economy in the advanced capitalist countries (Chapter 2).

3 This letter was obtained by Public Citizen's Global Trade Watch and was reproduced in the September, 1997 issue of *Multinational Monitor*, available online at www.essential.org/monitor/hyper/mm0997.10.html

4 Letter from the Business Roundtable addressed to President Clinton, Speaker Gingrich, Majority Leader Lott, and Minority Leader Daschle, dated 28 October, 1997, and signed by 45 major corporate CEOs. Letter reproduced at the web site of America Leads on Trade: www.fasttrack.org/about/brletter.html

5 This information was gleaned from the web site of the International Labor Organization: www.ilo.org/public/english/50normes/whatare/fundam/index.htm

6 The escalating magnitudes of global inequality over the last century or more suggest to me that we are witnessing not a cyclical repetition of discrete episodes of economic internationalization, but a cumulative process producing an increasingly hierarchic world.

7 Skepticism from the Third World regarding US labor's motivation in supporting proposals for trade-linked labor standards is, of course, understandable in light of the AFL–CIO's historical record of complicity in US imperial foreign policy which has secured US privilege at their expense (Sims, 1992). Whether the new AFL–CIO will indeed commit themselves to effective international solidarity—even if this implies eschewing imperial privilege and cozy relations with the Democratic Party—remains an open question. Nonetheless, to dismiss the issue of trade-labor linkages as nothing more than disingenuous protectionism is to lose sight of the contested character of both unions and the global economy. Supplanting competition with solidarity is a necessary step on the road to any democratizing global project, and trade-linked labor standards would inhibit a race to the bottom on the basis of coercive hyper-exploitation, enforced by competitive market pressures in the world economy (see, for example, Wachtel, 1998; Mayne and LeQuesne, 1999). Finally, it must be noted that the USA has a very poor record regarding adoption and fulfillment of core labor standards (International Confederation of Free Trade Unions, 1999), so that an effective trade-labor regime would hardly be a one-way street.

8 Along with Gary Burtless, Robert Lawrence and Robert Shapiro, Litan is an author of *Globaphobia*, a popular text aimed at debunking putatively misguided opposition to neoliberal globalization (Burtless et al., 1998).

9 Friedman is the author of what must surely be one of the worst books yet written on globalization. Eschewing evidence and analysis in favor of an accretion of facile metaphors and platitudes, Friedman glibly passes off as absolute truth the common sense of his informants in the global investor class, and seems to view even corporate commercial advertisements as unproblematic sources of wisdom about the contemporary world. So abject is Friedman's submission to the ideology of multinational capital that he refers to hedge fund managers as his "best intellectual sources" and happily describes himself as an information arbitrageur (Friedman, 1999a: 21–2).

References

Aaronson, S. A. (1996) *Trade and the American Dream*, Lexington, University Press of Kentucky.

Abraham, L. (1985) *Call It Conspiracy*, Wauna, WA, Double A Publications.

Action Canada Network (1993) *Setting a People's Agenda: Free Trade Alternatives*, Ottawa, Action Canada Network.

—— (n.d.) *NAFTA: Not Another Free Trade Agreement*, Ottawa, Action Canada Network.

AFL–CIO (1987) *The AFL–CIO's Foreign Policy*, Washington, D.C., AFL–CIO.

—— (1991) *Exploiting Both Sides: US–Mexico Free Trade*, Washington, D.C., AFL–CIO.

—— (1993) *Statement by AFL–CIO Executive Council on NAFTA*, Washington, D.C., AFL–CIO.

—— (1999) "Facts about Working Women," AFL–CIO web site: www.AFL-CIO.org/women/wwfacts.htm

Aglietta, M. (1979) *A Theory of Capitalist Regulation*, London, Verso.

Agnew, J. and S. Corbridge (1995) *Mastering Space*, London, Routledge.

Albelda, R. and C. Tilly (1997) *Glass Ceilings and Bottomless Pits*, Boston, South End Press.

Alexander, R. and P. Gilmore (1994) "The Emergence of Cross-Border Labor Solidarity," *NACLA Report on the Americas*, 28 (July–August): 42–8.

Alliance for Responsible Trade (1994) "A Just and Sustainable Trade and Development Initiative for the Western Hemisphere," Washington, D.C., Alliance for Responsible Trade.

Alternative Women-in-Development Working Group (1993) "Breaking Boundaries: Women, Free Trade and Economic Integration," Washington, D.C., Alt-WID.

America Leads on Trade (1997) "Business Community Launches Broad-Based Coalition to Support Renewal of Trade Negotiating Authority," Washington, D.C., America Leads on Trade.

Americas Watch (1993) "Letter to President Clinton," *News from Americas Watch* (October): 2–4.

Anderson, B. (1991) *Imagined Communities*, London, Verso.

Anderson, J. W. (1993) "Perot's Little Book of NAFTA Nonsense," *Washington Post National Weekly Edition* (13–19 September).

Anderson, S. and J. Cavanagh (1996) "CEOs Win, Workers Lose: How Wall Street Rewards Job Destroyers," Washington, D.C., Institute for Policy Studies.

Annan, K. (1999) "Address to the World Economic Forum in Davos," United Nations web site: www.un.org/news/press/docs/1999/199990201.sgsm6881.html

Arblaster, A. (1987) *Democracy*, Minneapolis, University of Minnesota Press.

Arnold, A. (1993) "Rich Get Richer, Poor Get Poorer under New Trade Pact," *Spotlight* (17 May).

Atlanta Constitution (1993) "Will Congress Be Wise Enough to Adopt NAFTA for America?" *Atlanta Constitution* (16 November).

Baker, Dean (1994) "Trade Reporting's Information Deficit," *EXTRA!* (November–December): 8–9.

—— (1998) "Profits Picture," Washington, D.C., Economic Policy Institute.

Baker, Dean and L. Mishel (1995) "Profits Up, Wages Down: Worker Losses Yield Big Gains for Business," Washington, D.C., Economic Policy Institute.

Baker, Donald (1996) "Perot Chooses Economist to Fill Reform Party Ticket," *Washington Post* (10 December).

Barkun, M. (1994) *Religion and the Racist Right*, Chapel Hill, University of North Carolina Press.

Barlett, D. and J. Steele (1992) *America: What Went Wrong?* Kansas City, Andrews and McMeel.

—— (1996) *America: Who Stole the Dream?* Kansas City, Andrews and McMeel.

Barrett, M. (1988) *Women's Oppression Today*, London, Verso.

Behr, P. (1994) "Son of NAFTA: Battle Lines Form over GATT," *Washington Post National Weekly Edition* (29 August–4 September).

Bello, W. (1998) "The End of a 'Miracle'," *Multinational Monitor* (January–February): www.essential.org/monitor/monitor.html

Bennett, D. (1995) *The Party of Fear*, New York, Vintage/Random House.

Bennett, J. (1995) "Buchanan in Unfamiliar Role," *New York Times* (31 December).

—— (1996) "Candidate's Speech Is Called Code for Controversy," *New York Times* (25 January).

Berke, R. (1999) "Judge Rejects Most Charges that Christian Group Played Illegal Role in Elections," *New York Times* (3 August).

Berlet, C. (1995) *Armed Militias, Right Wing Populism, and Scapegoating*, Cambridge, MA, Political Research Associates.

Berlet, C. and M. Lyons (1995) "Militia Nation," *The Progressive* (June): 22–5.

Bernard, E. (1999) "The Battle in Seattle: What Was That All About?" *Washington Post* (5 December).

Bernstein, J. and L. Mishel (1999) "Wages Gain Ground," Washington, D.C., Economic Policy Institute.

Black, D. (n.d.) "Pat Buchanan Stuns Establishment," Stormfront White Nationalist Resource Page: 204.181.176.4/stormfront/buchanan.htm

Block, F. (1977a) "The Ruling Class Does not Rule," *Socialist Revolution*, 33: 6–28.

—— (1977b) *The Origins of International Economic Disorder*, Berkeley, University of California Press.

Blustein, P. (1997) "Free Trade vs. Social Policy," *Washington Post* (19 September).

—— (1998) "The IMF Weathers the Storm," *Washington Post National Weekly Edition* (26 October).

Borosage, R. (1997) "Fast Track to Nowhere," *The Nation* (29 September): 20–2.

—— (1998) "Checking the IMF," *The Nation* (2 March): 4–5.

—— (1999) "The Global Turning," *The Nation* (19 July): 19–22.

Boston, R. (1996) *The Most Dangerous Man in America?* Amherst, NY, Prometheus Books.

Bowles, S. and R. Edwards (1993) *Understanding Capitalism*, New York, HarperCollins.

Bowles, S. and H. Gintis (1986) *Democracy and Capitalism*, New York, Basic Books.

Bowles, S., D. Gordon, and T. Weisskopf (1990) *After the Waste Land*, Armonk, M. E. Sharpe.

Bowles, S. and M. Larudee (1993) "A Low-Wage Game Plan," *New York Times* (15 November).

Boyer, P. J. (1999) "Burned," *The New Yorker* (1 November): 62–8.

Bradsher, K. (1994) "No Rest on Trade: In the Trenches," *New York Times* (3 October).

Brecher, J., J. B. Childs, and J. Cutler (eds) (1993) *Global Visions: Beyond the New World Order*, Boston, South End Press.

Brecher, J. and T. Costello (1994a) *Global Village or Global Pillage*, Boston, South End Press.

—— (1994b) "The Lilliput Strategy: Taking on the Multinationals," *The Nation* (19 December): 757–60.

Brecher, J. and B. Smith (1999) "In Focus: The Global Sustainable Development Resolution," Washington, D.C. and Albuquerque, Institute for Policy Studies and Interhemispheric Resource Center.

Brenner, J. (1993) "The Best of Times, the Worst of Times: US Feminism Today," *New Left Review*, 200: 101–59.

Brenner, R. (1998) "The Economics of Global Turbulence," *New Left Review Special Report on the Global Economy, 1950–98, 229.*

Brenner, R. and M. Glick (1991) "The Regulation Approach: Theory and History," *New Left Review*, 188: 45–119.

Bronfenbrenner, K. (1997) "We'll Close!: Plant Closings, Plant-Closing Threats, Union Organizing and NAFTA," *Multinational Monitor* (March): 8–13.

Brown, D. (1994) "Consumers Get More with GATT," *New York Times* (15 April).

Brown, R. (1994) "Trade Evolution Reflects the Global Village," *New York Times* (15 April).

Buchanan, P. J. (1992) "Speech to Republican National Convention," Dallas, Texas, reproduced at Buchanan for President web site: www.buchanan.org

—— (1993a) "NAFTA Threatens US Sovereignty," *Human Events* (18 September): 766.

—— (1993b) "America First—NAFTA Never," *Washington Post National Weekly Edition* (15–21 November).

—— (1994) "The Rise of Sovereignty Fears," Buchanan for President web site: www.buchanan.org

—— (1995a) "Where the Real Power Resides," *Washington Times* (8 February).

—— (1995b) "An American Economy for Americans," *Wall Street Journal* (5 September).

—— (1995c) Presidential Candidacy Announcement Speech, Buchanan for President web site: www.buchanan.org

—— (1996) "In Their Own Words," *New York Times* (8 March).

—— (1997) "Son of NAFTA," Buchanan for President web site: www.buchanan.org

—— (1998) *The Great Betrayal*, Boston, Little, Brown.

—— (1999) "It's Time for a New Patriotism," *New York Times* (26 October).

Buchanan for President (1996) "Pat Buchanan—Setting the Record Straight on Anti-Semitism."

Burgess, J. and S. Pearlstein (1999) "Protests Delay WTO Opening," *Washington Post* (1 December).

Burtless, G., R. Z. Lawrence, R. Litan, and R. Shapiro (1998) *Globaphobia*, Washington, D.C., Brookings Institution.

Business Roundtable (1991) "Building a Comprehensive US–Mexico Economic Relationship," New York, Business Roundtable.

Campbell, L. (1992) "Liberty Lobby in the Spotlight," *Chicago Tribune* (12 January).

Cantor, D. and J. Schor (1987) *Tunnel Vision*, Boston, South End Press.

Carre, F. and C. Tilly (1998) "Part-Time and Temporary Work: Flexibility for Whom?" *Dollars and Sense* (January–February): 22–5.

Carto, W. (1982) *Profiles in Populism*, Old Greenwich, CT, Flag Press.

—— (1993) "The Global Plantation," *Spotlight Special NAFTA Issue* (17 May).

Cavanagh, J. and S. Anderson (1993) "Europe Offers Practical Insight," *New York Times* (14 November).

Caves, R. and R. Jones (1981) *World Trade and Payments*, Boston, Little, Brown.

Center for Democratic Renewal (1994) "Willis Carto and the Liberty Lobby," Atlanta, CDR.

Clinton, W. J. (1998) "Address to the World Trade Organization," Geneva, US Mission.

—— (1999) "Remarks by the President to the International Labor Organization Conference," White House, Office of the Press Secretary.

Cohen, J. and N. Solomon (1993) "Mass Media Cheerleading Slants NAFTA Discussion," *Seattle Times* (13 November).

Cohen, S. D., J. R. Paul, and R. Blecker (1996) *Fundamentals of US Foreign Trade Policy*, Boulder, Westview.

Collier, A. (1994) *Critical Realism*, London, Verso.

Commager, H. S. (1958) *Documents of American History*, New York, Appleton-Century Crofts.

Cook, R. (1999) "Labor Protests against WTO," *Washington Post* (29 November).

Cooper, M. (1995a) "The Paranoid Style," *The Nation* (10 April): 486–92.

—— (1995b) "Cooper Replies [to Mullins and Harder]," *The Nation* (5 June): 808–9.

Cox, R. (1987) *Production, Power, and World Order*, New York, Columbia University Press.

Cunningham, S. and B. Reed (1995) "Balancing Budgets on Women's Backs," *Dollars and Sense* (November–December): 22–5.

Cypher, J. (1993) "The Ideology of Economic Science in the Selling of NAFTA," *Review of Radical Political Economics*, 25: 146–64.

Daniels, J. (1997) *White Lies: Race, Class, Gender, and Sexuality in White Supremacist Discourse*, London, Routledge.

Davey, M. (1996) "A Big Voice," *St. Petersburg Times* (9 June).

Davis, B. (1993) "In Debate over NAFTA, Many See Trade as a Symbol of Hardship," *Wall Street Journal* (20 October).

—— (1996a) "Bashing Big Business Becomes a Business for Talk Show Host," *Wall Street Journal* (16 May).

—— (1996b) "Perot Picks Choate," *Wall Street Journal* (11 September).

Davis, M. (1986) *Prisoners of the American Dream*, London, Verso.

Dees, M. and J. Corcoran (1996) *Gathering Storm: America's Militia Threat*, New York, HarperCollins.

DeGeorge, G. (1996) "For Pat Choate, Talk Radio Turns to Static," *Business Week* (4 November).

DeRosa, R. (1995) "Tuning in to High Wattage Talk Show Hosts," *USA Today* (1 February).

Development GAP (1992) "US Citizens' Analysis of the North American Free Trade Agreement," Washington, D.C., Development Group for Alternative Policies.

Diamond, S. (1995) *Roads to Dominion: Right Wing Movements and Political Power in the United States*, New York, Guilford.

Dicken, P. (1992) *Global Shift*, New York, Guilford.

Dionne, E. J. (1998) "Globalism with a Human Face," *Washington Post* (29 May).

—— (1999) "A Shift Is under Way to Try to Humanize the World's Commerce," *International Herald Tribune* (25 January).

Donahue, T. R. (1991) "The Case against a North American Free Trade Agreement," *Columbia Journal of World Business*, 26: 93–6.

Dornbusch, R. (1991) "North American Free Trade: What It Means," *Columbia Journal of World Business*, 26: 73–6.

Druck, D. (1993) "Not a Fair Trade Agreement," Council on Domestic Relations web site: www.logoplex.com/shops/cdr/cdr.html

Dryzek, J. (1996) *Democracy in Capitalist Times*, Oxford, Oxford University Press.

Dunne, N. (1994) "Clinton Pulls out Stops for Trade Deal Fast-Track," *Financial Times* (25 August).

Eagleton, T. (1991) *Ideology: An Introduction*, London, Verso.

Economic Policy Unit (1999) "Datazone: Share of Aggregate Income . . . 1947–1997," Washington, D.C., EPI.

Economist (1996) "Off-Piste in Davos," *The Economist* (10 February).

—— (1999) "Citizens' Groups: The Non-Governmental Order," *The Economist* (11–17 December).

Eddlem, T. (1992) "NAFTA: The Misnamed Treaty," *The New American* (28 December).

—— (1994) "Trading Away Our Sovereignty," *The New American* (7 March).

Editorial Board (1999) "Openness Deters Mayhem in Street," *Seattle Post-Intelligencer* (3 December).

Egan, T. (1995) "In Congress; Trying to Explain Contacts with Paramilitary Groups," *New York Times* (2 May).

Eisner, R. (1997) "A Free Trade Primer," *Wall Street Journal* (13 October).

Elliott, M. (1999) "The New Radicals," *Newsweek* (13 December).

Enloe, C. (1995) "The Globetrotting Sneaker," *Ms.* (March–April): 10–15.

Farrell, A. (1995) "Like a Tarantula on a Banana Boat: *Ms.* Magazine, 1972–1989," in *Feminist Organizations,* M. M. Ferree and P. Y. Martin (eds), Philadelphia, Temple University Press: 53–67.

Faux, J. and T. Lee (1992) "The Effect of George Bush's NAFTA on American Workers," Washington, D.C., Economic Policy Institute.

Feminist Majority (1997) "Women's Groups Demand Nike End Sweatshop Labor," *Feminist Majority Report* (Fall): www.feminist.org/research/report/93_twelve.html

Fenster, M. (1999) *Conspiracy Theories: Secrecy and Power in American Culture*, Minneapolis, University of Minnesota Press.

Fine, B. (1989) *Marx's Capital*, London, Macmillan.

Folbre, N. (1995) *The New Field Guide to the US Economy*, New York, New Press.

Frank, D. (1999) *Buy American: The Untold Story of Economic Nationalism*, Boston, Beacon Press.

Frank, E. (1999) "Bye Bye IMF? A New Blueprint for the Global Economy," *Dollars and Sense* (July–August): 13–14, 36.

Frantz, D. and M. Janofsky (1996) "Buchanan Drawing Extremist Support," *New York Times* (23 February).

Freeman, R. and J. Medoff (1984) *What Do Unions Do?* New York, Basic Books.

Freivogel, H. (1995) "Talking Tough: On 300 Radio Stations, Chuck Harder's Show Airs Conspiracy Theories," *St. Louis Post-Dispatch* (10 May).

Friedman, A. (1998) "Is Free Market a Casualty of the Economic Crisis?" *International Herald Tribune* (8 October).

Friedman, M. (1996) "Hong Kong vs. Buchanan," *Wall Street Journal* (7 March).

Friedman, S. (1992) "NAFTA as Social Dumping," *Challenge* (September–October): 27–32.

Friedman, T. (1993) "Adamant Unions Zero In on Clinton," *New York Times* (16 November).

—— (1999a) *The Lexus and the Olive Tree*, New York, Farrar Straus Giroux.

—— (1999b) "Senseless in Seattle," *New York Times* (1 December).

Gabriel, C. and L. Macdonald (1994) "NAFTA, Women, and Organizing in Canada and Mexico," *Millennium*, 23: 535–62.

Germain, R. and M. Kenny (1998) "Engaging Gramsci: International Relations Theory and the New Gramscians," *Review of International Studies*, 24(1): 3–21.

Gigot, P. (1993) "The Sucking Sound: Perot Fronts for Textile King," *Wall Street Journal* (25 June).

Gill, S. (1990) *American Hegemony and the Trilateral Commission*, Cambridge, Cambridge University Press.

Gladstone, B. (1996) "New Radio Network to Offer Full Diet of Populist Fare," National Public Radio *Morning Edition* (17 May). Radio Program Transcript #1870–11.

Gladwell, M. (1996) "Patrick J. Buchanan: History Conscious Fighter Focuses on Trade," *Washington Post* (26 January).

Goldfield, M. (1987) *The Decline of Organized Labor in the United States*, Chicago, University of Chicago Press.

—— (1997) *The Color of Politics*, New York, New Press.

Goodman, E. (1999) "Questions from Seattle: Whose World Is It?" *Boston Globe* (5 December).

Goodman, P. (1995) "Mistrustful Share Their Ideas Online," *Anchorage Daily News* (27 April).

Goodstein, L. (1999) "Coalition's Woes May Hinder Goals of Christian Right," *New York Times* (2 August).

Gordon, D. M. (1988) "The Global Economy," *New Left Review*, 168: 24–64.

—— (1996) *Fat and Mean*, New York, Free Press.

Gordon, D., R. Edwards, and M. Reich (1982) *Segmented Work, Divided Workers*, Cambridge, Cambridge University Press.

Gramsci, A. (1971) *Selections from the Prison Notebooks*, New York, International Publishers.

Gray, J. (1998) *False Dawn: The Delusions of Global Capitalism*, London, Granta.

Greenhouse, S. (1997a) "In Shift to Labor, Public Supports UPS Strikers," *New York Times* (17 August).

—— (1997b) "AFL–CIO Rallies against Clinton's New Free-Trade Pacts," *New York Times* (24 September).

—— (1997c) "Nike Supports Women in Its Ads, but not Its Factories, Groups Say," *New York Times* (26 October).

Greenhouse, S. and J. Kahn (1999) "US Effort to Add Labor Standards to Agenda Fails," *New York Times* (3 December).

Greider, W. (1993) "The Global Marketplace: A Closet Dictator," in *The Case against Free Trade*, R. Nader (ed.), San Francisco, Earth Island Press: 195–217.

—— (1997) *One World, Ready or Not*, New York, Simon and Schuster.

Grier, P. (1993) "GATT Debate Pales beside Drama of NAFTA," *Christian Science Monitor* (10 December).

Hall, J. (1993) "Labor's Lack of Logic," *Syracuse Post-Standard* (16 November).

Hall, S. (1988a) "The Toad in the Garden: Thatcherism among the Theorists," in *Marxism and the Interpretation of Culture*, C. Nelson and L. Grossberg (eds), Urbana, University of Illinois: 35–73.

—— (1988b) *The Hard Road to Renewal*, London, Verso.

—— (1996a) "The Problem of Ideology: Marxism without Guarantees," in *Stuart Hall: Critical Dialogues in Cultural Studies*, D. Morley and K.-H. Chen (eds), London, Routledge: 25–46.

—— (1996b) "On Postmodernism and Articulation," in *Stuart Hall: Critical Dialogues in Cultural Studies*, D. Morley and K.-H. Chen (eds), London, Routledge: 131–50.

—— (1997) "The Work of Representation," in *Representation: Cultural Representations and Signifying Practices*, S. Hall (ed.), London, Sage: 15–74.

Harder, C. (1994) "Trials and Tribulations at the Telford Hotel: A Brief History of For the People," *The News Reporter* (24 February).

—— (1995) "Reply [to Cooper]," *The Nation* (5 June): 778, 808.

Harris, W. and J. Levey (eds) (1975) *The New Columbia Encyclopedia*, New York, Columbia University Press.

Harrison, B. and B. Bluestone (1988) *The Great U-Turn*, New York, Basic Books.

Harvey, D. (1989) *The Condition of Postmodernity*, Oxford, Blackwell.

Heilbrunn, J. (1995) "On Pat Robertson: His Anti-Semitic Sources," *New York Review of Books* (20 April): 68–71.

Held, D. (1995) *Democracy and the Global Order*, Stanford, Stanford University Press.

Held, D., A. McGrew, D. Goldblatt, and J. Perraton (1999) *Global Transformations*, Cambridge, Polity.

Henwood, D. (1996) "Antiglobalization," *Left Business Observer* (January 22).

—— (1997a) "Earnings," *Left Business Observer* web site: www.panix.com/~dhenwood/Stats_earns.html

—— (1997b) "Dow 7000," *Left Business Observer*, 76 (February).

—— (1997c) "Does Globalization Matter?" *In These Times* (March 31): 14–16.

—— (1997d) "Measuring Privilege," *Left Business Observer*, 78 (July).

—— (1998a) "Asia Melts," *Left Business Observer*, 81 (January).

—— (1998b) "Crisis Update," *Left Business Observer*, 85 (September).

—— (1999) "LBO @ WTO," *Left Business Observer* web site: www.panix.com/~dhenwood/Seattle.html

Hernandez, R. and D. Sanchez (1992) *Cross-Border Links*, Albuquerque, Inter-Hemispheric Resource Center.

Hilliard, R. and M. Keith (1999) *Waves of Rancor: Tuning in the Radical Right*, Armonk, M. E. Sharpe.

Himmelweit, S. (1991) "Reproduction and the Materialist Conception of History: A Feminist Critique," in *The Cambridge Companion to Marx*, T. Carver (ed.), Cambridge, Cambridge University Press: 196–221.

Hirst, P. and G. Thompson (1996) *Globalization in Question*, Cambridge, Polity.

Hollings, E. (1993–4) "Reform Mexico First," *Foreign Policy*, 93: 91–103.

Hormats, R. (1996) "The High Price of Economic Isolationism," *Washington Post National Weekly Edition* (18–24 March).

Hudson, D. (1993) "American Dream Dead for People Out of Work," *Spotlight Special NAFTA Issue* (17 May).

Hufbauer, G. C. (1993) "NAFTA: Friend or Foe?" *New York Times* (15 November).

Hufbauer, G. C. and J. Schott (1993a) "Prescription for Growth," *Foreign Policy*, 93: 104–14.

—— (1993b) *NAFTA: An Assessment*, Washington, D.C., Institute for International Economics.

Hunt, M. (1987) *Ideology and US Foreign Policy*, New Haven, Yale University Press.

Ifill, G. (1993a) "Both Sides Assert Gain after Debate over Trade Accord," *New York Times* (11 November).

—— (1993b) "Americans Are Split on Trade Accord," *New York Times* (16 November).

International Confederation of Free Trade Unions (1999) "Internationally-Recognized Core Labor Standards in the United States," Geneva, ICFTU.

Isaac, J. (1987) *Power and Marxist Theory: A Realist View*, Ithaca, Cornell University Press.

Jackson, J. (1997) "Fast Track 1, Democracy 0: Trade Policy Isn't Open for Debate, Say Editorialists," *Extra!* (November), New York, Fairness and Accuracy in Reporting.

Janofsky, M. (1995) "Demons and Conspiracies Haunt a 'Patriot' World," *New York Times* (31 May).

Jasinowski, J. (1994a) "An Rx for US Manufacturers," *New York Times* (15 April).

—— (1994b) "Why Americans Can't Afford to Pull Back Now on GATT," *Christian Science Monitor* (28 November).

Jasper, W. (1992) *Global Tyranny . . . Step by Step*, Appleton, WI, Western Islands Publishers.

—— (1993) "The Free Trade Charade," *The New American* (27 December).

Jessop, B., K. Bonnett, S. Bromley, and T. Ling (1984) "Authoritarian Populism, Two Nations, and Thatcherism," *New Left Review*, 147: 32–60.

John Birch Society (1985) *Back to Basics*, Appleton, WI, John Birch Society.
—— (1996) *The New American Special Report: Conspiracy for Global Control*, Appleton, WI, John Birch Society.
Johnson, D. (1993) "Chicago on Trade Accord: Split along Class Lines," *New York Times* (14 November).
Judd, K. and S. M. Pope (1994) "The New Job Squeeze," *Ms.* (May–June): 86–90.
Kadetsky, E. (1994) "The Human Cost of Free Trade," *Ms.* (January–February): 12–15.
Kah, G. (1991) *En Route to Global Occupation*, Lafayette, LA, Huntington House Publishers.
Kamel, R. and A. Hoffman (eds) (1999) *The Maquiladora Reader*, Philadelphia, American Friends Service Committee.
Kantor, M. (1993) "Statement of Ambassador Mickey Kantor: NAFTA and the Perot–Choate Book," Washington, D.C., U.S. Trade Representative.
—— (1994) "Reaping Benefits from the Uruguay Round," *New York Times* (15 April).
—— (1997) "A Matter of Leadership," *Washington Post* (14 September).
Kapstein, E. (1996) "Workers and the World Economy," *Foreign Affairs* (May–June): 16–37.
Katson, T. (1994) *The Disaster that Is GATT 1994: The Ruling Elite's Plan for the Global Plantation*, Washington, D.C., Liberty Lobby.
Kazin, M. (1995) *The Populist Persuasion*, New York, Basic Books.
Khor, M. (1999) "The Revolt of Developing Nations," Penang, Malaysia, Third World Network web site: www.twnside.org.sg/souths/twn/title/revolt-cn.htm
Korten, D. (1996) "When Corporations Rule the World: An Interview with David Korten," in *Corporations Are Gonna Get Your Mama*, K. Danaher (ed.), Monroe, ME, Common Courage Press: 49–56.
Kraft, C. (1992) "A Preliminary Socioeconomic and State Demographic Profile of the John Birch Society," Cambridge, MA, Political Research Associates.
Kravis, I. and R. Lipsey (1992) "Sources of Competitiveness of the United States and of Its Multinational Firms," *Review of Economics and Statistics*, 74(2): 193–201.
Kristof, N. (1998) "Has the IMF Cured or Harmed Asia? Dispute Rages after Months of Crisis," *New York Times* (23 April).
Krugman, P. (1993a) "The Uncomfortable Truth about NAFTA," *Foreign Affairs*, 72: 13–19.
—— (1993b) "What Do Undergrads Need to Know about Trade?" *American Economic Association Papers and Proceedings*, 83(2): 23–6.
—— (1993c) "The Narrow and Broad Arguments for Free Trade," *American Economic Association Papers and Proceedings*, 83(2): 362–6.
—— (1996) "Ricardo's Difficult Idea," Paul Krugman's web site, web.mit.edu/krugman/www/ricardo.htm
—— (1999) "Enemies of the WTO: Bogus Arguments against the World Trade Organization," *Slate* (23 November): www.slate.com/dismal/99-11-23/dismal.asp
La Botz, D. (1992) *Mask of Democracy*, Boston, South End Press.
—— (1994) "Making Links across the Border," *Labor Notes* (August).
Laffey, M. (1991) "Ideology and the Limits of Gramscian Theory in International Relations," Paper presented at the annual Meeting of the International Studies Association.

Larrain, J. (1979) *The Concept of Ideology*, Athens, University of Georgia Press.
—— (1983) *Marxism and Ideology*, London, Macmillan.
—— (1996) "Stuart Hall and the Marxist Concept of Ideology," in *Stuart Hall: Critical Dialogues in Cultural Studies*, D. Morley and K.-H. Chen (eds), London, Routledge: 47–70.
Larudee, M. (1993) "Trade Policy: Who Wins? Who Loses?" in *Creating a New World Economy*, G. Epstein, J. Graham, and J. Nembhard (eds), Philadelphia, Temple University Press: 47–63.
Lee, T. (1993) "Happily Never Nafta," *Dollars and Sense* (January–February): 12–15.
Levinson, J. (1993) *The Labor Side Accord to the North American Free Trade Agreement*, Washington, D.C., Economic Policy Institute.
Lewis, C. and M. Ebrahim (1993) "Can Mexico and Big Business USA Buy NAFTA?" *The Nation* (14 June): 826–39.
Lewis, P. (1994) "Top International Trade Official Urges US to Approve Accord," *New York Times* (22 November).
Lind, M. (1995a) "Rev. Robertson's Grand International Conspiracy Theory," *New York Review of Books* (2 February): 21–5.
—— (1995b) "On Pat Robertson: His Defenders," *New York Review of Books* (20 April): 67–8.
Litan, R. (1999) "The Protesters Were Wrong, But Trade Means Compromise," *International Herald Tribune* (6 December).
Longworth, R. C. (1999) "Activist Groups Gain Influence in Global Body," *Chicago Tribune* (1 December).
Low, P. (1993) *Trading Free*, New York, Twentieth Century Fund.
Manvell, R. (1974) *Films and the Second World War*, South Brunswick, A. S. Barnes.
Marchand, M. (1996) "Selling NAFTA: Gendered Metaphors and Silenced Gender Implications," in *Globalization: Theory and Practice*, E. Kofman and G. Youngs (eds) London, Pinter: 253–70.
Marx, K. (1977a) *Capital* volume 1, New York, Vintage.
—— (1977b) "The Eighteenth Brumaire of Louis Bonaparte," in *Karl Marx: Selected Writings*, D. McLellan (ed.), Oxford, Oxford University Press: 300–325.
Marx, K. and F. Engels (1977) "The Communist Manifesto," in *Karl Marx: Selected Writings*, D. McLellan (ed.), Oxford, Oxford University Press: 221–47.
Masur, S. (1991) "The North American Free Trade Agreement: Why It's in the Interest of US Business," *Columbia Journal of World Business*, 26: 99–103.
May, M. (1990) "The Historical Problem of the Family Wage: The Ford Motor Company and the Five Dollar Day," in *Unequal Sisters*, E. C. DuBois and V. Ruiz (eds), London, Routledge: 275–91.
Mayne, R. and C. LeQuesne (1999) "Calls for a Social Trade," in *Global Trade and Global Social Issues*, A. Taylor and C. Thomas (eds), London, Routledge: 91–113.
McDowell, L. (1991) "Life Without Father or Ford," *Transactions of the Institute of British Geographers*, 16: 400–19.
McGaughey, W. (1992) *A US–Mexico–Canada Free Trade Agreement: Do We Just Say No?* Minneapolis, Thistlerose Publications.
McGinn, M. (1995) "How GATT Puts Hard-won Victories at Risk," *Ms.* (March/April): 15.

McLemee, S. (1994) "Spotlight on the Liberty Lobby," *Covert Action Quarterly*, 50 (Fall): 23–32.

McManus, J. (1994) "The War on Culture," *The New American* (12 December).

—— (1995a) *The Insiders: Architects of the New World Order*, Appleton, WI, The John Birch Society.

—— (1995b) "More 'Free Trade' Follies," *The New American* (9 January).

—— (1996) "Targeted for Destruction: Pat Buchanan's Campaign Has Raised the Ire of the Establishment," *The New American* (18 March).

McNally, D. (1995) "Language, History, and Class Struggle," *Monthly Review*, 47(3): 13–30.

Members of International Civil Society (1999) "Statement from Members of International Civil Society Opposing a Millenium Round," Friends of the Earth, UK web site: www.foe.co.uk/camps/susdev/stopround.html

Meyer, S. (1981) *The Five Dollar Day*, Albany, State University of New York Press.

Miller, J. (1998) "IMF Under Siege," *Dollars and Sense* (July–August): 9–10.

Mintz, F. (1985) *The Liberty Lobby and the American Right*, Westport, CT, Greenwood.

Mintz, J. (1996) "Air Force–German Alliance Draws Right-Wing Flak," *Washington Post* (28 May).

Mishel, L. (1997) "Behind the Numbers: Capital's Gain," *The American Prospect* (July–August): 71–3.

Mishel, L., J. Bernstein, and J. Schmitt (1997) *The State of Working America, 1996–97*, Armonck, M. E. Sharpe.

Moberg, D. (1999) "Bare Breasts, Green Condoms and Rubber Bullets," *Salon* (1 December): www.salon.com/news/feature/1999/12/01/wtoprotest/print.html

Moffett, M. and J. Opdyke (1993) "Perot's Stand against Trade Pact Isn't Shared by Businesses Owned by His Family," *Wall Street Journal* (6 July).

Moody, K. (1988) *An Injury to All: The Decline of American Unionism*, London, Verso.

—— (1991) "Whipsawing on a Continental Scale," *Labor Notes* (July).

—— (1994) "If NAFTA Don't Get You, Then the GATT Will," *Labor Notes* (February).

—— (1995) "AFL–CIO Takes a Walk as Congress Approves New Trade Pact," *Labor Notes* (January).

—— (1997a) *Workers in a Lean World*, London, Verso.

—— (1997b) "Towards an International Social-Movement Unionism," *New Left Review*, 225: 52–72.

Moody, K. and M. McGinn (1991) "From the Yukon to the Yucatan," *Dollars and Sense* (November): 10–12.

—— (1992) *Unions and Free Trade: Solidarity vs. Competition*, Detroit, Labor Notes Books.

Moore, M. (1997) *Downsize This!* New York, HarperCollins.

Mullins, E. (1992) *The World Order: Our Secret Rulers*, Staunton, VA, Ezra Pound Institute of Civilization.

—— (1993) "Secret of Rockefeller Fortune Is Part of Our Hidden History," *The Spotlight* (4 January).

Multinational Monitor (1997) "Buddy, Can You Spare $100,000?" *Multinational Monitor* (September) web site: www.essential.org/monitor/hyper/mm0997.10.html

Myerson, A. (1994) "In Trade-Pact War, Clashes Outside Capital Are Heavy," *New York Times* (24 November).

Nader, R. (ed.) (1993a) *The Case against Free Trade: GATT, NAFTA, and the Globalization of Corporate Power*, San Francisco, Earth Island Press.

—— (1993b) "Introduction: Free Trade and the Decline of Democracy," in *The Case Against Free Trade*, R. Nader (ed.), San Francisco, Earth Island Press: 1–12.

Nasar, S. (1993a) "A Primer: Why Economists Favor Free Trade Agreement," *New York Times* (17 September).

—— (1993b) "GATT's Big Payoff for the US," *New York Times* (19 December).

National Alliance (n.d.) "What Is the National Alliance?" National Alliance web site: www.natvan.com/what/what.html

Neal, T. M. (1997) "Business Leaders Gear Up Lobbying and Ad Campaign for Fast Track Bill," *Washington Post* (19 September).

Newsweek (1996) "The Hit Men," *Newsweek* (26 February).

New York Times (1993) "NAFTA and the National Interest," *New York Times* (17 November).

—— (1994) "For Freer Trade—And Better Jobs," *New York Times* (29 November).

—— (1996) *Special Report: The Downsizing of America*, New York, Times Books.

Nordheimer, J. (1996) "Buchanan Threatens Longtime Bipartisan Policy, Official Warns," *New York Times* (25 February).

North, G. (1985) "Prologue," in *Call It Conspiracy*, L. Abraham (ed.), Wauna, WA, Double A Publications: ix–vvii.

Nussbaum, K. (1998) "Women in Labor: Always the Bridesmaid?" in *Not Your Father's Union Movement*, J.-A. Mort (ed.), London, Verso: 55–68.

Open World Conference of Workers (1999) "Labor Alerts: Protect the ILO Conventions!" Washington, D.C., Campaign for Labor Rights.

Orme, W. (1993) "The NAFTA Debate: Myths vs Facts," *Foreign Affairs*, 72: 2–12.

Paulsen, M. (1999) "Buchanan Inc.," *The Nation* (22 November): 11–16.

Pearlstein, S. (1999a) "Trade Theory Collides with Angry Reality," *Washington Post* (3 December).

—— (1999b) "WTO Negotiators' Reach Far Exceeded Grasp of Complexities," *Washington Post* (5 December).

Perloff, J. (1988) *The Shadows of Power*, Appleton, WI, Western Islands Publishers.

Perot, R. and P. Choate (1993) *Save Your Job, Save Our Country*, New York, Hyperion.

Peterson, V. S. (1997) "Whose Crisis? Early and Post-modern Masculinism," in *Innovation and Transformation in International Studies*, S. Gill and J. Mittelman (eds), Cambridge, Cambridge University Press: 185–201.

Pettman, J. J. (1996) *Worlding Women: A Feminist International Politics*, London, Routledge.

Pfaff, W. (1999) "So Much for the Notion that Trade Can Do without Politics," *International Herald Tribune* (29 November).

Pierce, W. (1980) *The Turner Diaries*, pseudonym Andrew Macdonald, New York, Barricade Books.

—— (1992) "American Dissident Voices: Free Trade and the US Economy," Hillsboro, WV, National Vanguard Books/National Alliance. Audio recording.

—— (n.d.) "The New World Order, 'Free Trade', and the De-industrialization of America," National Alliance web site: www.natvan.com/natvan/n-wd-ord.html

Piper, M. (1995) "Broad-Spectrum Push for Populist Candidate," *The Spotlight* (24 July).

Pitcavage, M. (1996) "Other Things the Neo-Militiaperson Believes In," The Militia Watchdog web site: www.militia-watchdog.org

Public Citizen (1994) "Citizen Beware! Sovereignty and Democracy under Attack by the World Trade Organization," Washington, D.C., Public Citizen.

Reingold, J. (1997) "Executive Pay," *Business Week* (21 April).

Ridgeway, J. (1995) *Blood in the Face*, New York, Thunder's Mouth Press.

Roberts, R. (1994) *The Choice: A Fable of Free Trade and Protectionism*, Englewood Cliffs, Prentice Hall.

Robertson, P. (1991) *The New World Order*, Dallas, Word Publishing.

Robinson, I. (1993) *North American Trade as if Democracy Mattered*, Ottawa and Washington, D.C., Canadian Center for Policy Alternatives and International Labor Rights Fund.

—— (1995) "Globalization and Democracy," *Dissent* (Summer): 373–80.

Rodrik, D. (1997) *Has Globalization Gone Too Far?* Washington, D.C., Institute for International Economics.

Rosenbaum, D. (1999) "Tax-Exempt Status Rejected, Christian Coalition Regroups," *New York Times* (11 June).

Rosier, S. (1996) "Workers' Voices on the Air," *AFL–CIO News* (7 June).

Ross, A. (ed.) (1997) *No Sweat*, London, Verso.

Rowen, H. (1993a) "The Tide Is Turning," *Washington Post National Weekly Edition* (18–24 October).

—— (1993b) "What Kind of Democratic Party?" *Washington Post National Weekly Edition* (22–28 November).

—— (1993c) "The Job Ahead," *Washington Post National Weekly Edition* (6–12 December).

Runyan, A. S. (1996) "The Places of Women in Trading Places: Gendered Global/ Regional Regimes and Inter-nationalized Feminist Resistance," in *Globalization: Theory and Practice*, E. Kofman and G. Youngs (eds), London, Pinter: 238–52.

Rupert, M. (1995) *Producing Hegemony*, Cambridge, Cambridge University Press.

—— (1998) "Democracy, Peace: What's not to Love?" Paper presented at the workshop on Democracy, The Use of Force, and Global Social Change, Minneapolis, University of Minnesota.

Samuelson, R. J. (1994) "Why GATT Isn't Boring," *Washington Post National Weekly Edition* (27 December–2 January).

Sanders, B. (1999) "Global Sustainable Development Resolution," Office of Congressional Representative Bernie Sanders, VT, web site: www.house.gov/bernie/legislation/global/index.html

Sanger, D. (1988) "World Finance Meeting Ends with No Grand Strategy but Many Ideas," *New York Times* (8 October).

—— (1994a) "Clinton Pledges to Push for Vote on Trade Accord," *New York Times* (17 November).

—— (1994b) "House Approves Trade Agreement by a Wide Margin," *New York Times* (30 November).

—— (1994c) "Senate Approves Pact to Ease Trade Curbs," *New York Times* (2 December).

—— (1995) "Buchanan's Tough Tariff Talk Rattles GOP," *New York Times* (8 October).

—— (1998) "US and IMF Made Asia Crisis Worse, World Bank Finds," *New York Times* (3 December).

—— (1999) "After Clinton's Push, Questions about Motive," *New York Times* (3 December).

Sayer, A. (1992) *Method in Social Science: A Realist Approach*, London, Routledge.

Sayer, D. (1987) *The Violence of Abstraction*, Oxford, Blackwell.

—— (1991) *Capitalism and Modernity*, London, Routledge.

Schlefer, J. (1993) "History Counsels 'No' on NAFTA," *New York Times* (14 November).

Schmitt, E. (1998) "House Rejects Fast-Track Trade Bill," *New York Times* (26 September).

Schor, J. (1993) "The Great Trade Debates," in *Creating a New World Economy*, G. Epstein, J. Graham, and J. Nembhard (eds), Philadelphia, Temple University Press: 274–86.

Schwab, K. (1999) "Finding the Right Balance: Opening Address to Annual Meeting," Davos, World Economic Forum web site: live99.weforum.org/opening_ksc.asp

Schwab, K. and C. Smadja (1996) "Start Taking the Backlash against Globalization Seriously," *International Herald Tribune* (1 February).

—— (1999) "Globalization Needs a Human Face," *International Herald Tribune* (28 January).

Shaw, R. (1999) *Reclaiming America*, Berkeley, University of California Press.

Sims, B. (1992) *Workers of the World Undermined*, Boston, South End Press.

Sklair, L. (1997) "Social Movements for Global Capitalism: The Transnational Capitalist Class in Action," *Review of International Political Economy*, 4(3): 514–38.

Smith, P. (1997) *Millennial Dreams*, London, Verso.

Smith, R. (1993) "Beyond Tocqueville, Myrdal, and Harz: The Multiple Traditions in America," *American Political Science Review*, 87: 549–66.

Solomon, S. and M. Rupert (1999) "Historical Materialism, Ideology, and the Politics of Globalization," paper presented at the workshop on Historical Materialism and Globalization, Center for the Study of Globalization and Regionalization, University of Warwick.

Soros, G. (1998) *The Crisis of Global Capitalism*, New York, Public Affairs.

Southern Poverty Law Center (1999) *The World of "Patriots,"* Southern Poverty Law Center web site: www.splcenter.org/intelligenceproject/ip-4j1.html

Sparr, P. (1992) "How We Got into This Mess and Ways to Get Out," *Ms.* (March–April): 29–36.

Staples, B. (1999) "Unearthing a Riot," *New York Times Magazine* (19 December): 64–9.

Steele, R. W. (1979) "The Greatest Gangster Movie Ever Filmed: *Prelude to War*," *Prologue* (Winter): 220–35.

Stern, K. (1996) *A Force upon the Plain: The American Militia Movement and the Politics of Hate*, New York, Simon and Schuster.

Still, W. (1990) *New World Order: The Ancient Plan of Secret Societies*, Lafayette, LA, Huntington House Publishers.

Susskind, Y. (1998) "What's so Liberal about Neoliberalism?" *MADRE Speaks* (Fall): 3–8.

Sutherland, P. (1994) "From GATT to WTO," *New York Times* (15 April).

Swardson, A. (2000) "Entrance Fees to the Marketplace of Ideas," *Washington Post* (24 January).

Temple, C. (1997) "White House Pushes Fast Track," *The Spotlight* online edition (January, 1998): www.spotlight.org

Thomas, P. (1994) *Alien Politics: Marxist State Theory Retrieved*, London, Routledge.

Thomas, R. (1993) "The ABCs of the GATT Pact," *Newsweek* (27 December).

Tucker, J. (1993) "Globalists Celebrate Too Soon," *The Spotlight* (6 December).

—— (1994) "One World Closer with GATT," *The Spotlight* (10 January).

—— (1995) "Bought Think Tankers Beat Drums for One Worlders," *The Spotlight* (15 May).

Turner, G. (1996) *British Cultural Studies*, London, Routledge.

Uchitelle, L. (1997) "Gap between Full-Time and Part-Time Workers Has Widened," *New York Times* (8 August).

United Automobile Workers (1992) *Fast Track to Decline? North American Free Trade Agreement*, Detroit, UAW.

United Nations Development Program (1999) *Human Development Report*, New York, UNDP, Oxford University Press.

US Bureau of Labor Statistics (1997) "Union Members in 1996," Washington, D.C., US Department of Labor.

US Census Bureau (1996a) "Workers with Low Earnings, 1964 to 1990," Washington, D.C., US Department of Commerce.

—— (1996b) "A Brief Look at Postwar US Income Inequality," Washington, D.C., US Commerce Department.

USA*NAFTA (1993a) "Statement of Purpose," Washington, D.C., USA*NAFTA.

—— (1993b) "NAFTA, Our Economy, Our Future," Washington, D.C., USA*NAFTA.

—— (1993c) "NAFTA Myths and Realities: Focus on the Facts," Washington, D.C., USA*NAFTA.

van der Pijl, K. (1984) *The Making of an Atlantic Ruling Class*, London, Verso.

—— (1997) "Transnational Class Formation and State Forms," in *Innovation and Transformation in International Studies*, S. Gill and J. Mittelman (eds), Cambridge, Cambridge University Press: 118–33.

—— (1998) *Transnational Classes and International Relations*, London, Routledge.

Vickers, J. (1993) *Women and the World Economic Crisis*, London, Zed.

Vise, D. and L. Adams (1999) "Another Y2K Warning: FBI Advises Police Chiefs on Potential Millennium Violence," *Washington Post National Weekly Edition* (8 November).

Wachtel, H. (1990) *The Money Mandarins*, Armonk, M. E. Sharpe.

—— (1995) "Taming Global Money," *Challenge* (January–February): 36–40.

—— (1998) "Labor's Stake in the WTO," *The American Prospect* (March–April): 34–8.

Wallach, L. (1993) "Hidden Dangers of GATT and NAFTA," in *The Case against Free Trade*, R. Nader (ed.), San Francisco, Earth Island Press.

Washington Post (1993) "Why Vote for NAFTA?" *Washington Post National Weekly Edition* (8–14 November).

Weinstein, M. (1993) "Mr. Perot Attacks NAFTA: Inconvenient Facts Don't Trouble Him," *New York Times* (12 September).

Weisskopf, M. (1993) "In the Business of Promoting NAFTA," *Washington Post National Weekly Edition* (4–10 October).

Welch, R. (1986) "Republics and Democracies," Appleton, WI, John Birch Society.

Wilcox, C. (1996) *Onward Christian Soldiers? The Religious Right in American Politics*, Boulder, Westview.

Wills, G. (1995) "The New Revolutionaries," *The New York Review of Books* (10 August): 50–5.

Wolff, E. (1995) *Top Heavy*, New York, Twentieth Century Fund.

Wolff, R. and S. Resnick (1987) *Economics: Marxian versus Neoclassical*, Baltimore, Johns Hopkins University Press.

Wood, E. M. (1995) *Democracy against Capitalism*, Cambridge, Cambridge University Press.

World Bank (1995) *World Development Report: Workers in an Integrating World*, Oxford, Oxford University Press.

World Economic Forum (1996) "Creative Impatience Can Manage Problems of Globalization," (1 February). WEF web site: www.weforum.org/frames/press/am96/pr10ph.htm

—— (1997a) "Committed to Improving the State of the World," Geneva, WEF.

—— (1997b) "About the World Economic Forum," Geneva, WEF.

World Trade Organization (1995) *Trading into the Future*, Geneva, WTO.

—— (1998) *Trading into the Future*, second edition, Geneva, WTO.

Zeskind, L. (1996) "White-Shoed Supremacy," *The Nation* (10 June): 21–4.

Index